ENGLISH HISTORICAL FACTS
1485–1603

ENGLISH
HISTORICAL FACTS
1485–1603

Ken Powell and Chris Cook

ROWMAN AND LITTLEFIELD
TOTOWA, NEW JERSEY

First published in the United States 1977
by Rowman and Littlefield, Totowa, N.J.

First published 1977 by
THE MACMILLAN PRESS LTD
London and Basingstoke

Printed in Great Britain

Library of Congress Cataloging in Publication Data

Powell, K. G.
    English historical facts, 1485–1603.
    Bibliography: p.
    1. Great Britain—History—Tudors, 1485–1603—
Dictionaries.   I. Cook, Chris, 1945–   joint author.
II. Title
DA315.P68   942.05′03   77–7323
ISBN 0-87471-865-1

CONTENTS

PREFACE AND ACKNOWLEDGEMENTS

This volume has attempted to present, within a single medium-sized book, a reference work on Tudor history that will be of value to teachers, to students and to research workers in this important period of English history. Within this book we have attempted to bring together as many of the important historical facts as can be reasonably assembled. Inevitably, however, no book of this type can be entirely comprehensive. In some areas (such as royal finance or estimates of Tudor population) the data is unreliable or indeed non-existent. Reasons of space also dictate the amount of information that can be presented.

In any book of this sort, the compilers owe a deep debt both to existing published works and to individual scholars who have offered help and advice. The chapter on war, rebellion and diplomacy was compiled by Stephen Brooks. David Starkey and Lira Winston offered much informed advice. Dr. Anita Travers offered much valuable advice based on her expert knowledge of Tudor economic policy. A very special debt is owed to Professor A. G. Dickens, who gave very valuable advice at the outset. Professor Joel Hurstfield also offered advice on specialist points.

Finally, we would like to appeal to scholars and others working in this field to point out any omissions or errors in this book, so that the volume may be expanded or enlarged in future editions.

Ken Powell
Chris Cook

April 1977

1 CROWN AND CENTRAL GOVERNMENT

THE MONARCHY AND THE HOUSEHOLD

THE MONARCHY

BIOGRAPHICAL DETAILS OF THE TUDOR MONARCHS

Henry VII (1485–1509)

Born at Pembroke Castle, 28 January 1457, the son of Edmund Tudor (Earl of Richmond) and of Margaret Beaufort (great-granddaughter of John of Gaunt, Duke of Lancaster, the third son of King Edward III). Henry VII was proclaimed King on Bosworth Field by Sir William Stanley (22 August 1485). Subsequently crowned (30 October 1485) by the Archbishop of Canterbury (Cardinal Bourchier). On 18 January 1486, Henry married Elizabeth Plantagenet (born 11 February 1466), the eldest daughter of King Edward IV. Henry VII died on 21 April 1509 at Richmond.

The marriage produced the following children:

(1) *Arthur*: Prince Arthur was born on 20 September 1486. To his original title of Duke of Cornwall were added the style of Prince of Wales and Earl of Chester (29 November 1489). On 14 November 1501 he married the Infanta, Katherine of Aragon (daughter of Ferdinand V of Spain). Arthur died, without issue, on 2 April 1502.

(2) *Margaret*: Princess Margaret was born on 29 November 1489. She married King James IV of Scotland (8 August 1503). Her first child (James V, King of Scotland) was born on 15 April 1512. Her husband, James IV, died at Flodden Field (9 September 1513). Princess Margaret died on 18 October 1541.

(3) *Henry*: Prince Henry (Henry VIII after 1509) was born on 28 June 1491 at Greenwich. On the death of his brother (Prince Arthur) he assumed the title of Duke of Cornwall. Created Prince of Wales and Earl of Chester, 18 February 1504. For biographical details when King, see below.

1

(4) *Mary*:   Born in March 1496. She married King Louis XII of France on 9 October 1514. Louis XII died only a short time later (on 1 January 1515) and there were no children of the marriage. Mary was married a second time (on 13 May 1515) to Sir Charles Brandon, Duke of Suffolk. Mary died on 25 June 1533; Suffolk on 22 February 1545.

(5) *Edmund*:   Born 21/22 February 1499. Created Duke of Somerset, the young Prince died on 19 June 1500.

The other children of Henry VII also died in infancy.

Henry VIII (1509–47)

Born at Greenwich, 28 June 1491, the son of Henry VII and Elizabeth of York. Succeeded to the throne, 22 April 1509. Crowned on 24 June, 1509. Died, 28 January 1547. In all, Henry made six marriages. These were

(1) *11 June 1509, Katherine of Aragon*
Henry's marriage to Katherine, the widow of his deceased brother, Arthur, produced four children, who died almost at once, and Mary, who was born on 18 February 1516, and was crowned Queen of England on 30 November 1553. The marriage to Katherine was declared null and void on 23 May 1533. The marriage was subsequently 'utterly dissolved' in March 1534 by Act of Parliament (25 Hen. VIII c.22). Katherine herself died on 8 January 1536

(2) *25 January 1533, Anne Boleyn*
Anne Boleyn was the daughter of Sir Thomas Boleyn, subsequently created Earl of Wiltshire and Ormonde. The marriage to Henry was declared valid on 28 May 1533. There were two children of the marriage.
   (i) a son, the Duke of Cornwall, was born in November 1534, but died in infancy.
   (ii) Elizabeth, who acceded to the throne on 17 November 1558.
The marriage was declared invalid (17 May 1536) and Anne Boleyn was executed on 19 May 1536.

(3) *30 May 1536, Jane Seymour*
Jane Seymour was the daughter of Sir John Seymour. The Queen died on 24 October 1537, having given birth to a son, Edward VI (*q.v.*).

(4) *6 January 1540, Anne of Cleves*
Anne was the daughter of John, Duke of Cleves. Henry annulled the marriage on 9 July 1540. Anne died in Chelsea on 17 July 1557.

(5) *28 July 1540, Catherine Howard*
Catherine Howard was the daughter of Lord Edmund Howard and niece of the Duke of Norfolk. She was beheaded on 13 February 1542.

(6) *12 July 1543, Catherine Parr*
Catherine Parr was the daughter of Sir Thomas Parr of Kendal. She

survived the King's death, marrying for a second time (Lord Seymour of Sudeley, uncle of Edward VI). She died on 5 September 1548.

Note: Henry also had an illegitimate son, Henry Fitzroy. Born in 1519, he was created Duke of Richmond and Somerset in 1525. He died on 22 July 1536.

Edward VI (1547–53)

The son of Henry VIII and Jane Seymour, Edward was born on 12 October 1537 at Hampton Court. He acceded to the throne on 28 January 1547 and was crowned on 25 February 1547. Edward's maternal uncle, Edward Seymour, Earl of Hertford, was designated Protector on 31 January 1547. On 16 February 1547 he was created Duke of Somerset. Somerset's position was further recognised when, on 12 March 1547, he was formally appointed *personae regiae gubernator ac regnorum dominiorum et subditorum nostrorum protector*. Edward VI died, unmarried, at Greenwich on 6 July 1553.

Note: Lady Jane Grey

On Edward's death, an unsuccessful attempt was made to secure the crown for Lady Jane Grey. Jane Grey's claim to the throne was a device engineered by Northumberland to prevent Mary's accession and preserve his own control of the state. Lady Jane Grey was born on October 1537, the daughter of Henry Grey, Marquis of Dorset and Duke of Suffolk, and of Frances, the daughter of Mary Tudor and granddaughter of Henry VII. Brought up in the household of Catherine Parr, Jane was an intelligent girl and a pious Protestant. Her father's alliance with Northumberland led to her marriage (21 May 1553) to Lord Guildford Dudley, a younger son of the latter. When Edward VI died in July of that year, Jane was declared Queen (6 July 1553). Within a week, her 'reign' was over. Her father was pardoned, but she was tried and condemned for treason and beheaded on 12 February 1554.

Mary I (1553–58)

Mary was born at Greenwich on 18 February 1516, the daughter of Henry VIII and Katherine of Aragon. She acceded to the throne on 19 July 1553 and was crowned on 30 November 1553. On 25 July 1554 she married Philip II of Spain (son of the Emperor Charles V). Mary died, without issue, in London on 17 November 1558. She was buried at Westminster.

Elizabeth I (1558–1603)

The daughter of Henry VIII and Anne Boleyn, Elizabeth was born at Greenwich on 7 September 1533. She acceded to the throne on 17 November 1558. She was crowned on 15 January 1559. She died, unmarried, at Richmond on 24 March 1603 and was buried at Westminster. She was succeeded by her kinsman, James VI of Scotland, who ascended the throne as James I.

CHRONOLOGY OF MAJOR EVENTS CONCERNING THE TUDOR DYNASTY

28 Jan 1457	Henry VII born at Pembroke Castle
22 Aug 1485	Henry proclaimed King on Bosworth Field
30 Oct 1485	Henry crowned King by Cardinal Bourchier
18 Jan 1486	Henry's marriage to Elizabeth Plantagenet
20 Sep 1486	Birth of Prince Arthur
29 Nov 1489	Birth of the Princess Margaret
28 June 1491	Birth of Prince Henry (Henry VIII) at Greenwich
Mar 1496	Birth of Princess Mary
14 Nov 1501	Marriage of Prince Arthur to the Infanta Katherine of Aragon.
2 Apr 1502	Death of Prince Arthur, without issue
8 Aug 1503	Marriage of Margaret to King James IV of Scotland
21 Apr 1509	Death of Henry VII at Richmond
11 June 1509	Henry VIII's marriage to Katherine of Aragon
24 June 1509	Henry VIII crowned
15 Apr 1512	Birth of James V of Scotland
9 Sep 1513	Death of James IV at Flodden Field
9 Oct 1514	Marriage of Princess Mary to Louis XII of France
18 Feb 1516	Birth of Mary, daughter of Henry VIII
25 Jan 1533	Henry's second marriage to Anne Boleyn
23 May 1533	Henry's original marriage to Katherine of Aragon declared null and void
7 Sep 1533	Birth of Elizabeth at Greenwich
Mar 1534	By Act of Parliament (25 Henry VIII c. 22) Henry's marriage to Katherine of Aragon declared 'utterly dissolved'
8 Jan 1536	Death of Katherine of Aragon
17 May 1536	Henry's marriage to Anne Boleyn declared invalid
19 May 1536	Execution of Anne Boleyn
30 May 1536	Henry's third marriage, to Jane Seymour
22 July 1536	Death of Henry VIII's illegitimate son, the Duke of Richmond
12 Oct 1537	Birth of Edward VI
24 Oct 1537	Death of Jane Seymour
6 Jan 1540	Henry's marriage to Anne of Cleves
9 July 1540	Marriage with Anne of Cleves annulled
28 July 1540	Henry's marriage to Catherine Howard
13 Feb 1542	Catherine Howard beheaded
12 July 1543	Henry's marriage to Catherine Parr
28 Jan 1547	Death of Henry VIII; accession of Edward VI
31 Jan 1547	Somerset declared Protector
25 Feb 1547	Edward VI's coronation
5 Sept 1548	Death of Catherine Parr
21 May 1553	Marriage of Lady Jane Grey to Lord Guildford Dudley

6 July 1553	Death of Edward VI, unmarried, at Greenwich
19 July 1553	Accession of Mary to the throne
30 Nov 1553	Mary crowned Queen
12 Feb 1554	Lady Jane Grey beheaded
25 July 1554	Marriage of Mary and Philip II of Spain
17 July 1557	Death of Anne Boleyn
17 Nov 1558	Death of Mary; accession of Elizabeth
15 Jan 1559	Coronation of Elizabeth
24 Mar 1603	Death of Elizabeth at Richmond

A NOTE ON THE ROYAL STYLE

At the accession of Henry VII, no change was made from the royal style used by Henry VI. The first change under the Tudors came in 1521, when the title of *fidei defensor* was conferred by Pope Leo X on Henry VIII. After 1525, Henry became the first English monarch who formally adopted a number to his name.

A change occurred in 1541 when, by 33 Hen. VIII c. 1, Henry VIII was declared King (instead of Lord) of Ireland. By an Act in 1543 (35 Hen. VIII c. 3), which declared it to be High Treason to deprive the King of this style, Henry's formal title was as follows: *Henricus Octavus Dei Gratia Angliae, Franciae, et Hiberniae Rex, Fidei Defensor, et in terra Ecclesiae Anglicanae et Hibernicae supremum caput*. In English, this was 'Henry the Eighth, by the grace of God King of England, France, and Ireland, Defender of the Faith, and of the Church of England and of Ireland on earth the Supreme Head'.

Edward VI was styled the same as Henry VIII. Important changes occurred under Mary. The statute 35 Hen. VIII c. 3 was duly repealed by 1 and 2 Ph and M 8, and the claim to supremacy was thus dropped. By a proclamation of 27 July 1554 the royal style became: 'Philip and Mary, by the Grace of God King and Queen of England, France, Naples, Jerusalem and Ireland, Defenders of the Faith, Princes of Spain and Sicily, Archdukes of Austria, Dukes of Milan, Burgundy, and Brabant, Counts of Habsburg, Flanders and Tyrol.'

With the accession of Elizabeth, the royal style used was: 'Elizabeth, by the grace of God Queen of England, France and Ireland, Defender of the Faith . . .'

TUDOR PEERAGE CREATIONS

Henry VII

1485	Thomas Grey	Restored Marquis of Dorset
	John de Vere	Restored Earl of Oxford (extinct 1702)
	John Welles	Restored Lord Welles

5

	Sir John Radcliffe	Lord FitzWalter (beheaded 1498)
	William Beaumont	Restored Viscount Beaumont (extinct 1508)
	Henry Clifford	Restored Lord Clifford
1486	Philibert de Shaunde	Earl of Bath (extinct 1486)
	Sir Giles D'Aubeny	Lord D'Aubeny
1487	John Cheney	Baron Cheney of Shurland (extinct 1495)
	John, Lord Welles	Viscount Welles (extinct in 1523)
	Thomas Burgh	Lord Burgh of Gainsborough (extinct 1598)
1489	Thomas Howard	Restored Earl of Surrey
	Earl of Nottingham	Marquis of Berkeley (titles extinct, 1492)
1492	Robert Willoughby	Lord Willoughby de Broke
	Thomas Bullen	Baron Ormond
1495	Baron Ormond	Baron Rochford of Rochford
1504	Henry Pole	Lord Montague of Montague (beheaded 1538)
1505	Robert Ratcliffe	Restored Lord FitzWalter
1506	Charles Somerset	Baron Herbert of Gower
1507	William Conyers	Baron Conyers of Hornby
	John Zouche	Lord Zouche of Codnor (extinct 1605)

Henry VIII

1509	Henry Stafford	Earl of Wiltshire (extinct 1523)
	Thomas D'Arcy	Lord D'Arcy (attainted 1538)
1512	John Scroop	Lord Scroop of Upsall (extinct 1517)
1513	Earl of Surrey	Restored Duke of Norfolk (attainted 1546, restored again 1553, attainted again 1572; restored Earl of Arundel in 1603)
	Sir Charles Brandon	Duke of Suffolk (extinct 1551)
	Margaret Plantagenet	Countess of Salisbury (beheaded 1541)
	John Touchet	Restored Lord Audley of Helleigh
1514	Baron Herbert	Earl of Worcester
	Edward Stanley	Lord Monteagle
1515	George Manners	Lord Roos
1523	Henry Marney	Lord Marney of Marney (extinct 1570)
	Henry Stafford	Restored Baron Stafford
	Sir William Parker	Lord Morley
1524	Nicholas Vaux	Lord Vaux of Harrowden
	William Sandys	Baron Sandys of the Vyne

6

1525	Henry Fitzroy	Earl of Nottingham, and Duke of Richmond and Somerset (extinct 1536)
	Henry Brandon	Earl of Lincoln (extinct 1551)
	Lord Roos	Earl of Rutland
	Lord Clifford	Earl of Cumberland
	Lord Ormond and Rochford	Viscount Rochford
	Lord FitzWalter	Viscount FitzWalter
	Earl of Devonshire	Marquis of Exeter (attainted 1538, restored 1553)
1529	Lord Hastings	Earl of Huntingdon
	Andrew Windsor	Lord Windsor of Bradenham
	John Hussey	Lord Hussey of Sleaford (attainted 1537)
	Viscount Rochford	Earl of Wiltshire and Ormond (extinct 1538)
	Viscount FitzWalter	Earl of Sussex
	Thomas Wentworth	Baron Wentworth of Nettlested
	John Mordaunt	Baron Mordaunt of Thurvey
1533	Arthur Plantagenet	Viscount Lisle
	George Boleyn	Baron Rochford (attainted 1536)
	Anne Boleyn	Marchioness of Pembroke
	Henry FitzAlan	Lord Maltravers
1536	Francis Talbot	Lord Talbot
	Edmund Bray	Baron Bray of Eaton-Bray
	Lord FitzWarren	Earl of Bath
	Thomas Cromwell	Baron Cromwell of Wimbledon
	Gilbert Talbois	Baron Talbois of Kyme (extinct 1550)
	Sir Edward Seymour	Viscount Beauchamp of Hache
	Walter Hungerford	Lord Hungerford of Heytesbury (beheaded 1540)
1537	Sir William FitzWilliam	Earl of Southampton (extinct 1542)
	Viscount Beauchamp	Earl of Hertford
1538	Thomas Audley	Lord Audley of Walden (extinct 1554)
1539	Sir William Paulet	Baron St John of Basing
	William Parr	Baron Parr
	Lord D'Aubeny	Earl of Bridgewater (extinct 1548)
	John Russel	Lord Russel of Cheneys
1540	Lord Cromwell	Earl of Essex (beheaded 1540)
	Baron Cromwell of Wimbledon	Baron Cromwell of Okeham
1542	John Dudley	Baron Somerai, Basset and Teyes, and Viscount Lisle

7

1543	Baron Parr of Kendal	Earl of Essex
	William Parr	Baron Parr of Horton (extinct 1560)
	Thomas Wriothesley	Baron Wriothesley of Titchfield
	William Eure	Baron Eure of Wilton
1544	Edward Poynings	Lord Poynings (extinct 1560)
	Thomas Wharton	Lord Wharton of Wharton

King Edward VI

1547	Earl of Hertford	Baron Seymour of Hache, and the next day Duke of Somerset (attainted 1551)
	Earl of Essex	Marquis of Northampton (attainted 1553; restored 1559; extinct 1571)
	Viscount Lisle	Earl of Warwick
	Thomas Seymour	Lord Seymour of Sudley Castle (attainted 1549)
	Edmund Sheffield	Lord Sheffield of Butterwicke
	Richard Rich	Lord Rich of Leeze
	William Willoughby	Lord Willoughby of Parham
	Lord Wriothesley	Earl of Southampton (attainted 1601; restored 1603)
	John Lumley	Lord Lumley
	John Russell	Lord Russell
1548	George D'Arcy	Lord D'Arcy of Aston
	Lord St John of Basing	Earl of Wiltshire
1549	Lord Russell	Earl of Bedford
	Lord Ferrers of Chartley	Viscount Hereford
1550	Walter Paget	Baron Paget of Beaudesert (attainted 1586; restored 1603)
1552	Earl of Wiltshire	Marquis of Winchester
	Thomas Darcy	Baron Darcy of Chiche
	William Herbert	Lord Herbert of Cardiff, and Earl of Pembroke
	Marquis of Dorset	Duke of Suffolk (attainted 1553)
	Earl of Warwick	Duke of Northumberland (forfeited 1553)
	Lord John Dudley	Earl of Warwick (beheaded 1553)
	George Lord Talbot	Lord Talbot

Queen Mary I

1553	Edward Courtenay	Restored Earl of Devonshire, and Marquis of Exeter (extinct 1556)

8

	Thomas Howard	Restored Duke of Norfolk (attainted 1572, restored 1603)
	Edward North	Baron North of Kirtling
	Thomas Howard	Baron Howard of Effingham
	John Williams	Baron Williams of Thame (extinct 1559)
	Sir John Brudges	Baron Chandos of Sudley Castle
	Anthony Browne	Viscount Montague
	John Paulet	Lord St John of Basing
	Thomas Ratcliffe	Lord FitzWalter
1557	Thomas Percy	Restored Baron Percy, Poynings, Lucy, Bryan and FitzPaine; and next day Earl of Northumberland
	Sir Edward Hastings	Baron Hastings of Loughborough

Queen Elizabeth I

1559	William Parr	Restored Marquis of Northampton (extinct 1571)
	Edward Seymour	Restored Earl of Hertford, and Baron Beauchamp of Hacche
	Thomas Howard	Viscount Bindon of Bindon
	Henry Carey	Lord Hunsdon of Hunsdon
	Oliver St John	Lord St John of Bletso
	Henry Hastings	Lord Hastings
	Henry Stanley	Lord Strange of Knockyn
1562	Ambrose Dudley	Lord Lisle, and Earl of Warwick (extinct 1580)
1564	Robert Dudley	Baron Denbigh, and Earl of Leicester (extinct 1588)
1567	Sir Thomas Sackville	Lord Buckhurst of Buckhurst
1568	Thomas West	Baron Lawarr
1570	Sir William Cecil	Lord Burleigh of Burleigh
1572	Viscount Hereford	Earl of Essex (forfeited 1601; restored 1603)
	Lord Clinton	Earl of Lincoln
	William Paulet	Baron St John of Basing
	Henry Compton	Lord Compton of Compton
	Henry Cheney	Lord Cheney of Tuddington (extinct 1595)
	Henry Norreys	Baron Norreys of Rycote
1580	Philip Howard	Earl of Arundel
	Peregrine Bertie	Baron Willoughby of Eresby
1590	Ferdinando Stanley	Lord Strange of Knockyn
	Gilbert Talbot	Baron Talbot

9

	William Paulet	Lord St John of Basing
1597	Lord Howard of Effingham	Earl of Nottingham
	Thomas Howard	Baron Howard of Walden

CONTEMPORARY EUROPEAN SOVEREIGNS 1485–1603

(1) *The Papacy*

Innocent VIII (Giambattista Cibo)	1484–92
Alexander VI (Rodrigo Borgia)	1492–1503
Pius III (Francesco Todeschini)	1503 (Sep–Oct)
Julius II (Giulio della Rovere)	1503–13
Leo X (Giovanni de' Medici)	1513–21
Adrian VI (Adrian of Utrecht)	1522–3
Clement VII (Giulio de' Medici)	1523–34
Paul III (Alessandro Farnese)	1534–49
Julius III (Giovanni del Monte)	1550–5
Marcellus II (Marcello Cervini)	1555
Paul IV (Pietro Caraffa)	1556–9
Pius IV (Gian-Angelo de' Medici)	1559–65
Pius V (Michele Ghislieri)	1565–72
Gregory XIII (Ugo Buoncompagno)	1572–85
Sixtus V (Felix Peretti)	1585–90
Urban VII (Giambattista Castagna)	1590
Gregory XIV (Niccolo Sfondrato)	1590–91
Innocent IX (Gian-Antonio Fachinetto)	1591
Clement VIII (Ippolito Aldobrandini)	1592–1605

(2) *The Holy Roman Emperors* (House of Habsburg)

Frederick III	1440–93
Maximilian I	1493–1519
Charles V (died 1558)	1519–56
Ferdinand I	1556–64
Maximilian II	1564–76
Rudolf II	1576–1612

(3) *France*

Charles VIII	1483–98
Louis XII	1498–1515
Francis I	1515–47
Henry II	1547–59
Francis II	1559–60
Charles IX	1560–74
Henry III	1574–89
Henry IV	1589–1610

(4) *Portugal*

John II	1481–95
Manuel I	1495–1521
John III	1521–57
Sebastian	1557–78
Henry	1578–80

After 1580, Portugal was ruled by the Spanish Kings

Philip I (II of Spain)	1580–98
Philip II (III)	1598–1621

(5) *Spain*

  (a) *The Catholic Kings*

Isabella of Castille	1474–1504
Ferdinand of Aragon	1479–1516

  (b) *The House of Habsburg*

Charles I (V)	1516–58
Philip II	1558–98
Philip III	1598–1621

(6) *Sweden*

Gustavus I	1523–60
Eric XIV (deposed; died 1577)	1560–8
John III	1568–92
Sigismund (deposed; died 1632)	1592–1604
Charles IX	1604–11

(7) *Denmark and Norway*

Christian II (deposed; died 1559)	1513–23
Frederick I	1523–33
Christian III	1533–59
Frederick II	1559–88
Christian IV	1588–1648

(8) *The United Provinces*

William I (murdered)	1584
Maurice	1584–1625

(9) *The Ottoman Empire*

Mohammed II	1451–81	Selim II	1566–74
Bayezid II	1481–1512	Murad III	1574–95
Selim I	1512–20	Mohammed III	1595–1603
Suleiman I	1520–66	Ahmad I	1603–1617

11

(10) *Scotland*

James III	1460–88	James V	1513–42
James IV	1488–1513	James VI	1566–1625

THE HOUSEHOLD

OFFICIALS OF THE EXCHEQUER, 1485–1558

Introductory Note

During this period of significant Exchequer decline the real work in the Exchequer of Receipt was carried out by the Under-Treasurer and Chamberlains. The Chancellor's office, which originally developed from the clerkship of the Chancellor, was of minor importance at this time. The Chancellor's duties were restricted to the Upper Exchequer. The position of Treasurer was more nominal than real, and, under Henry VIII, commonly bestowed upon prominent members of the nobility.

Chancellors of the Exchequer

12 Oct 1485–28 May 1516	Sir Thomas Lovell
29 May 1516–n.a. 1527	John Bourchier (Lord Berners)
n.a. 1527–n.a. 1533	Robert Radcliffe
12 Apr 1533–29 July 1540	Thomas Cromwell (see p. 210)
Aug 1540–Dec 1558	Sir John Baker

Treasurers of the Exchequer

6 Dec 1484	Sir John Tuchet (Lord Audley)
14 July 1486	Sir John Dynham (Lord Dynham)
16 Jun 1501	Thomas Howard (Earl of Surrey)
4 Dec 1522	Thomas Howard (2nd Earl of Surrey and 2nd Duke of Norfolk)
10 Feb 1547	Edward Seymour (Earl of Hertford) (see p. 217)
3 Feb 1550	William Paulet (1st Earl of Wiltshire)
July 1572	William Cecil, Lord Burghley (see p. 209)
15 May 1599	Sir Thomas Sackville (1st Lord Buckhurst)

OFFICIALS OF THE HOUSEHOLD, 1485–1558

Treasurers of the Household

Oct 1485	Sir Richard Croft	May 1527	Sir William FitzWilliam
Aug 1492	Sir Thomas Lovell	Oct 1537	Sir William Paulet
Apr 1522	Sir Thomas Boleyn	Mar 1539	Sir Thomas Cheyney

Cofferers

1485–8	John Payne	June 1509–May 1527	John Shirley
1488–1509	William Cope	May 1527–Apr 1564	Edmund Peckham

Comptrollers of the Household

1485	Richard Edgecumbe	1540	John Gage
1492	Roger Tocotes	1547	William Paget
1498	Richard Guildford	1550	Anthony Wingfield
1509	Edward Poynings	1552	Richard Cotton
1520	Henry Guildford	1553	Robert Rochester
1526	William FitzWilliam	1557	Thomas Cornwallis
1532	William Paulet	1558	Thomas Parry
1537	John Russell		

Great Masters or Lords Stewards of the Household

1485	John Radcliffe	1540	Charles Brandon
1488	Robert Willoughby	1545	William Paulet
1490	William Stanley	1550	John Dudley
1506	George Talbot	1553	Henry FitzAlan

Treasurers of the Chamber

Apr 1484–Nov 1485	Edmund Chaderton
Nov 1485–Aug 1492	Sir Thomas Lovell
Aug 1492–Feb 1521	Sir John Heron
Feb 1521–May 1523	John Micklowe
May 1523–Jan 1524	Edmund Peckham
Jan 1524–Apr 1528	Sir Henry Wyatt
Apr 1528–Oct 1545	Sir Brian Tuke
Nov 1545–Feb 1546	Sir Anthony Rous
Feb 1546–Oct 1558	Sir William Cavendish
Oct 1558–	Sir John Mason

Keepers of the Jewel House

Sir William Tyler	Sep 1485–14 Sep 1486
Sir Henry Wyatt	14 Sep 1486–Jan 1522
Sir Thomas Wyatt	21 Oct 1525–10 Apr 1526
Robert Amadas	20 Apr 1526–6 Apr 1530
Sir John Williams	6 Apr 1530–12 Apr 1532
Thomas Cromwell	12 Apr 1532–29 July 1540
Sir John Williams	Spring 1536–1 May 1544
Sir Anthony Rous	1 May 1544–29 Sep 1545
Anthony Aucher	29 Sep 1545–

13

Chief Butlers of England

Sir John Fortescue	26 Sep 1485–28 July 1501
Sir Robert Southwell	12 Nov 1504–30 Mar 1514
Sir John Daunce	25 July 1515–30 Sep 1517
Sir Edward Belknap	30 Sep 1517–Mar 1521
Sir John Hussey	1 June 1521–1537
Sir Francis Brian	14 Sep 1535–

THE PRIVY COUNCIL

EVOLUTION AND POWERS

Sir John Fortescue provided a sound indication of the composition of the fifteenth-century Council when he wrote that it was 'chose off grete princes, and off the greteste lordes off the lande, both spirituelles and temporellis, and also off other men that were in grete auctorite and offices'.[1]

The Council described by Fortescue was a reflection of the power structure of England, containing representatives of the great secular magnates and of the episcopacy. Kings had always surrounded themselves with advisers and these advisers had included both the great men whose advice they could ill afford to ignore and humbler men of talent, selected purely for their abilities. Every monarch was circumscribed in the choice of his counsellors – those who broke the rules often came to unfortunate ends – but the right to choose them remained his and his alone. The Council governed under the monarch – it was *his* Council. It was sometimes convenient for disgruntled subjects to believe that a monarch was being misled by his counsellors and many who disliked the religious changes of the 1530s blamed not Henry VIII but the 'naughty harlots' around him – as a Norfolk man described the Council.[2] This particular subject had no doubt that 'the government' which was taking actions of which he disapproved consisted of both King and Council.

Medieval Councils were large bodies and it was difficult for them to remain in constant assembly. The bishops, magnates and others had their own interests to look after and in general the Council met at Westminster only during the legal terms. The advice, administrative expertise and judgement it offered was however necessary throughout the year and often the monarch had to hand only those members who were royal officers or members of the Household. In the absence of the rest of the Council these men constituted a body reduced in size but not in competence. If especially difficult matters were under discussion it was possible for action to be deferred until all members were present but this was not an inevitable course and indeed the Council often deputed small 'sub-committees' to deal with matters demanding lengthy investigation. A small group of men could often work more quickly and effectively and recognition of this fact prompted Thomas Cromwell's reform of the Council and establishment of the Privy Council as the supreme executive in the 1530s. Henry VII had followed medieval precedent by surrounding himself with a large Council – forty to fifty was the usual attendance at meetings – selected on traditional lines. The breakdown of government in the mid-fifteenth century had brought the Council under magnate domination. Henry Tudor placed at his side only those he trusted and thought able, whether the traditional nobility, clerics (like Bishop Fox) or civil servants (like Sir Reginald Bray). This large Council, which could have become unwieldy and ineffective, was made more flexible by the gradual separation of its judicial functions. The councillors who sat in Star Chamber and Requests were drawn from the larger Council, as were the 'inner ring' of advisers who accompanied the King on his progresses through England.

Henry VIII inherited this large Council from his father but his very different personality led him to place an unprecedented amount of power in the hands of Thomas Wolsey. Wolsey was not especially interested in conciliar government but his unpredictable governmental genius produced proposals, the Eltham Ordinances of 1526, for a smaller Council of about twenty. The proposals sank when Wolsey first lost interest and then fell from power. But by the mid-1530s Thomas Cromwell had created a new small Council, the Privy Council, very much on these lines. In 1536 the Privy Council had nineteen members and this new executive instrument soon caused the demise of the wider Council, which had lost its *raison d'être* (some individuals were referred to for a brief period as 'ordinary councillors'). Most of the new Privy Council were office-holders, professional royal servants sitting as a board of management under the chairmanship of the King. As principal secretary Cromwell gathered a vast concentration of power into his own hands and often took the initiative in government from the Council, whose business he personally superintended and organised.

Cromwell's fall in 1540 was a profoundly significant event in the history of the Privy Council, which now began to record its deliberations in a minute book. For the first time a permanent clerk was appointed to serve the Council. The judicial and administrative work of the Council, two very distinct functions, were from henceforth permanently separated, although Privy Council members still sat in both Council and Star Chamber. It was simply that 'the two aspects of the work done by these men were embodied in separate institutions'.[3] Both Star Chamber and Requests had emerged from the judicial sessions of the Council, but it was never truly a court of law, despite its right to initiate legal action and refer criminal matters to other courts. The removal of Cromwell might have offered a new measure of governmental initiative to the Council, yet the reigns of Edward VI and Mary produced large and ineffective Councils which reflected the weakness of the Crown. Quite early in Edward's reign the Council, increasingly the instrument of faction, numbered forty; and its inability to act effectively led to the establishment of a number of committees, which were the only reliable means of dealing rapidly with the King's business. Efforts at reform were made but the divisions within the Council's ranks made agreement on its reconstitution impossible.

The reign of Mary saw no attempt at reform: the Council grew in numbers and declined in efficacy. In effect the Queen took decisions on the advice of a few trusted confidants, most notably Reginald Pole. As a result her administration assumed a character increasingly out of touch with the nation. When Elizabeth came to the throne she made a deliberate decision to return to the concept of a small group of reliable advisers. The Elizabethan Privy Council usually numbered about a dozen and between 1559 and 1603 only fifty-eight individuals served as members. Between 1509 and 1527 exactly twice that number had served Henry VIII.[4] The omnicompetent, omniscient Elizabethan Privy Council was an important factor in the great revival of the Tudor monarchy under Elizabeth. It was the means whereby the monarchy was able to function successfully and the vital link between Crown and Parliament, Crown and country. The Privy Council governed England and concerned itself with everything that went on within the realm of the Queen. With a newly augmented bureaucratic machinery, it was often able to act with a measure of efficiency surprising in an England which lacked a permanent civil service. The success of the Council was inevitably linked to the fact that its members were involved in English society and government at every level. Because most councillors were landed magnates, the Council had access to the services of a large number of retainers throughout the country. All Privy Councillors were Justices of the Peace, most in a number of shires, many were Lords Lieutenant with a finger on the political pulse of the regions. Throughout the reign councillors sat in Parliament, representing the interests of the Queen in a period when opposition in Parliament was growing.

The work of the Privy Council can be gauged by a study of its recorded 'acts' – the agenda for its meetings. Meeting at Westminster in February 1566 it discussed the provisioning of the troops in Ireland, the release of certain prisoners in the Tower on bail, the licensing of the French Ambassador's butcher to sell meat in Lent, and a warrant to finance children's plays at Court. In August 1562, meeting at Greenwich, the Council discussed cases of fraud in Wiltshire, the problem of gipsies in Oxfordshire and military levies in Essex. At St James's Palace in November 1564, the matters on the agenda included the selling of prohibited wares by various traders, the state of the Kent garrisons, the repair of the pier at Scarborough and the arrest of an Oxford doctor for recusancy.[5] In obtaining the implementation of its decisions the Council made use of a large and varied range of agencies throughout England, prominent among them the Justices and Lords Lieutenant. The J.P.s were closely controlled by the Council. When Elizabeth came to the throne many counties were in the hands of predominantly Catholic justices and a definite programme of dismissal and replacement was carried out where

16

necessary. In Norfolk sixteen of forty-two justices were removed from office and within a few years attempts were made to further reduce their numbers.[6] In many shires it remained difficult to obtain a prompt execution of government orders and sometimes especially difficult local conditions demanded extraordinary measures.

The regional Councils were one example of the extension of the Council's work through a special agency. The Third Earl of Huntingdon, while President of the Council in the North, received a constant stream of orders from the Council in London about such miscellaneous topics as the regulation of market trading at Leicester, piracy at Hull, recusancy, the suppression of disorder and the raising of musters. Conversely Huntingdon often asked the Council for advice on a variety of issues and generally acted as agent of the Council rather than as an independent agent.[7] The special ecclesiastical commissions, like that set up in the dioceses of Bristol and Gloucester in 1574, were similarly under the close supervision of the Privy Council, whence they derived their authority. The Council did not interfere in the workings of the Bristol and Gloucester commission but was on several occasions called upon by the commission to use its supreme authority to punish powerful local offenders. The arrogance of a landowner who was influential in Gloucestershire was usually much reduced when he was called to appear in London before the Queen's Council.[8]

On many occasions the Privy Council was the scapegoat for the bad judgement of the Queen herself, although she was often genuinely in need of advice on difficult issues. In 1570 Elizabeth came to the Council for advice on the treatment of Mary Stuart: 'She assured them that she herself was free from any determined resolution and that she would first hear their advice and thereupon make choice of what she would think meetest for her honour.'[9] In most cases the Council offered the best advice that the Queen could receive but the increasing conservatism of the latter part of the reign gripped the Council as much as the monarch. Throughout the Tudor period and especially during Elizabeth's reign the Council was often guilty of mismanagement, petty factionalism and of both interfering with the laws of the realm and at the same time frequently failing to achieve its aims. Its role as a political arena for the manoeuvrings of the Cecils, Walsingham, Leicester, Essex and the other politicians of the period was in no small part a cause of its decline as an organ of government. The purpose of the Privy Council was 'the preservation of ... good subjects in quytnes amonge themselves'[10] and government by Privy Council was authoritarian government. The decline of the Privy Council was part and parcel of the general decline of the Tudor system.

NOTES

1. J. Fortescue, *The Governance of England*, ed. C. Plummer (Oxford, 1885) p. 145.
2. G. R. Elton, *Policy and Police* (Cambridge, 1972) p. 306.

3. G. R. Elton, *Studies in Tudor and Stuart Politics and Government* (Cambridge, 1974) I, p. 320.

4. Calculated by M. B. Pulman: *The Elizabethan Privy Council in the Fifteen-Seventies* (Berkeley, U.S.A., 1971) pp. 13, 17.

5. *A. P. C.*, *VIII, 1558–70*, ed. J. R. Dasent (London, 1893) *passim*.

6. A. Hassell-Smith, *County and Court: Government and Politics in Norfolk, 1558–1603* (Oxford, 1974) pp. 80–2.

7. C. Cross, *The Puritan Earl: The Life of Henry Hastings, Third Earl of Huntingdon, 1536–1595* (London, 1966) *passim*.

8. F. D. Price, *The Commission for Ecclesiastical Causes in the Dioceses of Bristol and Gloucester, 1574* (Bristol and Gloucestershire Archaeological Society, n.d.) pp. 18–20.

9. C. Read, *Lord Burghley and Queen Elizabeth* (London, 1960) p. 21.

10. Pulman, *op. cit.*, p. 249.

CHRONOLOGY

THE PRIVY COUNCIL 1485–1603

1487   'Star Chamber' Act gave widespread powers to the Council to act in matters of sedition and corruption.

1526   Wolsey's Eltham Ordinances proposed a reduced Council of about twenty members.

1534–6   Cromwell's reforms produced the true Privy Council.

1540   Minutes began to be kept and a Clerk of Privy Council was appointed.

1552   The Privy Council set up a special commission to examine the King's financial problems.

1553   Edward VI proposed a reform of the Privy Council to expedite the handling of important business.

1553   Mary set up a number of special committees to deal with business usually the concern of the whole Council.

1559   The accession of Elizabeth brought an immediate reduction in the size of the Privy Council.

1582   The first of many attempts was made to limit the amount of private business coming before Privy Council – it was largely unsuccessful and private suits clogged proceedings increasingly.

THE SEALS AND THE SECRETARY

THE SEALS

Tudor government was monarchical government – the monarch actually ruled – as English government had been throughout the medieval centuries. The Tudor period saw the dramatic revival of the monarchy after the tragic debacle of the 1450s and 1460s and this revival was characteristically founded on both innovation and the enlightened use of precedent. Kings had always in fact been obliged to take into account the views of their more powerful subjects and the *curia* (or Council) always contained both magnates and the king's selected personal advisers. Such was the case in Tudor England. The principal officer of the Anglo-Norman kings was the Chancellor, who kept the great seal (needed to authenticate royal orders). The characteristic development of the later middle ages was the growth in the use of the privy seal, a means of making administration more flexible after the great seal had become 'institutionalised' with an office of clerks. The privy seal itself underwent a similar process of institutionalisation: hence the development of the signet. The advantage of the privy seal and the signet was that they enabled the monarch to by-pass the Chancellor's office (the Chancery) and govern in a more personal fashion. (Richard II attempted to govern in an arbitrary manner by the use of his signet.) The great seal always remained the final instrument of government, but was activated via the signet and privy seal. Apart from its use as the actual instrument of government the great seal was needed to validate royal grants of land and of offices – grants of land, in particular, were much more numerous after the dissolution of the monasteries in the 1530s.

In the early fifteenth-century the Council was at the peak of its powers as a policy-making, administrative and judicial body. Thereafter government fell into the hands of the civil servants and ministers, the king's picked men, as the monarchy reasserted itself. Under Edward IV and Henry VII the Council was effectively managed by the ministers, who were backed by their departments. The greatest of these departments was Chancery, which was rapidly developing, within the same period, into a great law court with legal personnel. Its legal business rose steadily in volume, from an average of 553 cases per annum in 1475–85 to 770 per annum during Wolsey's tenure of the office of Lord Chancellor.[1] (For the Chancery as a law court, see pp. 44–5.) The Tudors stabilised the office of Lord Chancellor with the long tenures of Morton, Warham and Wolsey. The latter was the last Chancellor to be the monarch's chief officer and later holders of the office were lawyers. The Chancellor became the chief legal officer of the Crown – and remains so to the present day. Only under Mary was there a brief reversion to the old idea of a clerical Chancellor, Stephen Gardiner in particular being the central figure in government.

The Tudor period saw in fact the decline of the seals as governmental instruments. For long periods under Elizabeth there was no Lord Chancellor and the office of Lord Privy Seal was held by men whose chief source of power lay in their tenure of another office, that of Secretary of State. Use of the seals became ever more formalised and the proliferation of government departments with their own seals undermined the old system still further.

NOTE
1. N. Pronay, 'The Chancellor, the Chancery, and the Council at the End of the Fifteenth Century', in *British Government and Administration: Studies Presented to S. B. Chrimes*, ed. H. Hearder and H. R. Loyn (Cardiff, 1974) p. 89.

LORD CHANCELLORS (AND KEEPERS) 1485–1603

1485	Thomas Rotherham, Archbishop of York
1485–7	John Alcock, successively Bishop of Worcester and of Ely
1487–1500	John Morton, Archbishop of Canterbury (see p. 216)
[1500–2	Henry Deane, Archbishop of Canterbury, Keeper]
[1502–4	William Warham, successively Bishop of London and Archbishop of Canterbury, Keeper (see p. 219)]
1504–15	William Warham
1515–29	Thomas Wolsey, successively Bishop of Bath and Wells, Lincoln, Durham, Archbishop of York, Cardinal (1515) and Papal Legate *a latere* (1518) (see p. 220)
1529–32	Sir Thomas More (see p. 215)
[1532–3	Sir Thomas Audley, Keeper]
1533–44	Sir Thomas Audley (1st Lord Audley, 1538)
1544–7	Thomas Wriothesley, 1st Lord Wriothesley (1st Earl of Southampton, 1547)
[1547	William Paulet, 1st Lord St John, Keeper]
1547–51	Richard Rich, 1st Lord Rich
[1551–2	Thomas Goodrich, Bishop of Ely, Keeper]
1552–3	Thomas Goodrich
1553–5	Stephen Gardiner, Bishop of Winchester (see p. 212)
1556–8	Nicholas Heath, Archbishop of York
[1558–79	Sir Nicholas Bacon, Lord Keeper]
1579–87	Sir Thomas Bromley
1587–91	Sir Christopher Hatton (see p. 214)
[1592–6	Sir John Puckering, Lord Keeper]
[1596–1603	Sir Thomas Egerton, Lord Keeper (1st Lord Ellesmere, 1603)]

SOURCE Sir Maurice Powicke and E. B. Fryde (eds), *Handbook of British Chronology.*

KEEPERS OF THE PRIVY SEAL 1485–1603

1485–7	Peter Courtenay, Bishop of Exeter
1487–1516	Richard Fox, successively Bishop of Exeter, Bath and Wells, Durham and Winchester (see p. 212)
1516–23	Thomas Ruthall, Bishop of Durham
1523	Sir Henry Marny, 1st Lord Marny
1523–30	Cuthbert Tunstal, Bishop of London (see p. 218)
1530–6	Thomas Boleyn, 1st Earl of Wiltshire and Ormonde.
1536–40	Thomas Cromwell, 1st Lord Cromwell (1st Earl of Essex, 1540) (see p. 210)
1540–2	William FitzWilliam, 1st Earl of Southampton
1542–55	John Russell, 1st Lord Russell (1st Earl of Bedford, 1550)
1555	William Paget, 1st Lord Paget
1559?–72	William Cecil (1st Lord Burghley, 1571) (see p. 209)

1572–3   William Howard, 1st Lord Howard of Effingham
1573–6   Sir Thomas Smith (Secretary of State, 1572–6)
1576–90   Sir Francis Walsingham (Secretary of State, 1573–90) (see p. 219)
1590–8   Lord Burghley
1598–1603 Robert Cecil (see p. 209)

SOURCE *Handbook of British Chronology* (op. cit.).

THE SECRETARY

The government of modern Britain is carried on by ministers, or Secretaries of State, who are the Queen's ministers with special responsibility for particular aspects of government, such as defence or education. The system was developed in the Tudor period to replace the old system of government by seals and is one of the major administrative legacies of the Tudor age. Up to the 1530s the Secretary was the king's personal secretary, a trusted adviser who kept the signet but was not on a level with the great officers of state. Secretaries were by no means inevitably members of the Council. Between 1533 and 1540 Thomas Cromwell made the office of Secretary the principal and central office of all government, while the Chancellorship was pushed firmly into a subordinate, principally judicial, role. William Cecil was Cromwell's greatest successor in the office. After Cromwell's removal in 1540, there were usually two Secretaries and it was not until the late Elizabethan period that it was formally accepted that one was very much the assistant of the other.

The office of Secretary was for a long period only very vaguely defined and its place in the government depended largely on the individuals who held it. Sir Thomas Smith was such an abject failure in 1548–9 and offended both the main 'parties' in the state so effectively that he was forced to resign and was gaoled for a period.[1] William Petre on the other hand provided unspectacular but efficient continuity in administration at a time of political instability.[2] Nicholas Faunt, an aide of Walsingham, who attempted to define the Secretary's work in the early 1590s admitted that the office was characterised by 'variety and uncertainty'.[3] The chief function of the Secretary was that of a link between Crown and Council, Crown and Parliament, Crown and people. He was also head of the diplomatic service and general guardian of the peace of the realm. The Secretary was the manager of the Council and drew up its agenda. Robert Beale, who produced a 'Treatise of the Office of a Counsellor and Principal Secretary to her Majesty', advised that the Secretary should ensure that Council meetings did not waste time on trivial matters: they should deal only with 'such things as shall be propounded unto them'.[4] Cromwell and the Cecils were plainly the central continuous personalities in the Council for long periods, although their power rested not on primacy in the Council through political means but on the fact that they had the monarch's trust. From the 1540s the Secretaries were instructed to attend both Houses of Parliament regularly, here again almost personifying the Crown interest.

The Secretaries were never peers and when William Cecil became Lord Burghley he ceased to be Secretary – although still a key figure in the state. The Secretaries had precedence over peers and over all the officials of the Household. Their official salaries were not great, but it was accepted that Tudor officials might legitimately derive financial benefits from office-holding. Although William Petre's salary in 1555 was only £100 he derived from his office an income of over £1000.[5] The greatest of the Tudor Secretaries were both ingenious managers and skilful politicians, but they had to be efficient bureaucrats too. At the centre of their task lay the Tudor balance between government which was purely monarchical and government which rested on a Council responsible to the country as a whole and subject to the growing pressure of Parliament. The Secretary was the pivot of government and Robert Cecil candidly defined the ingredients of success in the office along these lines:

A secretary must either conceive the very thought of a king, which is only proper to God, or a king must exercise the painful office of a secretary, which is contrary to majesty and liberty; or else a prince must make choice of such a servant of such a prince as the prince's assurance must be his confidence in the secretary and the secretary's life his trust in the prince.[6]

NOTES

1. M. Dewar, *Sir Thomas Smith* (London, 1964) p. 36ff.
2. See F. G. Emmison, *Tudor Secretary* (London, 1961).
3. Nicholas Faunt, 'A Discourse touching the Office of Principal Secretary of State', in *E.H.R.*, xx (1903) p. 500.
4. Robert Beale, 'Treatise of the Office of a Counsellor and Principal Secretary to her Majesty', in C. Read, *Mr. Secretary Walsingham* (Oxford, 1925) I, p. 424.
5. Emmison, op. cit., p. 322.
6. Robert Cecil, 'The State and Dignity of a Secretary of State's Place', cited by F. M. G. Evans, *The Principal Secretary of State* (Manchester, 1923) p. 59.

SECRETARIES OF STATE

1485 Dr Richard Fox (see p. 212)	1528 Dr Stephen Gardiner (Bishop of Winchester from 1531,
1487 Dr Owen King	see p. 212)
1500 Dr Thomas Ruthall	
1516 Dr Richard Pace	1533 Thomas Cromwell (see p. 210)
1526 Dr William Knight	

PRINCIPAL SECRETARIES

1540–4	Sir Thomas Wriothesley	1548–9	Sir Thomas Smith
1540–3	Sir Ralph Sadler	1549–50	Sir Nicholas Wotton
1543–8	Sir William Paget	1550–3	Sir William Cecil (see
1544–57	Sir William Petre		p. 209)

1553	Sir John Cheke	1577–81	Thomas Wilson
1553–8	Sir John Bourne	1586–7	William Davison
1557–8	Sir John Boxall	1596–1603	Sir Robert Cecil (see
1558–72	Sir William Cecil	1600	p. 209)
1572–6	Sir Thomas Smith		John Herbert
1573–90	Sir Francis Walsingham (see p. 219)		

SOURCE   F. M. G. Evans, *The Principal Secretary of State* (Manchester, 1923).

ROYAL FINANCE

TUDOR FINANCIAL ADMINISTRATION

CHRONOLOGY OF MAJOR EVENTS

1491   Henry VII levies a benevolence.

1492   Customs yield estimated at £3700.

1503   A regular Master of the Wards appointed, with supporting organisation, to make certain of this source of revenue.

1508   Short-lived office of Surveyor of the King's Prerogative.

1512   Experiment of the Graduated Poll Tax.

1514   Wolsey's first Subsidy.

1515   The Act concerning the King's General Surveyors (6 Hen. VIII c. 24). This Act only operated from one Parliament to the next. Made permanent in 1535.

1523   Wolsey's 'anticipation' offers easier terms to those agreeing to pay taxes earlier than Parliament had stipulated.

1525   Wolsey's 'Amicable Grant' abandoned because of violent opposition.

1528   Sir Brian Tuke appointed Treasurer of the Chamber; growing complexity of the internal organisation of the office.

1531   *Praemunire* fine imposed on clergy raised £118,000.

1536–40   Vesting of all monastic property in the Crown.

1536   An Act establishing the Court of Augmentations (27 Hen. VIII c. 27).

1540   By the Act 32 Hen. VIII c. 45, First Fruits and Tenths constituted a Court; in the same year (32 Hen. VIII c. 46) the Court of Wards and Liveries was responsible for feudal revenue.

1542   By the act of 33 Hen. VIII c. 39, the General Surveyors reduced to the status of a Court.

1545   Benevolence levied by Henry VIII.

1547   General Surveyors and Augmentations were combined into one office (Second Court of Augmentations).

1554   After lengthy discussion, all the new Courts absorbed into the Exchequer.

1558	New Book of Rates for Customs.
1583	New Book of Rates introduced.
1590	New Book of Rates introduced.

PRINCIPLE OFFICE-HOLDERS CONCERNED WITH FINANCE

CLERKS OF THE HANAPER IN THE CHANCERY

20 Sep 1485	William Smith	16 July 1532	Thomas Cromwell
1 Jan 1505	Simon Stalworth	26 July 1540	Sir Ralph Sadler
29 July 1509	William Lupton	Sep 1545–	Sir John Hales and
13 June 1513	Roger Lupton and Sir John Heron	end of reign	Sir Ralph Sadler
30 Sep 1514	Sir John Heron		
10 July 1526	Thomas Hall		

CONTROLLERS OF THE MINT

Oct 1485	Nicholas Flynt	Mar 1542	Hugh Aglionby
May 1488	Sir Henry Wyatt	27 May 1544	Robert Broke
c. 1536	John Walley	28 May 1544	Sir Edmund Peckham
Sep 1537	Peter Mewtas		(to 1 Jan 1551)

THE COURT OF AUGMENTATIONS

Chancellors

24 Apr 1536	Sir Richard Rich (to 1 May 1544)	24 Apr 1544	Sir Edward North (to end of 1547)

Treasurers

24 Apr 1536	Thomas Pope	31 Mar 1544	Sir John Williams
17 Mar 1540	Sir Edward North		

General Surveyors

2 Jan 1547　Sir Thomas Moyle and Walter Mildmay

THE COURT OF WARDS AND LIVERIES

Master of the King's Wards

9 Dec 1503	Sir John Hussey	22 May 1526	Sir Thomas Englefield
14 June 1513	Sir Thomas Lovell	3 Nov 1526	Sir William Paulet
24 Jan 1518	Sir Richard Weston	26 July 1540	Sir William Paulet
8 Dec 1520	Sir Edward Belknap	1542	John Hynde

Surveyors of Liveries

c.1514	Sir Thomas Neville	Apr 1535	Sir Richard Rich
Sep 1529	Sir Robert Norwich	c.1537	John Hynde

Receiver-General

2 Aug 1540	Philip Paris	30 Jan 1545	John Beaumont
26 Feb 1544	Richard Lee		

Attorney

Aug 1540	Thomas Polsted	May 1546	Richard Goodrich
Feb 1541	John Sewster	Jan 1547	Nicholas Bacon

COURT OF THE GENERAL SURVEYORS OF THE KINGS LANDS

General Surveyors

c.May 1542	Sir John Daunce	Nov 1542	Sir Richard Southwell
c.May 1542	Sir Richard Pollard	Dec 1545	William Daunce
c.May 1542	Sir Thomas Moyle	Dec 1545	Sir Walter Mildmay

COURT OF FIRST FRUITS AND TENTHS

Chancellor

4 Nov 1540–	Sir John Baker

Attorneys

28 Jan 1541	John Carell	12 June 1543	Robert Chidley

Treasurers

c.Mar 1535	John Gostwick	20 Oct 1549	William Peter
21 Apr 1545	Wimund Carew		

Auditors

20 Nov 1540	Richard Mody	15 Nov 1540	Thomas Leigh

MISCELLANEOUS FINANCIAL REVENUE STATISTICS

CUSTOMS REVENUE

Year	Estimated Revenue	Year	Estimated Revenue
1505	£27,000	1559	£83,000
1540	£40,000	1590	£100,000

REVENUE FROM CROWN LANDS

Year	Yield (estimated)	Year	Yield (estimated)
1491	£3700	c.1540	c.£125,000
1509	£25,000	c.1600	c. £60,000

INCOME FROM WARDS LANDS UNDER CROWN MANAGEMENT
1485–1509

1487	£353	1505	£5422
1491	£343	1506	£5626
1494	£1588	1507	£6163
1504	£3003		

SOURCE   Dietz, p. 31.

EXPENDITURES IN THE EXCHEQUER DURING THE REIGNS OF
HENRY VIII, EDWARD VI AND MARY: 1509–58

	£		£
1509	39,766	1534	37,106
1510	46,054	1536	37,234
1511	57,937	1537	38,246
1512	46,717	1538	38,279
1513	36,964	1540	20,200
1515	51,974	1542	30,402
1516	50,745	1543	26,443
1517	34,517	1545	116,584
1519	52,306	1546	178,083
1520	46,421	1547	105,655
1521	45,387	1548	78,980
1523	34,786	1549	80,444
1524	32,467	1550	61,810
1525	38,506	1551	86,058
1526	34,174	1552	66,541
1527	43,622	1553	43,820
1529	34,228	1554	90,331*
1530	31,974	1555	151,100
1531	34,817	1556	246,274
1532	38,935	1557	293,152
1533	37,789	1558	334,340

* In this year the Augmentations Court, and the Court of First Fruits and Tenths were merged with the Exchequer.

SOURCE   Dietz, p. 216.

2 PARLIAMENT

INTRODUCTORY NOTE

'By the early sixteenth century, Parliament was an accepted part of the constitution, a known and established element in the king's government, though not as yet a regular or necessary part.' (G. R. Elton, *The Tudor Constitution*, p. 228).

During the period from 1485 to 1603, crucial developments took place in the evolution of the place of Parliament in public life. The importance of the 1529 Reformation Parliament, the growth in the sheer size and composition of Parliament, its increasing emphasis on its procedure and privileges, all reflected this. But at the outset of the Tudor period, the role of Parliament must not be exaggerated. In 1485, it was accepted that Parliament met only occasionally, when it was required for a special purpose such as the granting of money. Parliaments met only rarely and for short periods (see p. 35). By the end of the Tudor period, the place of Parliament had been transformed. This chapter attempts to set out in tabular form the main changes and developments.

COMPOSITION

When Henry VII became King in 1485, the House of Commons was already of considerable size. Some 37 counties and 111 boroughs returned 296 members. Thus the Commons had gradually grown over the preceding years, as successive reigns had seen small additions to the numbers of constituencies.

Growth of Composition of the Commons 1272–1509

Year	Counties	Boroughs	Total
Death of Edward I (1307)	74	160	234
Death of Edward II (1327)	74	172	246
Death of Edward III (1377)	74	194	268
Death of Henry VI (1461)	74	210	284
Death of Edward IV (1483)	74	222	296
Death of Henry VII (1509)	74	222	296

The 37 counties represented were the ancient counties of England, less the counties palatine of Chester and Durham and Monmouth.

27

Between 1272 and 1483, the following boroughs had been enfranchised:

Edward I (1272–1307)

Bedford	Bridport	Stafford	Grimsby
Reading	Shaftesbury	Ipswich	London
Wallingford	Wareham	Dunwich	Norwich
Wycombe	Colchester	Southwark	King's Lynn
Cambridge	Gloucester	Bletchingley	Yarmouth
Launceston	Hereford	Reigate	Northampton
Liskeard	Leominster	Guildford	Newcastle
Lostwithiel	Huntingdon	Chichester	Wilton
Truro	Nottingham	Horsham	Downton
Bodmin	Oxford	Lewes	Calne
Helston	Shrewsbury	Shoreham	Devizes
Carlisle	Bridgnorth	Arundel	Chippenham
Derby	Bristol	Bramber	Malmesbury
Exeter	Bath	Warwick	Cricklade
Totnes	Wells	Appleby	Great Bedwyn
Plympton East	Taunton	New Sarum	Ludgershall
Barnstaple	Bridgwater	Canterbury	Worcester
Tavistock	Winchester	Rochester	Scarborough
Dorchester	Southampton	Leicester	York
Lyme Regis	Portsmouth	Lincoln	

Edward II (1307–27)

Weymouth	Midhurst	East Grinstead
Melcombe Regis	Steyning	Kingston

Edward III (1327–77)

Maldon	Sandwich	Romney
Hastings	Hythe	Rye
Dover	Newcastle-under-Lyme	Winchelsea

Two boroughs (Dartmouth and Old Sarum) were restored.

Henry VI (1422–61)

Gatton	Hindon	Wootton Bassett
Heytesbury	Westbury	

Three boroughs (Windsor, Plymouth and Coventry) were restored.

Edward IV (1461–83)

Grantham, Ludlow, Wenlock
One borough (Stamford) was restored.

The boroughs returning members to Parliament in 1485 at the start of the Tudor period are set out below.

BOROUGH REPRESENTATION IN PARLIAMENT IN 1485

Constituency	No. of members	Constituency	No. of members
Appleby (Westmorland)	2	Helston (Cornwall)	2
Arundel (Sussex)	2	Hereford (Herefordshire)	2
Barnstaple (Devon)	2	Heytesbury (Wilts)	2
Bath (Somerset)	2	Hindon (Wilts)	2
Bedford (Beds)	2	Horsham (Sussex)	2
Bletchingley (Surrey)	2	Hull (Yorks)	2
Bodmin (Cornwall)	2	Huntingdon (Hunts)	2
Bramber (Sussex)	2	Hythe (Kent)	2
Bridgnorth (Salop)	2	Ipswich (Suffolk)	2
Bridgwater (Somerset)	2	King's Lynn (Norfolk)	2
Bridport (Dorset)	2	Launceston (Cornwall)	2
Bristol (Glos)	2	Leicester (Leics)	2
Calne (Wilts)	2	Leominster (Herefordshire)	2
Cambridge (Cambs)	2	Lewes (Sussex)	2
Canterbury (Kent)	2	Lincoln (Lincs)	2
Carlisle (Cumberland)	2	Liskeard (Cornwall)	2
Chichester (Sussex)	2	London (Middx)	4
Chippenham (Wilts)	2	Lostwithiel (Cornwall)	2
Chipping Wycombe (Bucks)	2	Ludgershall (Wilts)	2
Colchester (Essex)	2	Ludlow (Salop)	2
Coventry (War)	2	Lyme Regis (Dorset)	2
Cricklade (Wilts)	2	Maidstone (Kent)	2
Dartmouth (Devon)	2	Maldon (Essex)	2
Derby (Derbyshire)	2	Malmesbury (Wilts)	2
Devizes (Wilts)	2	Marlborough (Wilts)	2
Dorchester (Dorset)	2	Melcombe Regis (Dorset)	2
Dover (Kent)	2	Midhurst (Sussex)	2
Downton (Wilts)	2	Much Wenlock (Salop)	2
Dunwich (Suffolk)	2	Newcastle upon Tyne (Northumberland)	2
East Grinstead (Sussex)	2	Newcastle-under-Lyme (Staffs)	2
Exeter (Devon)	2	New Romney (Kent)	2
Gatton (Surrey)	2	New Windsor (Berks)	2
Gloucester (Glos)	2	Northampton (Northants)	2
Grantham (Lincs)	2	Norwich (Norfolk)	2
Great Bedwyn (Wilts)	2	Nottingham (Notts)	2
Great Yarmouth (Norfolk)	2	Old Sarum (Wilts)	2
Grimsby (Lincs)	2	Oxford (Oxon)	2
Guildford (Surrey)	2	Plymouth (Devon)	2
Hastings (Sussex)	2		

29

Constituency	No. of members	Constituency	No. of members
Plympton East (Devon)	2	Taunton (Somerset)	2
Poole (Dorset)	2	Tavistock (Devon)	2
Portsmouth (Hants)	2	Totnes (Devon)	2
Reading (Berks)	2	Truro (Cornwall)	2
Reigate (Surrey)	2	Wallingford (Berks)	2
Rochester (Kent)	2	Wareham (Dorset)	2
Rye (Sussex)	2	Warwick (War)	2
Salisbury (Wilts)	2	Wells (Somerset)	2
Sandwich (Kent)	2	Westbury (Wilts)	2
Scarborough (Yorks)	2	Weymouth (Dorset)	2
Shoreham (Sussex)	2	Wilton (Wilts)	2
Shrewsbury (Salop)	2	Winchelsea (Sussex)	2
Southampton (Hants)	2	Winchester (Hants)	2
Southwark (Surrey)	2	Wootton Bassett (Wilts)	2
Stafford (Staffs)	2	Worcester (Worcs)	2
Stamford (Lincs)	2	York (Yorks)	2
Steyning (Sussex)	2		
			222

For representation by county, see p. 33–4.

Under the Tudors, membership of the Commons rose swiftly, from 296 in 1509 to 460 by 1603, a rise of 56 per cent. Whilst some of these additions were the result of the calling of M.P.s from such areas as Wales and Chester (and Calais for the brief period 1536–58), by far the most important factor was the enfranchisement of new and restored English boroughs.

The extent of this activity can be seen in the table below:

Creation of new seats, 1509–1603

Reign	Method of Creation	Counties	Boroughs	Total
	In existence in 1509	74	222	296
Henry VIII	Prerogative Charters	—	14⎫	341
	Acts of Parliament	16	15⎭	
Edward VI	Prerogative Charters	—	34	375
Mary I	Prerogative Charters	—	23	398
Elizabeth I	Prerogative Charters	—	62	460

The 62 new members created under Elizabeth's reign are a remarkable total since no new boroughs were created after 1586. The reasons for this remarkable expansion – at one time believed to be an attempt by the Crown to 'pack' Parliament – have now been established as coming from the boroughs themselves. The pressure came from landed gentlemen keen to enfranchise those places in which they had influence. The novel desire to enter Parliament, and the 'invasion' of Parliament by the country gentry, were features of the period.

The result of this activity in the composition of the Commons is set out below:

House of Commons Membership, 1509–1603

Year	Counties	Boroughs	Total
Death of Henry VII (1509)	74	222	296
Death of Henry VIII (1547)	90	251	341
Death of Edward VI (1553)	90	285	375
Death of Mary I (1558)	90	308	398
Death of Elizabeth I (1603)	90	370	460

Divided into county and borough seats, the changes from 1509 to 1603 were as follows:

Counties
Under Henry VIII the counties of Chester and Monmouth were given 2 seats each in Parliament and each of the 12 Welsh counties was granted 1 member each.

Boroughs
Of the 148 borough seats created by the Tudors, 15 were the result of legislation under Henry VIII bringing in Chester, Monmouth, and the Welsh boroughs; all the rest were due to royal charters. The full list was as follows:

Boroughs enfranchised under Henry VIII

Berwick upon Tweed	2	Monmouth (Mon)	1
(Northumberland)		Newport (Cornwall)	2
Buckingham (Bucks)	2	Orford (Suffolk)	2
Chester (Cheshire)	2	Preston (Lancs)	2
Lancaster (Lancs)	2	Thetford (Norfolk)	2

Boroughs enfranchised under Edward VI

Boston (Lincs)	2	Heydon (Yorks)	2
Bossiney (Cornwall)	2	Lichfield (Staffs)	2
Brackley (Northants)	2	Liverpool (Lancs)	2
Camelford (Cornwall)	2	Mitchell (Cornwall)*	2
Grampound (Cornwall)	2	Penryn (Cornwall)	2

31

Peterborough (Northants)	2	West Looe (Cornwall)	2
Petersfield (Hants)	2	Westminster (Middx)	2
Saltash (Cornwall)	2	Wigan (Lancs)	2
Thirsk (Yorks)	2		

* Also known as St Michael's and Midshall.

Boroughs enfranchised under Mary I

Abingdon (Berks)	1	Knaresborough (Yorks)	2
Aldborough (Yorks)	2	Morpeth (Northumberland)	2
Aylesbury (Bucks)	2	Ripon (Yorks)	2
Banbury (Oxon)	1	St Albans (Herts)	2
Boroughbridge (Yorks)	2	St Ives (Cornwall)	2
Castle Rising (Norfolk)	2	Woodstock (Oxon)	2
Droitwich (Worcs)	2	*Less* two members for	
Higham Ferrers (Northants)	1	Maidstone, disfranchised	

Boroughs enfranchised under Elizabeth I

Aldeburgh (Suffolk)	2	Maidstone (Kent)	2
Andover (Hants)	2	Minehead (Somerset)	2
Berealston (Devon)	2	Newport (Isle of Wight)	2
Beverley (Yorks)	2	Newton (Lancs)	2
Bishop's Castle (Salop)	2	Newtown (Isle of Wight)	2
Callington (Cornwall)	2	Queenborough (Kent)	2
Christchurch (Hants)	2	Richmond (Yorks)	2
Cirencester (Glos)	2	St Germains (Cornwall)	2
Clitheroe (Lancs)	2	St Mawes (Cornwall)	2
Corfe Castle (Dorset)	2	Stockbridge (Hants)	2
East Looe (Cornwall)	2	Sudbury (Suffolk)	2
East Retford (Notts)	2	Tamworth (War)	2
Eye (Suffolk)	2	Tregony (Cornwall)	2
Fowey (Cornwall)	2	Whitchurch (Hants)	2
Haslemere (Surrey)	2	Yarmouth (Isle of Wight)	2
Lymington (Hants)	2		

GEOGRAPHICAL DISTRIBUTION OF CONSTITUENCIES

The ancient boroughs were, for the most part, seaports, county towns, and fortified places that had received franchises or liberties by royal charter conferring special privileges. The majority of those represented in the parliaments of Henry VIII were in the south, west, and east of England, where most of the thriving towns were to be found. The new creations of the Tudor period only served to reinforce this geographical concentration, although Yorkshire and Lancashire rose to achieve much higher representation.

County	Total representation 1509	Represented 1603
Bedfordshire	4	4
Berkshire	8	10
Buckinghamshire	4	8
Cambridgeshire	4	4
Cheshire	—	4
Cornwall	14	44
Cumberland	4	4
Derbyshire	4	4
Devon	16	18
Dorset	16	18
Durham	—	—
Essex	6	6
Gloucestershire	6	8
Hampshire	8	26
Herefordshire	6	6
Hertfordshire	2	4
Huntingdonshire	4	4
Kent	16	18
Lancashire	2	14
Leicestershire	4	4
Lincolnshire	10	12
Middlesex	6	8
Monmouthshire	—	4
Norfolk	8	12
Northamptonshire	4	10
Northumberland	4	8
Nottinghamshire	4	6
Oxfordshire	4	8
Rutland	2	2
Shropshire	10	12
Somerset	10	12
Staffordshire	6	10
Suffolk	6	14
Surrey	12	14
Sussex	26	26
Warwickshire	6	6
Westmorland	4	4

County	Total representation 1509	Represented 1603
Wiltshire	34	34
Worcestershire	4	6
Yorkshire	8	26

In 1485, the counties with 10 or more representatives were as follows (with 1603 figures in second column).

1485		1603	
Wiltshire	34	Cornwall	44
Sussex	26	Wiltshire	34
Kent ⎫		Sussex ⎫	
Devon ⎬	16	Hampshire ⎬	26
Dorset ⎭		Yorkshire ⎭	
Cornwall	14	Devon ⎫	
Surrey	12	Dorset ⎬	18
Lincolnshire ⎫		Kent ⎭	
Shropshire ⎬	10	Lancashire ⎫	
Somerset ⎭		Suffolk ⎬	14
		Surrey ⎭	
		Lincolnshire ⎫	
		Norfolk ⎬	12
		Shropshire ⎪	
		Somerset ⎭	
		Berkshire ⎫	
		Northants ⎬	10
		Staffordshire ⎭	

Some regional increases are set out below

	1485	1603	% increase
Devon and Cornwall	30	62	206
Dorset, Wiltshire, Somerset	60	64	6
Home Counties (Sussex, Kent, Surrey, Hants)	62	84	35
Lancashire and Yorkshire	10	40	400
East Anglia (Norfolk and Suffolk)	14	26	86

At the outset of the Tudor period, the sessions of Parliament were infrequent; long intervals separated each session. And, as has been emphasised, continuous parliamentary government was neither expected nor desired. Not least, indeed, by the members themselves, for whom an extended Parliament was a chore for them and a burden to their constituents. Thus, the most striking feature of sessions of Parliament during the Tudor period was their brevity and their separation by long intervals.

As the table below shows, in the 38 years during which Henry VIII reigned, only nine Parliaments were held. From December 1515 to April 1523, there was no Parliament at all.

PARLIAMENTARY SESSIONS 1509–1603*

Monarchs	When met	When dissolved	Duration		
			Y.	M.	D.
Henry VIII	21 Jan 1509	23 Feb 1509	0	1	2
	4 Feb 1511	4 Mar 1513	2	1	0
	5 Feb 1514	22 Dec 1515	1	10	17
	15 Apr 1523	13 Aug 1523	0	3	29
	3 Nov 1530	4 Apr 1536	5	5	1
	8 June 1536	18 July 1536	0	1	10
	8 Apr 1539	24 July 1540	1	2	26
	16 Jan 1541	29 Mar 1544	3	2	13
	23 Nov 1545	31 Jan 1547	1	2	8
Edward VI	4 Nov 1547	15 Apr 1552	4	5	11
	1 Mar 1553	31 Mar 1553	0	1	0
Mary	5 Oct 1553	6 Dec 1553	0	2	1
	2 Apr 1554	5 May 1554	0	1	3
	12 Nov 1554	16 Jan 1555	0	2	4
	21 Oct 1555	9 Dec 1555	0	1	18
	20 Jan 1557	17 Nov 1557	0	9	28
Elizabeth	23 Jan 1558	8 May 1558	0	3	16
	11 Jan 1562	2 Jan 1567	4	11	22
	2 Apr 1571	29 May 1571	0	1	27
	8 May 1572	18 Mar 1580	7	10	10
	23 Nov 1585	14 Sep 1586	0	9	21
	29 Oct 1586	23 Mar 1587	0	4	23
	4 Feb 1588	29 Mar 1588	0	1	25
	19 Nov 1592	10 Apr 1593	0	4	22
	24 Oct 1597	9 Feb 1598	2	3	16
	7 Oct 1601	29 Dec 1601	0	2	22
James I	19 Mar 1603	9 Feb 1611	7	10	21

* British Imperial Calendar.

Not only were Parliaments infrequent, but the turnover of members appears to have been large. Statistics for the mid-Tudor period show a remarkable percentage of new members.

Percentage of new members by Parliament*

Parliament	% new members
Mary's 2nd Parliament	76
Mary's 3rd Parliament	70
Mary's 4th Parliament	$73\frac{1}{2}$
Mary's 5th Parliament	81
Elizabeth's 1st Parliament	75

* SOURCE *English Historical Review*, XXIII, p. 645.

FRANCHISE AND QUALIFICATIONS

COUNTY FRANCHISE

By a statute of 1430 (8 Hen. VI c. 7) the county franchise was restricted to persons resident in the county having freehold to the minimum value of 40s per annum. Those eligible for election (according to a statute of 1445, 23 Hen. VI c. 14) were to be 'notable knights of the same counties for which they are to be chosen' or persons of similar substance. Effectively, only persons with land of the annual value of £20 were thus eligible.

BOROUGH FRANCHISE

Originally, the borough franchise had probably rested with all those entitled to describe themselves as burgesses (i.e. those free inhabitants of the borough who paid the proper dues and were enrolled at the court leet). By 1485, however, the tendency had already extensively developed to limit the franchise to a more selective and oligarchic system. The new boroughs which were granted charters by the Tudors often vested the franchise in a very small body – the later the charter, the more oligarchic the borough constitution.

OFFICERS OF THE HOUSE

THE SPEAKER

Date of Election	Name	Constituency
8 Nov 1485	Sir Thomas Lovell (d. 1524)	Northamptonshire
10 Nov 1487	Sir John Mordaunt (d. 1504)	Bedfordshire
14 Jan 1489	Sir Thomas FitzWilliam (d. 1495)	Yorkshire
18 Oct 1491	Sir Richard Empson (d. 1510)	Northamptonshire
15 Oct 1495	Sir Robert Drury (d. 1536)	Suffolk
19 Jan 1497	Sir Thomas Englefield (d. 1514)	Berkshire
26 Jan 1504	Edmund Dudley (see p. 211) (1462–1510)	Staffordshire

Date of Election	Name	Constituency
23 Jan 1510	Sir Thomas Englefield (d. 1514)	Berkshire
5 Feb 1512	Sir Robert Sheffield (d. 1518)	Lincolnshire
6 Feb 1515	Sir Thomas Neville (d. 1542)	Kent
16 Apr 1523	Sir Thomas More (see p. 215) (1478–1535)	Middlesex
5 Nov 1529	Sir Thomas Audley (1488–1544)	Essex
9 Feb 1533	Sir Humphrey Wingfield (d. 1545)	Great Yarmouth
9 Jan 1536	Sir Richard Rich (1496–1567)	Colchester
28 Apr 1539	Sir Nicholas Hare (d. 1557)	Norfolk
19 Jan 1542	Sir Thomas Moyle (d. 1560)	Kent
4 Nov 1547	Sir John Baker (d. 1558)	Huntingdonshire
2 Mar 1553	Sir James Dyer (1512–82)	Cambridgeshire
5 Oct 1553	Sir John Pollard (d. 1557)	Oxfordshire
2 Apr 1554	Sir Robert Brooke (d. 1558)	City of London
12 Nov 1554	Sir Clement Higham (d. 1570)	West Looe
21 Oct 1555	Sir John Pollard (d. 1557)	Chippenham
20 Jan 1558	Sir William Cordell (d. 1581)	Suffolk
25 Jan 1559	Sir Thomas Gargrave (1495–1579)	Yorkshire
12 Jan 1563	Thomas Williams (1513–66)	Exeter
1 Oct 1566	Richard Onslow (1528–71)	Steyning
2 Apr 1571	Sir Christopher Wray (1524–92)	Ludgershall
8 May 1572	Sir Robert Bell (d. 1577)	Lyme Regis
18 Jan 1581	Sir John Popham (1531–1607)	Bristol
23 Nov 1584	Sir John Puckering (1544–96)	Carmarthen
29 Oct 1586	Sir John Puckering (1544–96)	Gatton
4 Feb 1589	Thomas Snagge (1536–92)	Bedford
19 Feb 1593	Sir Edward Coke (1552–1634)	Norfolk
24 Oct 1597	Sir Christopher Yelverton (1535–1612)	Northamptonshire
27 Oct 1601	Sir John Croke (1553–1620)	City of London

CLERK OF THE PARLIAMENTS

1485	Morgan, J.	1543	Paget, W.
1496	Hatton, R.	1543	Knight, T.
1509	Taylor, J.	1550	Mason, Sir J.
1523	Tuke, B.	1551	Mason, Sir J.
1531	Tuke, Sir B.	1551	Spilman, F.
1531	North, E.	1574	Spilman, F.
1540	Soulement, T.	1574	Mason, A.
1541	Paget, W.	1597	Smith, T.

37

GENTLEMAN USHER OF THE BLACK ROD

1485	Marleton, R.	1554	Norris, J.
1489	Assheton, R.	1554	Norris, W.
1495	Assheton, R.	1591	Wingfield, A.
1495	Dennys, H.	1593	Bowyer, S.
1513	Compton, W.	1598	Coningsby, R.
1528	Norris, Sir H.	1605	Coningsby, Sir R.
1536	Knyvett, A.	1605	Pollard, G.
1543	Hoby, P.		

CLERK OF THE CROWN IN CHANCERY 1481–1603

c.1481	Ive, R.	1537	Pope, T.
1485	Ive, R.	1538	Pope, T.
1485	Bacheler, G.	1538	Lucas, T.
1487	Bacheler, G.	1544	Martin, E.
1487	Clerk, C.	1546	Martin, E.
1504	Porter, W.	1546	Powle, T.
1522	Pexsall, R.	1601	Coppin, G.

THE GROWTH OF PRIVILEGE AND PROCEDURE

CHRONOLOGY OF KEY EVENTS

1513   Strode's Case formally recognised that the Commons and its business, as part of the High Court of Parliament, were privileged against inferior courts of the realm.

1515   The Speaker empowered by Act of Parliament (6 Hen. VIII c. 16) to license members to absent themselves. Previously this power had lain with the Crown.

1523   Speaker More's request for free speech. The first known request by a Speaker on this theme.

1534   Beginning of period of Thomas Cromwell's 'management' of elections.

1536   The Canterbury election. The town was compelled, on orders from Thomas Cromwell, to reverse its election and instead choose two nominees of the Crown.

1543   Ferrers' Case. The Commons released one of its members, George Ferrers, a burgess of Plymouth, by despatching their own serjeant-at-law, claiming that his mace was sufficient authority to secure release.

1553   Commons declared that Alexander Nowell, being now a prebendary of Westminster, and thus having a voice at Convocation House, could not be a member.

1555   Discussion by Commons of a Bill prohibiting any paid servant or

38

dependant of the Crown from sitting as a member. Nothing came of this discussion.

1571 (5 April) Case of Thomas Clark and Anthony Bull. Both men, non-members of the House, committed to the serjeant's ward for 'presuming' to enter the Commons.

1571 Strickland's Case.

1572 (30 June) Lord Cromwell's Case. Established that the Lords could similarly protect themselves from arrest.

1576 Peter Wentworth's (burgess for Tregony) famous speech for liberty (8 February). Subsequent punishment and commitment to the Tower (9 February). Queen remits sentence (12 March).

1576 Smalley's Case. The case (in February 1576) involved Edward Smalley, a servant of Arthur Hall, the burgess for Grantham. Smalley engineered his own arrest for a debt really incurred by Hall. Hall moved for privilege to free his servant. After initial reluctance by the Commons, Smalley was duly freed by warrant of the mace. The Commons, however, committed Smalley to the Tower until the debt was paid.

1581 Commons establishes its claim to judge the qualifications of elected members. Arthur Hall's case occurred in the same year. Hall, attacking the Commons as 'a new person in the Trinity' in two pamphlets published in 1579–80, was fined, imprisoned and expelled from the House (14 February).

1584 Parry's Case. After speaking in very violent terms against the Bill against Jesuits, Parry was sequestered and forced to submit (17 December).

1584 Finnies' Case. An attempt by Viscount Bindon to claim privilege for his servant, Robert Finnies, failed. The case marked a sensible corrective on the number of those who could claim privilege as a 'servant' of a Member.

1585 Richard Cook's Case (February). Court of Chancery refuted Commons claims over subpoenas.

1586 Case of the disputed Norfolk election: Commons decided in favour of the disputed first election. Beginning of the custom to appoint Standing Committees at the opening of each parliament to decide disputed elections.

1587 Peter Wentworth's questions. Arrest of Wentworth and other members for their unconstitutional dealings before the opening of Parliament.

1589 Commons' decision to award writs of *supersedeas* in cases where members have writs of *nisi prius* brought against them.

1589 (15 February) Sir Edward Hoby's motion to preserve the secrecy of the House's proceedings.

39

1593   Fitzherbert's Case (April 1593). Established the point that privilege did not extend to members who, though elected, were not technically members (Thomas Fitzherbert had been arrested for debt at the Queen's suit before his return had been received by the Sheriff).

1604   Goodwin's Case. Commons had to assert its right to settle questions of disputed election.

3 THE JUDICATURE AND THE COURTS

INTRODUCTION

England under the Tudors was a society striving for law and order, for the secure peaceful background to people's lives which has been frequently seen, in previous and later centuries, as the basic prerequisite of a civilised society. But, as at other periods, the Tudor thirst for order claimed many victims and pursued its own ends regardless of some of the most basic human values. Fifteenth-century society in England had felt the weakening influence of the vacuum at its summit – the monarchy. The first task of the Tudor monarchy was to restore the power and prestige of the Crown. From this followed the general reassertion of royal government throughout the realm: once more the monarch ruled England.

In Utopia, Thomas More related, there were but few laws, and no lawyers. The contrast with sixteenth-century England was startling. Life was becoming ever more bound up with the rule of law: more laws – and more lawyers (largely to handle the private suits of the increasingly litigious English). At the basis of all law lay the concept of authority, set by God in the person of the monarch. The 1547 *Book of Homilies*, an excellent source for the official ideology of the age, suggested the result of removing rulers: 'No man shall ride or go by the highway unrobbed, no man shall sleep in his own house or bed unkilled, no man shall keep his wife, children and possessions in quietness, all things shall be common . . .' The law existed, then, to protect lives and property. It also existed to maintain the hierarchical structure of society and the total uniformity of thought, word and deed on which that structure seemed to rest. Thence came the (to modern minds) 'innocent' victims: Thomas More, Prior Houghton, Edmund Campion, John Penry and many others. Obedience, claimed the Tudor propagandists, was the greatest virtue. Preachers relayed the message from innumerable pulpits throughout the land. The obedience due to princes was of the same order as the unquestioning subservience owed by wives to husbands, children to parents, and servants to masters. Terror of disorder, fear of the mob – stimulated by the occasional riots and risings which did occur and by reports of the horrors of Continental Anabaptism – was a basic component of the psychological make-up of the

41

middle and upper classes of Tudor England. Draconian penalties threatened wrongdoers. Nobody took seriously the pretence that the law provided fair treatment for rich and poor. If a man killed his master he died horribly. If a master killed his servant the means could very often be found to acquit him of the charge.[1] If Tudor government was government by consent, as some have claimed, the consent was that of the ruling classes. Since the overwhelming desire of the latter was for peace and order, they secured a convenient and lasting détente with the Crown, which lasted right up to the 1630s. The landed élite and, in towns, the great merchants and tradesmen, provided the Lords Lieutenant, sheriffs and justices who were, for most of the time, the visible representatives of the law.

In recent years, considerable attention has been given to the whole question of consent in Tudor society.[2] The myth of mass popular support, say for the Henrician Reformation, has been exploded in favour of a complex picture where zealous support, outright opposition, sullen acquiescence and complete apathy all mingle. The flowering of law, of legal institutions and of the legal profession, undoubtedly produced a less openly violent, more regulated society. What has still to be determined is the extent to which a more regulated society is a more just society. The thought that 'Tudor thinking and practice on the law subordinated everybody, the king included, to the rule of law'[3] can have been little comfort to the victims of a Cromwell or a Walsingham. The institutional and ideological structure of the Tudor legal system reflected a rigidly authoritative society. Justice was a commodity all too often available only to those with the funds to purchase it.

NOTES

1. For examples, see F. G. Emmison, *Elizabethan Life: Disorder* (Chelmsford, 1970) pp. 155–6.

2. See the relevant essays in J. Hurstfield, *Freedom, Corruption and Government in Elizabethan England* (London, 1973).

3. G. R. Elton, 'The Rule of Law in sixteenth-century England', *Studies in Tudor and Stuart Politics and Government* (Cambridge, 1974) I, p. 277.

THE ANCIENT COURTS

KING'S BENCH

Law in Tudor England was, as it had been from Saxon times, the King's law. The King's law was common to all his realm – hence 'common' law. For centuries the King, assisted by his Council or *curia*, was the ultimate source of justice and cases were heard before the King in Council. The *curia*, in other words, assumed a judicial function as a court *coram rege*. The growth of King's Bench as a separate court began as early as the twelfth century and in 1178 Henry II appointed five judges to hear cases. In 1268 presidency of the court was given to a chief justice.

The jurisdiction of King's Bench originally extended only to those matters touching the rights of Crown and subjects. But the fact that King's Bench was the highest court in the land resulted inevitably in the extension of its powers. Since it was superior to all other courts (and could remove cases from them by writs such as *habeas corpus* and *quo warranto*) it developed into a sort of appeal court, retrying cases where there was suspicion of an erroneous verdict. (For most of the Tudor period appeal above King's Bench lay only to Parliament.) The criminal jurisdiction was normally exercised by assizes under commission of oyer and terminer. In the sixteenth century, the court developed a thriving civil jurisdiction, taking advantage of the fact that trespass was in theory a criminal offence, which undermined the authority of the Court of Common Pleas.

CHIEF JUSTICES OF KING'S BENCH

1485	William Huse	1553	Thomas Bromley
1495	John Finieux	1555	William Portman
1526	John FitzJames	1557	Edward Saunders
1539	Edward Montagu	1559	Robert Catlin
1545	Richard Lyster	1574	Christopher Wray
1552	Roger Cholmley	1592	John Popham

COMMON PLEAS

'Common pleas' were civil suits between subjects. Under the terms of Magna Carta (1215), these suits were not to be heard *coram rege* (that is, before the King, wherever he might be) but at Westminster before specially appointed judges. By 1272 (when a Chief Justice of Common Pleas was appointed) the Court of Common Pleas had attained identity as an independent court. It was the establishment, indeed, of this court at Westminster which established there the chief centre of English law. The growth of a new legal profession was given new impetus.

The jurisdiction of the Court of Common Pleas covered all civil actions and it was superior to and a source of appeal from all local and minor courts. Appeal from Common Pleas lay to King's Bench. Common Pleas was the busiest court of later medieval England – and also the slowest. Its delays encouraged the encroachments of King's Bench on its business during the Tudor period.

CHIEF JUSTICES OF COMMON PLEAS

1485	Thomas Bryan	1535	John Baldwin
1500	Thomas Wood	1545	Edward Montagu
1502	Thomas Frowyk	1553	Richard Morgan
1506	Robert Read	1554	Robert Brooke
1519	John Ernle	1558	Anthony Browne
1521	Robert Brudenell	1559	James Dyer
1531	Robert Norwich	1582	Edmund Anderson

CHANCERY

The office of Chancellor began as a sort of private secretaryship to the monarch, usually the preserve of clerics. The Chancellor wrote letters, drew up charters, treaties and so on and sealed them with the King's Seal – the Great Seal of the realm. The Chancery office thus arose as a place where the monarch's official records were kept. Its legal importance lay in the fact that action in the Royal courts was begun with the issue by Chancery of a writ. From this function grew the Court of Chancery, the Lord Chancellor's Court. It was a court of equity, that is, of appeal and petition, designed to remedy the deficiencies in the Common Law. At first, the Chancellor, by the later middle ages the Crown's chief officer, sat in judgment personally in cases where the Common Law had failed to reach a satisfactory conclusion or was unable to act at all. Thus at first Equity supplemented the Common Law and was not a rival to it. The Chancellor sought to administer natural justice when the Common Law failed to do so. Chancery's attraction (and it was clogged with business in the Tudor period) lay in the fact that it was less rigid and dogmatic in its approach than the Common Law courts. It also had to hand methods outside the Common Law, such as the right to bind all appearing in it to oath. Sir Thomas More (Chancellor 1529–32) was himself a Common lawyer and the gradual formalisation of the business of Chancery by lawyers reduced its flexibility and its effectiveness. But Chancery survived even the fierce assault of the Common lawyers in the reign of James I. Writs were not used but bills, setting out the details of the plaintiff's writ. Examination on oath and the use of a right to subpoena defendants and witnesses were inevitably aids to speedier verdicts. While Chancery was influenced by Roman (or civil) law principles, its proceedings were not out of keeping with the spirit of Common Law; and basically it survived because it worked.

Lord Chancellors: See above p. 20.

The Court of Chancery was usually presided over, in the absence of the Chancellor, by the Master of the Rolls.

MASTERS OF THE ROLLS

1485 Robert Morton, later Bishop of Worcester
1486 David William
1492 John Blythe, later Bishop of Salisbury
1494 William Warham, later Archbishop of Canterbury (see p. 219)
1502 William Barnes, later Bishop of London
1504 Christopher Bainbridge, later Archbishop of York
1508 John Yonge, later Dean of York
1516 Cuthbert Tunstal, later Bishop of London and Durham (see p. 218)
1522 John Clerke, later Bishop of Bath and Wells
1523 Thomas Hannibal
1527 John Taylor, Archdeacon of Derby and Buckingham

1534 Thomas Cromwell (see p. 210)
1536 Christopher Hales
1541 Sir Robert Southwell
1550 John Beaumont
1552 Sir Robert Bowes
1553 Sir Nicholas Hare
1557 Sir William Cordell
1581 Sir Gilbert Gerrard
1594 Sir Thomas Egerton

EXCHEQUER

This Court was in origin a financial office of the Crown, concerned with the collection of Royal revenues. (The name is derived from Latin *scaccarium* – a chess-board – because of the system of accounting in squares.) The collection of revenues inevitably involved disputes and the Exchequer assumed a legal role as a Common Law court dealing with financial cases. Thus the Court of Exchequer began to develop apart from the revenue-collecting office and in 1579 was constituted as a court of law on the same lines as King's Bench and Common Pleas with all its officers drawn from the legal profession. The Exchequer of Pleas, as the Court was properly known, was presided over by the Lord Treasurer (or Chancellor of the Exchequer) and a number of judges (or 'Barons'). During the Tudor period, the court developed an equity side and dealt with cases similar to those usually brought to Chancery.

The *Court of Exchequer Chamber* developed from the custom of judges from all the courts meeting in Exchequer Chamber to discuss legal issues. In 1585 a court of this name was established as a court of appeal from King's Bench. Another, separate, court of this name was set up in 1589 to look into complaints about the workings of the Court of Exchequer.

CHIEF BARONS OF THE COURT OF EXCHEQUER

1485	Humphrey Starkey	1553	David Brook
1486	William Hody	1558	Clement Heigham
1522	John FitzJames	1559	Edward Saunders
1526	Richard Broke	1577	Robert Bell
1529	Richard Lyster	1577	John Jeffrey
1545	Roger Cholmley	1578	Roger Marwood
1552	Henry Bradshaw	1593	William Periam

THE CONCILIAR COURTS

STAR CHAMBER

The development of the Common Law courts out of the Royal Council did not deprive that body of all its legal functions. The Council represented, in very comprehensible terms, the prerogative of the Crown. But the law courts, once established, were reluctant to yield back to the Council any of their powers. An attempt, for example, in 1366 by the Council to reverse a judgment of Common Pleas was unsuccessful and the Council never gained the right to reverse decisions of the Courts. Parliament itself became the ultimate court of appeal. But it was recognised that the Council had certain rights of jurisdiction, often in matters where the Common Law was unable to act or offered no certain remedy. It was established that trial by jury was essential in matters touching life or property but beyond this the Council might act freely in a wide variety of cases. In 1388 the Council examined numbers of heretics, assuming a role usually that of the Church courts. The penalties which could be imposed were fines and imprisonment, although prisoners could be passed on to other courts.

During the fifteenth century, the Council met for judicial purposes – quite separate from its normal meetings – in the Star Chamber at the Palace of Westminster. It was a body which could divert its attentions to new issues confronting English society and in the later fifteenth century sporadic outbreaks of lawlessness and riot were dealt with – 'Maintenances, Oppressions, or other Outrages of any persons in the Country . . . at the Suit of the Party'.[1] Many more outrages must have been avoided by the swift justice often obtainable in the Star Chamber. It was justice available to a wide section of the population – in 1483 a clerk was appointed for the purpose of registering the petitions of 'poor persons'.[2]

Professor Elton points out that 'the Privy Council and Star Chamber were two aspects of essentially the same body of men . . .'[3] So the Tudor Star Chamber – the Council sitting in a judicial contest – was essentially a continuation of medieval tradition. Star Chamber was not *founded* in 1487, when an Act authorised it to 'punish divers misdemeanours'. It grew in stature under Wolsey and by 1540 was indelibly separate from the Privy Council. Its normal composition was the Privy Councillors plus the two Chief Justices.[4]

These 'divers misdemeanours' included 'riots and unlawful assemblies', and a special committee was to be set up to make inquiries into such occurrences.

CHRONOLOGY OF EVENTS

1504   The Statute of Liveries authorised proceedings to be taken in Star Chamber.

1529   An Act was passed setting up a further committee of the type authorised in 1487, but the results are uncertain.

1540   The Court was given a more formal existence by the appointment of its own Clerk, who kept a minute book distinct from that of the Privy Council.

1586   A decree of the Chamber introduced a system of censorship over printers.

REQUESTS

'A poor man's chancery',[5] a court offering equitable jurisdiction to the impecunious, the Court of Requests grew out of the Royal Council as a rival to the Common Law courts of the Crown. Requests was a civil court covering private matters, on the basis of equity and conscience, in a fairly efficient and speedy manner (which attracted plaintiffs, not only always poor ones). At first councillors had been deputed to hear poor men's suits – Henry VII continued this Yorkist practice – but the court developed under Henry VIII as a separate entity with its own staff of civil lawyers – the Masters of Requests.

The business of the Court of Requests was concerned with rights – especially rights of trade and land-holding. It thus covered the same sphere of legal practice as the Court of Common Pleas, which strove to undermine its popular rival. The Court of Requests had in fact never been given a statutory basis – but then neither had the authority of Star Chamber depended on express statute. Both drew authority from the King's Council.

Thomas Smith called Requests 'the poore man's Court because there he should have right without paying any money'; and indeed the extensive jurisdictional rights of the court over land-holding seem to have annoyed magistrates such as Francis Russell, Earl of Bedford, who wrote to the Masters of Requests to complain about their hearing a case relating to a Hertfordshire manor.[6] The speedy workings of the Court, which made it a cheap source of justice, attracted plaintiffs unable to pour large sums into litigation. Its procedure, wrote Sir Julius Caesar, sometime Master of Requests, 'was altogether according to the process of summary causes in the Civill Law'.[7] It was based on bill, subpoena and commission: Lambarde reported that 'the usual process is by privy seal . . . attachment and writ of rebellion if the contumacy of the defendant do so deserve; in the rest of the proceeding, the course is not so much different from the order of the Chancery.'[8]

ADMIRALTY

The growth of trade in later medieval Europe, which brought large numbers of foreign ships and merchants to England, created the need for a system of jurisdiction covering the activities of the mercantile class. Throughout most of the medieval period, disputes about trade and maritime affairs had been mostly handled at local level by courts existing in the chief ports (for example, Bristol and the Cinque Ports). There was no central court, although there were international 'common laws' of the sea. The so-called 'Judgments of Oleron', derived from a port in Guienne, came to be accepted throughout the Northern seas and formed the basis of English admiralty law. Local compilations of maritime law, like the 'Red Book' of Bristol, were based on the same formula. Thus a system of law outside the Common Law was arising slowly to meet the needs of merchants. Many of those involved in trade, naturally, were foreigners and thus the basis of admiralty law was Roman or civil law.

The term 'admiral' in England does not appear to pre-date the fourteenth century. A proper court of judges concerned with maritime law was in existence by 1357, piracy being among its chief concerns. While the court was at first primarily criminal in its jurisdiction, it soon began to develop as a civil court. (Initially it is more correct to talk of 'courts', for there were a number, amalgamated under a Lord High Admiral in the early fifteenth century.) Sitting at Doctors' Commons, it shared most of its practising civil lawyers with the ecclesiastical courts – it was not uncommon for one man to be Dean of Arches and Judge of the Court of Admiralty. In both, civil law was administered, although in 1536 the criminal jurisdiction of the Court was transferred to special commissions administering common law. As a civil court, the Admiralty Court continued to gain importance throughout the Tudor period – an age of maritime enterprise. In fact, the court appeared to be gaining a monopoly of all important commercial cases, even those relating solely to England and not involving foreigners. Concurrent with this development was the increasing flow into the common law courts of commercial cases formerly dealt with by local courts. The attempt by the Common lawyers to reduce the status of the Court of Admiralty went on into the seventeenth century.

HIGH COMMISSION

It must not be forgotten that, alongside the various secular common law and conciliar courts, there existed an alternative system of justice administered by the Church. The Church courts were by no means confined to 'religious' issues, although they did try cases of heresy and disbelief. Their jurisdiction extended over all sorts of 'moral' offences, including sexual matters, and matrimonial and testamentary disputes. Action in the Church courts could be 'office' (that is, taken by the Court against a person or persons) or 'instance' (person against person). Canon Law, the international law of the Roman Church, was administered and this provided only for spiritual punishments – the ultimate being excommunication. However, while the Church courts lacked the power to touch property or life, they could enrol the support of the secular power. Thus a condemned heretic could be burned at the stake after trial by an ecclesiastical court. The Church courts survived the Reformation and continued to handle a great mass of business throughout the Tudor period. They were disliked by laymen for their defence of the clerical interest – for example, over tithes and other dues – but continued to attract cases of defamation, adultery, fornication and all the other offences they had dealt with in pre-Reformation England. Before the Reformation ultimate appeal from the English Church courts (which were organised on a diocesan basis) lay to Rome but this was removed by the Act of Appeals of 1533. From 1534 ultimate appeal lay to the Crown via Chancery.

High Commission came into existence as a result of the Royal Supremacy. Henry VIII's so-called 'Caesaro-Papism' gave the Crown super-episcopal as well as administrative control of the Church – the King could declare on doctrine and theology. It was inevitable that even Henry VIII would seek to delegate certain aspects of the supremacy to others and special commissions were appointed by the King, acting as Supreme Head, to deal with specific areas of Church affairs. Thomas Cromwell was, in the same way, Henry's personal deputy, his 'vicegerent' in spiritual matters. Out of these commissions grew the established Court of High Commission.

Elizabeth established an ecclesiastical commission by statute to deal with 'errors, heresies, crimes, abuses, offences, contempts and enormities, spiritual and ecclesiastical'. For several decades this commission, while sitting more or less permanently, was not constituted as a formal court, but it seems to have become such by about 1580. High Commission was a 'popular' court, in the sense that lay-people used it as a short-cut across the endless delays of the diocesan courts, but it was by the end of Elizabeth's reign a body bitterly hated by the Puritan wing of the English Church. The 1559 statute had envisaged the use of High Commission's powers mainly against Romanists but Whitgift turned it into a weapon against the party of further reform. The preacher John Udall, gaoled for sedition in 1590, was among its victims (having been handed over to assizes).[9] The Court became increasingly hated by the Puritans, especially as it was used by Laud in the 1630s. It was abolished in 1641.

NOTES

1. Cited by A. Harding, *The Law Courts of Medieval England* (London, 1973) p. 107.
2. Ibid.
3. Elton, *The Tudor Constitution* (Cambridge, 1960) p. 159.
4. For a discussion of the procedure of the Court, see Elton, op. cit. pp. 167–71.
5. A. Harding, *The Law Courts of Medieval England* (London, 1973) p. 107.
6. Cited by I. S. Leadam, *Select Cases in the Court of Requests, 1497–1569* (London: Selden Society, 1898) pp. xv, xvi.
7. Ibid., p. xxi.
8. Cited by G. R. Elton, *The Tudor Constitution* (Cambridge, 1960), p. 188.
9. P. Collinson, *The Elizabethan Puritan Movement* (London, 1967) p. 407. For an example of the repressive use of High Commission under Whitgift, see Collinson, pp. 403–16.

4 LOCAL GOVERNMENT

INTRODUCTION

'In the Elizabethan period most of the population did not come into direct contact with the central authorities at all. For the great majority of the Queen's subjects it was local officials, especially the justices of the peace, who determined their fates.'[1]

The history of local government in the Tudor period serves as a corrective to an uncritical acceptance of the supposed 'revolution' in government. Central government depended on local officials to implement statutes and proclamations issuing from London. The greater burden of the work devolved on the J.P.s. In the past, many historians claimed that the office of justice was virtually created by the Tudors as a central feature of local government. But the origins of the office must be sought as far back as the twelfth century, when Archbishop Hubert Walter first enlisted the services of local knights to assist overworked royal justices. Clearly concepts of major governmental change in Tudor England need to be balanced with the recognition that ancient and well-proved institutions continued to function as before. Tudor local government was a complex system, or rather an unsystematic and developing mesh of overlapping jurisdictions, constantly subject to redefinition and to interaction with central government. Ancient local courts based on hundreds or wapentakes still existed in the seventeenth century and these divisions retained some importance in administration.[2] Neither were manorial courts (courts leet and baron) defunct: run by manorial stewards, they administered a local law based on custom. Courts leet were responsible for presenting offenders to higher authority – in theory they possessed no rights of judgment. Courts baron possessed powers over land-holding and the respective rights of lord and tenant. In practice, the two fused, often becoming amalgamated with ancient hundred courts. Their powers were considerable: 'Serious offenders were of course excluded, but these were comparatively rare. It was the minor breaches of the peace which disturbed the everyday life of the community, and these could be brought into court by jury presentments and punished by fines. . . No aspect of community life was too trivial for the attention of the court, and little escaped its notice.'[3]

Manorial courts were still often the principal judicial and civil institutions in innumerable small communities, but for centuries the greater towns had possessed zealously guarded rights of self-government under royal charter. These rights excluded the interference of county magnates – a city like Gloucester had its own sheriffs and was immune from the jurisdiction of the sheriff of Gloucestershire. Within the larger towns, oligarchical régimes administered justice to the minority of Englishmen who lived in towns in the same way as the landed gentry ruled the shires. Both town and country were subject to an alternative system of law and administration based on the courts of the Church, administered by archdeacons and the legal officers of the bishops. Church courts met in every cathedral town and in other towns within the diocese, and were increased in number by the creation of new bishoprics under Henry VIII. These ecclesiastical courts survived the Reformation and retained a wide jurisdiction extending beyond purely 'religious' matters (like heresy) to cover all kinds of moral offences, including sexual misdemeanours, as well as the probate of wills. Moreover, the business of the Church courts grew in volume after the Reformation in pace with the general growth of litigation. Perhaps the most important aspect of the work of these courts was to give legal sanction to the system of tithes and fees which financed the State Church. In the 1640s Common lawyers led the agitation against the Church courts.[4]

The law administered by all the secular courts (and, after the Reformation, by the Church courts) was that flowing from the monarchy. Local government was the means whereby the will of the monarch was imposed on the population. Tudor governments sought to carry out major changes in English society and it is significant that the drive towards a 'modern', centralised state ruled by a monarchy with augmented, even despotic, powers was halted only by the determined resistance of a large section of the ruling élite in the reign of Charles I. Many contemporary European states – for example Spain – possessed permanent, trained and salaried officials to implement government in the localities, but the Tudors had no civil service of this type. For this reason it was of the highest importance that the interests of the Crown and the ruling class usually coincided. Lawrence Stone claims that the 'tacit agreement' which existed between Crown and ruling class resulted in a steady growth of local particularism alongside that of the power of the central government.[5] What united monarch and local oligarchy was the desire for stable government, the defence of the realm against invaders, the suppression of sedition, rebellion and unorthodoxy, the protection of property and traditional rights, and the acquiescence of the mass of the people in return for their protection and the paternal care they received from their betters. The Tudor monarchy's aides in the provinces were not so much the traditional aristocracy (although the greater magnates often occupied positions of honour) as the broad gentry class, individuals whose status, wealth and education varied widely. It has been suggested that the gentry class was given extensive administrative powers as a counter to the power of the magnates. There is some truth in this generalisation. In the North and the Welsh Marches the government of Henry VIII extended its influence by means of special 'councils', which undermined the powers of the magnates. The Councils of the North and of the Marches were based on fifteenth-century prototypes but were formally constituted in the 1530s to deal with the problems of remote and lawless regions long dominated by dangerously powerful aristocrats. The size of the areas under the control of these bodies – the Council in the Marches was responsible for all Wales plus six border shires of England (Cheshire was excluded after 1569) – demanded firm and inspired leadership. The Council in the North was especially successful in the later Elizabethan period, when Henry Hastings, Earl of Huntingdon, held the presidency.

The existence of the regional Councils made government in the North of England and Wales somewhat different in form from that prevailing in most of England. In most shires, the sheriff was, under the early Tudors, the most important royal official. The importance of the sheriffs was in decline, partly on account of the failure of their predecessors in mid-fifteenth-century England to halt the decay in government.[6] The rise of the Lords Lieutenant and the J.P.s was a major factor in the decline of the sheriffs but the office continued to be an essential one sought after by substantial men – despite the fact that it was 'burdensome and expensive' and lacked effective power.[7] The sheriff's duties were mainly legal: empanelling juries, ensuring the safekeeping of prisoners, carrying out sentences. But he was often, especially before the reign of Elizabeth, entrusted with a variety of other duties, including the collection of taxes and subsidies, the suppression of sedition and the arrest of religious dissenters. The sheriffs were used extensively by Thomas Cromwell in the enforcement of the legislation of the 1530s. Cromwell was convinced, Professor Elton reports, that 'everything turned on the gentry . . . he depended in the last resort on the willingness, prejudices and private ends of men over whom he had no hold except what general adjurations and general warnings could add to general loyalty and the desire to stand well with the fountain of patronage'.[8]

The other local offices held under the Crown and existing unchanged throughout the period included those of coroner, escheator (concerned with the feudal rights of the Crown), and customer (collector of customs dues). At the same time, the new jurisdictions of the centrally-based 'courts' of wards and augmentations impinged on the fields of the older officials. By the reign of Elizabeth, the most notable local servant of the Crown was the Lord Lieutenant. The title 'lieutenant' had been used of the men sent to the regions to organise defence under Henry VIII and Edward VI. Even under Elizabeth, the office long remained a temporary *ad hoc* arrangement, becoming only gradually established on a permanent basis. War with Spain in the 1580s led to the appointment of lieutenants for many shires and many of those appointed went on to hold the office for life. Some of the lieutenancies lapsed with the deaths of the incumbents. The office was not at first invariably associated with a single shire, and some lieutenants held office in more than one county. Thus, the office was a recognition of the continued importance of the landed aristocracy in the regions and an annexation of their military might to the protection of the state in a period when the desire for stability united Crown and magnates. The Lords Lieutenant were the formal leaders of the localities: in Wiltshire the Earls of Pembroke were the usual holders of the office for almost a century. In Gloucestershire the office became the preserve of the Lords Chandos.[9] The tenure of the lieutenancy by men of this stature inevitably meant that much routine work was handed down to humbler deputies drawn from the gentry class. Deputy lieutenants were first appointed early in Elizabeth's reign and there were often as many as six for one county: the deputies could serve only in one county despite their service to a superior who might hold office in a number. The duties of the lieutenants were largely military – drawing up a 'muster roll' of able-bodied men able to bear arms in time of war, keeping an account of arms in stock, maintaining supplies of those weapons and of gunpowder, bringing together the defensive resources of the shire when the need arose. Men with appropriate financial resources were expected and obliged to provide themselves with weapons appropriate to their station – clergy were not exempt – while the less affluent were provided with arms from public stocks. The difficulties of raising musters and the reluctance of men to leave homes and crops to serve as soldiers are shown clearly in Shakespeare's *Henry IV*. In early seventeenth-century Gloucestershire, it was estimated that there were over 18,000 able-bodied men but only one in nine had received military training.[10] The non-military duties of lieutenants were many, including the collection of loans and taxes and the enforcement of religious orthodoxy. The growth of the office of Lord Lieutenant must be counted a significant innovation in Tudor local government, and a beneficial one too.

The novel requirements of Tudor government prompted administrative experiments. The ancient ecclesiastical parish, of which there were several hundred in the average county, was utilised as a unit of civil administration. Local rates, the church rate and poor rate, financed the work of local officials. The established posts of church-warden and constable continued to exist but new parochial offices were now created to carry out new legislation: surveyors of highways and overseers of the poor worked under the supervision of the justices. The latter were fast becoming the key figures in local government. They were, explained Thomas Smith in his *De Republica Anglorum* (1565), 'men elected out of the nobility, higher and lower, that is the dukes, marquises, barons, knights, esquires, and gentlemen, and of such as be learned in the law, such and in such number as the prince shall think fit, and in whom for wisdom and discretion he putteth his trust . . .'[11]

From obscure origins, the office of justice developed during the thirteenth and fourteenth centuries to become an established feature of county government, first established by statute in 1327. In 1361 the title 'justice' was formally given to those known before as 'keepers of the peace'. By the Tudor period, the office was considered essential to good order in the realm. J.P.s' powers were held under royal commissions of the peace and formed a useful counter to magnate domination, although how far this was deliberate policy is open to question. J.P.s were simply the obvious choice of governments seeking local knowledge and the help of local leaders. To be chosen for the honour of serving in the commission of the peace was an accomplishment valued by the Tudor gentry. To be excluded was a mark of some dishonour, evidence that a man was not a respected member of the county community. J.P.s did not have to be expert at law, although increasing numbers of gentry were in any case receiving a legal education at the Inns of Court. Those men who were legally trained were usually named as members of a quorum and the more important sessions could not proceed without a member of the quorum being present. One justice, often the Lord Lieutenant, was selected as *custos rotulorum*, keeper of the rolls or records, while a clerk of the peace was usually available to give advice to all. The number of J.P.s increased in every shire during the Tudor period. In Wiltshire, there were thirty in 1562, fifty-two in 1600.[12] Status counted more than considerations of profit: four shillings a day was the usual attendance allowance in the Elizabethan period. Most justices were in any case men of substance. The essential qualities of a justice were that he 'should have sufficient living and countenance and not be utterly discreditable even if a fool'.[13] The principal function of the J.P.s was the maintenance of the law, the preservation of social order in a society where violence was not far beneath the surface. This concern united men who might disagree violently, for example on religion: Catholics often served as justices in a competent and uncontroversial manner. But in Lancashire, where most of the gentry were Catholics, it was very difficult to find any to enforce the recusancy laws.[14] J.P.s possessed wide powers of search, arrest and imprisonment. Criminals were brought to trial at the quarterly meeting of the justices – Quarter Sessions. Certain crimes had to be reserved for the Assizes, which took place in the county towns – Quarter Sessions were held in most sizeable places. But the majority of offences could be immediately dealt with and the sessions possessed full powers to sentence, including the death penalty. But hanging was an infrequent penalty to judge from studies of the East Riding of Yorkshire and of Gloucestershire.[15] The most common offence brought before Gloucestershire justices seems to have been the procreation of bastards, while in East Yorkshire theft cases outnumbered all others.[16] Fines and whippings were the commonest punishments. In all shires, a minority of justices did most of the work: the greater land-holders were usually inactive. Sessions usually lasted a day but could extend over several.

The most important functions of the J.P.s were not related to criminal justice but involved wide jurisdiction in the fields of trade and industry, taxation and social welfare. The administrative work of the J.P.s centred on the Quarter Sessions but much routine business was naturally carried on outside these occasions. The efficiency of this work was hampered by the lack of able subordinates at parish level: constables, wardens and overseers could be as incompetent as Dogberry and Verges in *Much Ado About Nothing*. Poverty and vagrancy, words given solid and frightening form by the armies of rootless beggars infesting the roads and towns of Tudor England, were potentially dangerous and disruptive forces. Tudor governments tried to control the problems arising from the economic changes of the period and the breakdown of a co-operative, communal society in favour of one based on competition. Whipping beggars and sending them on to the next parish was no solution. Existing charitable institutions and the newly-founded hospitals and almshouses could not contain all the deserving poor: the rootless were usually excluded from establishments that catered chiefly for aged and retired householders (who enjoyed quite comfortable conditions).

The able-bodied, masterless poor appeared a frightening menace and received ruthless treatment. Tudor reform of the poor law took due account of these problems, official policy gradually arriving at the recognition that support for the sick and old, and work for others, could only be provided by society as a whole. The J.P.s were given the job of implementing the reforms. The Acts of 1536 and 1563 were major turning-points in official attitudes to poverty. In 1536 the parishes were for the first time given responsibility for the poor within their bounds. But not until 1563 could J.P.s compel householders to pay contributions to poor relief. The economic crisis of the 1590s necessitated more radical steps. The thorny problem of the mass of vagrants, unable to find work, cut off from communities and families, and wandering about the land in a way which alarmed the respectable, remained serious. It had become established that an attempt should be made to find work for these unfortunates. In 1598, despite the passage of another Act allowing whipping and gaoling of beggars, another statute demonstrated an advance in official thinking. Compulsory rates were to be used to buy materials for paupers to perform useful work and, in the absence of sufficient parochial funds, the whole shire was to provide finance. Poor-houses, 'houses of correction', were to be built to house paupers. Destitutes who preferred to wander the highways rather than work in a closely supervised manner were to be rounded up. Perhaps it was the recovery of the economy, rather than the quality of the legislative machinery, which enabled the Elizabethan poor law to survive into the next century and beyond. The poor law could only work at all because the ruling class assented to its provisions and were enthusiastic for the 'social engineering' involved. The 1598 reforms stemmed from Commons pressure, just as the 1563 Statute of Artificers was, in its final form, the product of M.P.s' demands for a more comprehensive measure than that at

55

first suggested.[17] This Act was a clear demonstration, in fact, of the social conservatism of the landed classes in the face of inflation and the steady if slow growth of industry and trade. The Act stipulated that all unemployed men were to be forced to work on the land. Entry to trades was made harder and wage rates were to be carefully regulated to eliminate market forces. This was an impressive attempt at control of the economy, but was obviously difficult to enforce. The task of attempting to enforce it was given to the hard-worked J.P.s.

The special importance of the reign of Elizabeth in the development of local government is no accident. The age saw the emergence of the English provinces, with a new sense of identity evident in the taste for local history and antiquities. Whether there was such a phenomenon as 'the rise of the gentry' or not, it is certainly the case that in every shire a class of wealthy, well-informed, well-educated gentlemen was emerging in the late sixteenth century. This class, aided by the growing ranks of the professional and commercial classes, was instrumental in the formation of a system of local government which was to survive in essence for over four centuries.

NOTES

1. A. G. R. Smith, *The Government of Elizabethan England* (London, 1967) p. 85.
2. G. C. F. Forster, *The East Riding Justices of the Peace in the Seventeenth Century* (East Yorkshire Local History Society, 1973) pp. 9–10.
3. W. B. Willcox, *Gloucestershire: a Study in Local Government, 1590–1640* (1940) pp. 291–2, 304.
4. For the importance of tithes, see J. E. C. Hill, *Economic Problems of the Church* (Panther ed., 1971) pp. 77–131.
5. L. Stone, *The Causes of the English Revolution: 1529–1642* (London, 1972) pp. 63–4.
6. G. R. Elton, *England under the Tudors* (London, 1955) p. 58.
7. A. G. R. Smith, op. cit., p. 86.
8. G. R. Elton, *Policy and Police* (Cambridge, 1972) p. 382.
9. J. Hurstfield, 'County Government c.1530–c.1660' in *Victoria County History of Wiltshire*, v (1957) p. 81; W. B. Willcox, op. cit., p. 73.
10. Ibid., p. 80n.
11. Cited by G. R. Elton, *The Tudor Constitution* (Cambridge, 1960) pp. 456–7.
12. J. Hurstfield, op. cit., p. 89.
13. A. L. Rowse, *The England of Elizabeth* (London, 1950) p. 343.
14. For evidence of the effects of religious divisions on the workings of the Commission of the Peace in Sussex, see R. B. Manning, *Religion and Society in Elizabethan Sussex* (Leicester, 1969) pp. 238–71.
15. W. B. Willcox, op. cit., pp. 66–7; G. C. F. Forster, op. cit., pp. 44–5.
16. W. B. Willcox, op. cit., p. 67; G. C. F. Forster, op. cit., p. 41.
17. S. T. Bindoff, 'The Making of the Statute of Artificers' in *Elizabethan Government and Society . . .*, ed. S. T. Bindoff, J. Hurstfield, C. H. Williams (London, 1961) *passim*.

JUSTICES OF THE PEACE

1487 A Bail Act allowed J.P.s for the first time to receive bail from suspected offenders awaiting trial. This measure led to the abandonment of 'mainprize', a form of bail by personal surety without cash guarantee.

1489   An Act passed this year reinforced the powers of the justices by re-iterating their general authority in their shires.

1495   An Act against Extortion by sheriffs allowed J.P.s to convict sheriffs of misdeeds. This was a clear affirmation of the government's faith in the superior ability of justices to enforce a fair legal system.

The Beggars Act authorised the punishment of vagabonds by means of the stocks.

1501   J.P.s had been given no special powers under the 1495 Act: now they were ordered to pay special attention to the problem of vagrants, whom they were authorised to punish.

1504   The Act against Retainers empowered J.P.s to seek out offenders, thus demonstrating the official view that the justices were a useful counterweight to local magnates.

1522   A statute was passed forbidding J.P.s to issue warrants for arrest on suspicion.

1531   A new Beggars Act drew an important distinction between the 'idle', able-bodied poor and the sick and old: the first were to be apprehended by the justices and whipped, the latter were to be given licences to beg.

Another measure of the same year made the county authorities responsible for repairs to bridges within their borders.

1536   The Beggars Act (which originated from proposals made by William Marshall, an aide of Thomas Cromwell) established the principle that the parishes, supervised by the J.P.s, should find work and alms for the poor. Contributions for this purpose were voluntary.

1542   Closer government supervision of J.P.s was made possible by an instruction to judges of assize to hear complaints about their work.

1543   The court of King's Bench began to receive regular transcripts of all Quarter Sessions proceedings. This measure was another safeguard against corruption and maladministration.

1555   An Act was passed redefining the powers of justices to offer bail.

A Licensing Act gave J.P.s the responsibility for the licensing of alehouse-keepers.

Parishes became responsible for road repairs, under the ultimate super-vision of the J.P.s.

1563   A new Beggars Act introduced an element of compulsion into the poor rate – weekly contributions were to be paid by those able to do so, and those refusing to pay were to be called before the justices and ordered to pay. Gaol sentences could be imposed on those who still refused to pay.

The Artificers Act gave J.P.s further supervisory powers – all adult males were to work on the land except tradesmen who had served seven-year apprenticeships. J.P.s were to also compile and enforce local wage rates.

1572 A new Act for poor relief gave J.P.s the duty to assess the fair poor rate contributions of all, to ensure payment, and to appoint overseers of the poor in each parish. They were again ordered to deal severely with vagrants, who could face death if arrested a third time.

1576 Some provision for the able-bodied poor was made in a statute of this year. Justices were to see that stocks of raw materials were everywhere maintained to provide useful work in houses of correction.

1577 Justices were empowered to collect local contributions for the maintenance of the inmates of prisons.

1581 William Lambarde's study of the work of the J.P.s – *Eirenarcha* – was published.

1590 A thorough reform of the commission of the peace took place: the duty of the justices to hold regular sessions, hear cases, take sureties, keep records and generally to inquire into all matters in their competence was reiterated. The slight reduction in the jurisdiction of J.P.s in more serious crimes was apparent in a clause reserving serious felonies for judges of assize.

1593 Men who had sustained crippling injuries in war were put under the care of local J.P.s, who were to levy rates for their support.

1598 An Act for the Punishment of Rogues and an Act for the Relief of the Poor – both to be implemented by the J.P.s – together formed an important new approach to the problem of poverty. 'Rogues' were to be whipped, sent home and then put to work. Compulsory rates were to be used by local overseers to provide for the aged and sick and to buy raw materials for other paupers to work usefully. J.P.s were to select the overseers and Quarter Sessions were to build workhouses.

1601 The Act passed this year mostly repeated the provisions of that of 1598.

REGIONAL COUNCILS

INTRODUCTION

The accession to power of Henry Tudor in 1485 was followed by a steady recovery of the power and prestige of the central government. The most obvious change was that, following an era of war and political instability, a long period of peace and stable government began. After Henry had succeeded in crushing a series of dynastic revolts, the Tudor claim to the throne was confirmed and the first Tudor monarch was able to hand on to his heir a greatly strengthened and enhanced inheritance of power. Under Henry VIII, the Tudor monarchy became the central factor in a revolution affecting the lives of all its subjects. This revolution was based on a reinvigorated and much enlarged system of law and administration, novel not only in its methods but also in its aims. It succeeded in large part because it was based too on consent – not the consent of the nation as a whole but that of the ruling class which provided the commissioners, justices and lieutenants to implement it. At the centre of the kingdom was the glorious personality of the monarch, set at the centre of the panoply and show of the Tudor court, a figure not only symbolic of earthly power but possessed too of a profound spiritual and magical aura. It was from those regions far remote from the court, from Parliament and the Star Chamber, that the major threats to the peace of Tudor England came – most notably in 1536, 1549 and 1569. Wales, the far West and the North were isolated regions resistant to change – religious, social, cultural and economic as well as political.

In the North, the problems facing Tudor governments were extremely complex, but the basic issue was a simple one of national security. England needed a system of government in this region which was capable of withstanding invasion from Scotland. Over the previous five centuries, English kings had ceded extensive powers to those magnates who were able to muster the necessary armed force for this very purpose. The Bishop of Durham ruled in princely fashion a palatinate, the independence of which was not totally extinguished until the nineteenth century. In the baronies, honours and liberties which covered much of the remainder of England north of the Trent, Royal authority was strictly limited in practice by the rights of the lords and their servants to administer justice – the sheriffs were virtually powerless. As a county palatine in the hands of the Crown, Lancashire was a special case but elsewhere subjects looked more to local lords than to the king for justice. Among Northern families, two reigned supreme for much of the fifteenth and sixteenth centuries – the Percies and the Nevilles, Earls of Northumberland and Westmorland respectively. The creation of a Wardenship of the Marches in the early fifteenth century did nothing to alter this situation, neither was it the aim of any fifteenth-century king so to do. The two great families dominated the North and numerous lesser families ruled under them, seeking from them profit, privilege and patronage. The political scene there was not unresponsive to national politics – the Nevilles rose and declined in influence under Edward IV. Edward's awareness of the dangers inherent in dependence on these king-making magnates prompted his creation of a new office, that of Lieutenant in the North, which was given to his brother, Richard of Gloucester, in 1482. Two years later, Richard, now king, established a Council in the North based on Royal authority and entrusted with supreme overall authority in the region. The Council, already in existence from the time of

Richard's own rule in the North, was presided over by a Lieutenant – John de la Pole, Earl of Lincoln – although the office of Warden (now Warden-General) of the Marches was given to the Earl of Northumberland. A year after the Tudor coup of 1485, the latter replaced Lincoln. In 1489, he was 'furiously and cruellie murthered' by a mob at Thirsk, Yorkshire.[1]

In the government of the North, as elsewhere, the reign of Henry VII saw no startling innovations. Thomas Howard, Earl of Surrey, replaced Northumberland and held office for ten years, his chief task being the government of Yorkshire, while Princes Arthur and Henry were in succession given the honorific title of Warden-General of the Marches. In reality, power rested with the Lieutenant and his aides and there was no Royal council of the sort which had existed under Richard III.[2] By the time Henry VIII came to the throne in 1509 the very notion of a 'King's Council in the North' was moribund and the dissolution of the existing body was merely a belated recognition of that fact. R. R. Reid's contention that the revival of conciliar government by Wolsey was 'simply . . . part of the policy of securing closer control over the outlying parts of the realm which was forced on the Crown by the resistance offered in 1523 and 1525 to the heavy taxation required to meet the cost of the war with France and Scotland' may not be far from the truth.[3] Certainly war conditions stimulated a new concern over the government of the North. In 1525 a council of 17 members, mainly lawyers, was constituted under the formal presidency of Henry VIII's bastard son Henry 'Fitzroy' (d. 1536), who was created Duke of Richmond. At first the Council had full jurisdiction over all the Northern shires, excepting only the Durham Palatinate, but in 1527–8 military control of the Marches was again hived off and given to the Earl of Northumberland and to Lord Dacre. Except in judicial matters, where it was fast acquiring a reputation for efficient and fair treatment of cases, the Council's powers were now limited to Yorkshire. Richmond's Council was one of 'the temporary and personal councils which had fitfully governed the north since Edward IV's day'[4] but after the fall of Wolsey the origins of a permanent Royal Council began to emerge. In 1530, Cuthbert Tunstal, Bishop of Durham, became 'President of the Council in the North parts' – a permanent body of Royal officials under the headship of a leading ecclesiastical civil servant. Seven years later, after an interval which had seen the startling eruption of regional revolt in the Pilgrimage of Grace, a rising into which members of the existing Council had been inevitably swept, decisive action was taken by Thomas Cromwell to remould the government of the five Northern counties. There was to be a permanent King's Council under a Lord President, consisting both of the principal magnates and gentry of the region and of Royal officials, usually lawyers, meeting regularly and possessed of overall administrative and judicial authority. At first, the Council was instructed to meet in all the chief towns of its region, but later settled at York. To that city over the next century came thousands of prisoners awaiting trial for felony and treason and people involved in civil suits of every description. The duties of the President lay in his responsibility to the monarch for the good order of the North, the implementation of legislation there and the efficient despatch of legal business. Clearly, the office demanded men of exceptional qualities. Tunstal, again in command from 1537 to 1538 was not an ideal choice. Robert Holgate, a controversially Protestant ex-monk and staunch Henrician who was Bishop of Llandaff (Archbishop of York from 1544), has been described as 'the first of the great Lords President'.[5] His long term of office (1538–50) saw the problem of the North 'solved at last' and, despite war with Scotland and internal rebellion, Holgate could justly claim 'that there was never anye man that had cause to compleane for lacke of justice . . .'[6] Holgate's removal from office resulted from his adherence to Protector Somerset and the desire of John Dudley to buy the support of the Catholic Earl of Shrewsbury, Francis Talbot, who held the Presidency until 1560. The decline in influence of the Council during the 1550s was to some extent offset by the efforts of Thomas Gargrave, its Vice-President (d. 1579).

During the reign of Elizabeth, the Council was to become a more important feature of English government than ever before – as the driving force behind England's Northern defences, the link between regional administration and an ever more complex mass of parliamentary legislation, and the source of cheap and swift justice and equity for the Queen's Northern subjects. The indecisive Presidencies of Henry Manners, Earl of Rutland (1561–3), Dr Thomas Young, Archbishop of York (1564–8), and Thomas Radcliffe, Earl of Sussex (1568–72) provided little evidence of the inspired leadership required: Young was particularly unpopular and notably corrupt. The 1569 rebellion in the North was a turning-point: its aftermath saw the end of the Percies and Nevilles, their clients and followers, as a potent political force. The Neville lands passed to the Crown after the flight of the Earl of Westmorland; in 1572 the Earl of Northumberland was executed for treason. In August of the same year, a new President was appointed: Henry Hastings, Puritan zealot, cousin to the Queen, and third Earl of Huntingdon. Huntingdon's arrival at York in November 1572, initiated a long era of conscientious, incorruptible, paternalistic rule in the North. The authority of the President embraced trade, industry, religion and the welfare of the poor. Huntingdon sat at assizes, intervened in Parliamentary elections, acted as intermediary between Privy Council and local courts, between lord and tenant. Under him the Council became a more representative body (wisely including members of families hitherto noted for their Catholicism) and a more efficient organ of government. The power and prestige of the Council reached its zenith during Huntingdon's presidency, and his influence as patron of the Reformation in the North can scarcely be exaggerated: he 'cast down Catholicism not so much out of a love of destruction . . . as to build anew. . . . Huntingdon must

61

be held in no small way responsible for the religious development of the north in the latter part of the sixteenth century'.[7] His death in 1595 marked the end of the Council's greatness. Although it continued as a busy and efficient legal institution under Archbishop Hutton, Thomas, Lord Burghley (Robert Cecil's elder brother), and their Stuart successors its day had passed if only because the pressing circumstances which had brought it into being had passed too. The formal abolition of the Council in 1641, soon after the execution of its last President, the Earl of Strafford, was an inevitable concomitant of the destruction of the Stuart monarchy.

Many of the conditions which made Northern England an area with special problems for Tudor governments applied equally to Wales and its borders. Much of Wales was hilly and remote: 'hideous after a sort to behold, by reason of the turning and crooked by-ways and craggy mountains', as Camden described Radnorshire.[8] It possessed curious laws and customs. Murder was a crime open to compensation through the system of *galanas* – evidence of 'the kind of primitive, accommodating attitude towards crime which undermined the whole principle of justice, little tempered by mercy, which [the English] regarded as the only possible basis of a well-ordered society'.[9] The Welsh had their own language and culture. 'Theire harpers and crowthers singe them songs of the dooings of theire ancestors ... Here alsoe they spende theire time in hearinge some part of the lives of ... prophets and saincts of that cuntrie', wrote an English visitor to an early seventeenth-century *eisteddfod*.[10] After the Reformation, many Englishmen (and Welsh reformers like John Penry) deplored the state of religion in Wales, her people 'utterly destitute of Goode's holy woorde ... in the like, or reyther more darcknes and ignorance, then they were in the tyme of Papistrye'.[11] But most serious, from a Tudor viewpoint, was the lack of political and administrative organisation and the instability of Wales. Unlike the North, Wales was historically a nation but had lost its freedom in the thirteenth century. Subsequently English institutions, notably legal institutions, had been imposed in the six shires of the Principality – Anglesey, Caernarvon, Flint, Merioneth, Cardigan and Carmarthen, while a similar legal and governmental system applied in the Crown lordships of Pembroke and Glamorgan. Elsewhere, power rested with the magnates, the Marcher lords, whose domains were independent of Royal justice. Even more than the North, Wales was a land where land-holding, lineage and the ability to muster arms were the props of power. Towns were few in number, small, poor and alien in culture (Welshmen had been forbidden to hold land or property in towns). The Glyndŵr rising and the instability of Wales during the civil wars of the late fifteenth century prompted action from the energetic régime of Edward IV, who created his heir Prince of Wales in 1471 and appointed a council which was soon entrusted with substantial responsibilities in Wales and the border. (The Prince was also formally Lord of the county palatine of Cheshire;

Shropshire, Worcestershire, Herefordshire and Gloucestershire constituted the 'Marches'.) But above all the council remained the Prince's own household and, with his accession (as Edward V) and death and the usurpation of his uncle Richard of Gloucester in 1483 it ceased to exist. In 1493, Henry VII's heir Arthur was given similar powers and a new council, under the presidency of Bishop William Smith, was based at Ludlow, the centre of Arthur's earldom of March. After the Prince's death (1501) the council continued 'as a loosely organized commission, with the power of punishing crime in the Principality and the border shires'[12] until its authority was reinforced by Wolsey in 1525. In the North, Henry Fitzroy served as figurehead for a reformed council, in the Marches Princess Mary was chosen and her councillors were to be headed by John Veysey, lawyer Bishop of Exeter. The council was given considerable powers, exercising a commission of oyer and terminer, hearing private suits and receiving petitions, but made little impact under the uninspired presidency of Veysey.

Thomas Cromwell's plans for Wales went far beyond anything envisaged by Wolsey and in 1536 an act of union dissolved all Marcher lordships, created the new counties of Monmouth, Brecon, Radnor, Montgomery and Denbigh, and imposed an English system of administration and representation, with J.P.s, lieutenants and Welsh M.P.s at Westminster. Two years earlier, Dr Rowland Lee, a servant of Wolsey and friend of Cromwell, had been given the bishopric of Coventry and Lichfield and the Presidency of the Council in the Marches. (Lee, who was 'not affable to anye of the walshrie', disliked the idea of giving power to the Welsh gentry, as justices, on account of their poverty and supposed ignorance.) The Act of Union gave the Council a general, if vague, authority over Wales and the border counties (Bristol was excluded in 1562 and Cheshire in 1569). In practice, it could try any criminal offence, including treason, possessed the duty to enforce the ever-growing body of legislation concerning trade, commerce and welfare, and exercised judgment in civil cases of every conceivable description. It possessed full powers to fine, execute and even torture. Moreoever, it was 'even more than its northern brother, a local Star Chamber and Chancery',[13] because the 1536 Act of Union had given it prerogative powers. Thus the Council in the Marches was 'a starre Chamber and Chauncerie Corte for Wales', handling, usually with some degree of efficiency and speed, both criminal and civil business – the absence of a jury made for swift deliberation – and firmly backing up the *status quo* in religion. Local officials throughout Wales and the Marches were subject to its supervision (indeed it had a vital advisory role in the selection of J.P.s, sheriffs and lords lieutenant) and it had an important function in economic matters. Its military duties were above all related to the defence of the coasts.

By the end of the Tudor period, the Council consisted of 38 members and, as in the Council of the North, by this period the local gentry outnumbered the lawyers and other Royal officials. Thus the Council, for long an alien body, became more 'Welsh', more representative of the region over which its authority extended. Many members were rarely seen at meetings of the Council, a fact which increased the importance of its permanent officials, the poet Fulke Greville being the most famous among them, and reinforced the necessity for sound leadership. Rowland Lee's remarkably energetic Presidency (1534–43) was long remembered in Wales and was followed by the inconclusive terms of office of Bishop Richard Sampson (Lee's successor at Coventry and Lichfield) and of his successors, the Earls of Warwick and Pembroke and Bishops Heath and Bourne. Elizabeth replaced Bourne, a fanatical Marian and Bishop of Bath and Wells, with Lord Williams of Thame who soon gave way to Sir Henry Sidney. Sidney's long presidency was marked by serious attempts at an increase in efficiency and a reduction in corruption but was marred by bitter factional squabbling within the Council (Sidney was well known as a protégé of the Earl of Leicester).[14] In fact, the authority and importance of the Council was declining fast. The Elizabethan period saw no cataclysm in Wales to parallel the 1569 Northern rebellion – although the general nervousness of the government meant that great priority was still accorded to the choice of a President in the Marches. In 1586, Henry Herbert, 2nd Earl of Pembroke, was selected. Despite his desire for reform, Herbert's impulsive nature led him to quarrel with the lawyers and the officials of the Council and his feud with the Earl of Essex, who had great influence in late Elizabethan Wales, began a period of fruitless factional dispute. Essex's fall and execution came soon after the death of Pembroke but by 1601 there was plenty of evidence to suggest that strong government was again needed in Wales. The Presidency of Lord Zouche failed to totally meet this need: 'Factions were formed; disputes broke up the Council; and vested interests could not be overcome.'[15] Nevertheless, despite its eclipse as a political institution, the Council continued as a chiefly judicial body up to the Civil War and was restored at the Restoration, being finally abolished in 1689.

The Councils in the North and the Marches were established – on the basis of existing institutions – by a government anxious to secure a uniform system of law and administration throughout the realm. Their responsibilities extended over especially troublesome regions, a definition which, in 1539, seemed to apply equally to south-western England in the aftermath of the Exeter Conspiracy (in 1538, Henry Courtenay, Marquess of Exeter, had been executed together with the Countess of Salisbury and two of her sons). A Council of the West, under Lord Russell and consisting of eighteen members, was established and its duties included significantly that of taking action against speakers of seditious words and those who 'invent rumours or commit any such offences, not being treason, whereof inconvenience may grow'.[16] The end of the crisis in the West led to the abolition of the council.

NOTES
1. R. R. Reid, *The King's Council in the North* (London, 1921) p. 76.
2. S. B. Chrimes, *Henry VII* (London, 1972) p. 98.
3. R. R. Reid, op. cit., p. 101.
4. G. R. Elton, *England under the Tudors* (London, 1955) p. 176.
5. A. G. Dickens, *Robert Holgate: Archbishop of York and president of the King's Council in the North* (York, 1955) p. 11.
6. R. R. Reid, op. cit., p. 165; A. G. Dickens, op. cit., p. 11.
7. C. Cross, *The Puritan Earl: the Life of Henry Hastings, Third Earl of Huntingdon 1536-1595* (London, 1966) pp. 247, 269.
8. Cited by A. L. Rowse, *The England of Elizabeth* (London, 1950) p. 71.
9. G. D. Owen, *Elizabethan Wales* (Cardiff, 1962) p. 171.
10. Cited by A. H. Dodd, *Studies in Stuart Wales* (Cardiff, 1952) p. 13.
11. J. Penry, *Three Treatises Concerning Wales* (ed. D. Williams, Cardiff, 1960) p. xi.
12. P. Williams, *The Council in the Marches of Wales under Elizabeth I* (Cardiff, 1958) p. 11.
13. G. R. Elton, *The Tudor Constitution* (Cambridge, 1960) p. 199.
14. For the influence of faction in the Council, see P. Williams, op. cit., ch. xi.
15. Ibid., p. 311.
16. G. R. Elton, *Policy and Police* (Cambridge, 1972) p. 298.

OFFICERS OF THE COUNCIL IN THE NORTH

LIEUTENANTS AND HIGH COMMISSIONERS IN THE NORTH PARTS

1484–5 *John de la Pole, Earl of Lincoln.* Heir to the Duke of Suffolk, de la Pole served as Lord Lieutenant of Ireland and was among Richard III's closest aides. He survived the fall of his master, but rebelled against Henry VII and was killed at the battle of Stoke in 1487.

1485–6 *Richard Fitzhugh, Lord Fitzhugh.* Chosen by Henry VII, Fitzhugh was made constable of the castles of Richmond, Middleham, and Barnard and custodian of the Neville lands.

1486–9 *Henry Percy, 4th Earl of Northumberland.* After being released from gaol and restored to his earldom by Edward IV, Percy was given a number of offices including the wardenship of the East and Middle Marches. Richard III made him Chamberlain of England, Warden-General of the Marches and justice of the peace and restored to him all the forfeited Percy lands; but he deserted Richard at Bosworth and found favour with Henry Tudor. He was murdered in 1489.

1489–99 *Thomas Howard, Earl of Surrey.* Heir to John, 1st Duke of Norfolk, and created Earl of Surrey in 1483, he was a prominent supporter of the York-ist party and became Lord Steward of the Household in 1483. His restoration to favour by Henry VII in 1489 and appointment as Lieutenant and deputy-warden in the Marches initiated a long career as courtier, diplomatist and soldier. In 1510, Surrey became Earl Marshal and after his victory at Flodden (1513) was created Duke of Norfolk (1514). He died in 1524.

1499–1502 *William Senhouse (Sever).* Senhouse, a Benedictine monk, was

65

abbot of St Mary's, York, 1485–1502, Bishop of Carlisle, 1495–1502, and Bishop of Durham 1502–5. He died in 1505.

1502–7 *Thomas Savage.* A staunch Lancastrian and trusted servant of Henry VII, Savage was rewarded for his services by appointment as Bishop of Rochester (1492). In 1496, he was translated to London and in 1501 became Archbishop of York. He died in 1507.

1507–9 *Margaret Beaufort, Countess of Richmond.* See p. 207.

1525–30 *Henry Fitzroy, Duke of Richmond.* See p. 3.

PRESIDENTS OF THE KING'S COUNCIL IN THE NORTH
1530–3 *Cuthbert Tunstal, Bishop of Durham.* See p. 218.

1533–6 *Henry Algernon Percy, 6th Earl of Northumberland.* Born c.1502, he entered the Council in 1522, was made Warden of the East and Middle Marches in 1527 and Sheriff of Northumberland in 1532. In 1536, the Earl, heavily burdened with debts, surrendered his lands to the King in return for an annuity of £1000. He was too ill to play much part in the suppression of the Pilgrimage of Grace, resigned his office late in 1536, and died the following year.

1536–7 *Thomas Howard, 3rd Duke of Norfolk.* See p. 214. Norfolk served as Lieutenant and supervised the defeat of the rebels and the subsequent Royal vengeance. In fact, he was never President in title, but served as supreme Royal agent in the North for about nine months before the appointment of Tunstal in the autumn of 1537.

LORDS PRESIDENT OF THE KING'S COUNCIL IN THE NORTH
1537–8 *Cuthbert Tunstal.*

1538–50 *Robert Holgate.* Holgate, a Cambridge graduate and Gilbertine monk, was given the see of Llandaff in 1537 and soon after was recommended by Tunstal to Cromwell as 'a man veray mete to serve the Kinge in these partes' (i.e. the North). A moderate Protestant and keen educationalist, Holgate was Archbishop of York from 1544 to 1554, when he was deprived for marriage. Holgate died in 1555.

1550–60 *Francis Talbot, 5th Earl of Shrewsbury.* Prominent as a courtier and soldier (especially on the Borders – he was appointed Lieutenant-General in the North in 1544), Shrewsbury's religious views were distinctly conservative and he was pushed into office by the Earl of Warwick, who made himself Warden of the Marches and High Steward of Durham and reduced the Council's powers. Shrewsbury's abilities as a time-server kept him in office until his death but his lazy and careless attitude towards the Council's work could have been disastrous if it had not been for the work of Sir Thomas Gargrave.

1561–3 *Henry Manners, 2nd Earl of Rutland.* Rutland had succeeded his father in 1543 and had subsequently held office as constable of Nottingham Castle (1547), Warden of the East and Middle Marches (1549), and Lord Lieutenant of Lincolnshire and Nottinghamshire (1551). A favourite of Queen Elizabeth, he took a determined attitude to his work in the North and began work on making the King's Manor a more habitable residence (his predecessor had resided at Sheffield). His death in 1563 deprived the Council of a potentially active President.

1564 *Ambrose Dudley, 2nd Earl of Warwick.* Warwick, fourth son of the Duke of Northumberland, had been given his earldom by Elizabeth in 1561. A zealous Puritan, he was well known as a military commander and in 1564 was commanding an English force at Le Havre. According to Reid, 'on his return it was found that his health had been so shattered by the campaign that he could not endure the cold of a northern winter', and he immediately resigned the Presidency.

1564–8 *Thomas Young.* Dr Young, a Welshman, educated at Oxford, was appointed Bishop of St David's in 1559, a recognition of his exile under Mary. Little more than a year later, he became Archbishop of York. Said by Sir John Harrington to be of 'a drossie and unworthy part', Young is commonly claimed as the worst of the Presidents. His slovenly rule came at a dangerous period, on the eve of the 1569 rebellion.

1568–72 *Thomas Radcliffe, 3rd Earl of Sussex.* Sussex's long career as courtier, soldier and ambassador included a period of service (1557–64) as Lord Deputy of Ireland. His antipathy to the Earl of Leicester (especially at the time of the proposed Anjou marriage) made him a controversial figure in Elizabethan politics. Sussex's term of office saw the successful destruction of the rebel earls but contemporaries gave him little credit for this achievement and the last two years of Sussex's presidency were spent away from the North. Replaced by Huntingdon, he was given high office at Court as Chamberlain to the Queen and died in 1583.

1572–95 *Henry Hastings, 3rd Earl of Huntingdon.* Huntingdon had succeeded his father in 1560. An ardent puritan, he was not only the most powerful man in Leicestershire but cousin to the Queen too – he possessed no lands in the North. His energetic and precise conception of his office made him an ideal President and one well able to work closely and harmoniously with the central government: Queen Elizabeth praised his 'vigilant and watchful care'. The very length of Huntingdon's presidency gave him a unique insight into Northern affairs and his religious zeal drove him to campaign vigorously against Catholicism (between 1582 and 1595 thirty priests and eight lay-people, including Margaret Clitheroe of York, were executed for their beliefs). Huntingdon's death (in December 1595) was a severe blow to the Council and precipitated a struggle for control between the Earl of Essex and Robert Cecil.

1596–9 Matthew Hutton. A former Master of Pembroke Hall and Regius Professor of Divinity at Cambridge, Hutton was made Dean of York in 1567 and Bishop of Durham in 1589 with the backing of Lord Burghley. Early in 1596, he was promoted to both the leadership of the North and the Archbishopric of York, but was not given the formal title of President. (Despite the patronage he had received from the Cecils, Hutton had become an ally of Essex.) In 1599, Robert Cecil secured Hutton's forced retirement, ostensibly on the grounds of old age (he was seventy) and ill health.

1599–1603 Thomas Cecil, 2nd Lord Burghley, later Earl of Exeter. Elder brother to the Queen's chief minister, Robert Cecil, William Cecil's heir was a man of no more than mediocre abilities. Nevertheless, his appointment suited Robert Cecil well, especially in view of the impending negotiations over James VI of Scotland's claim to the English throne. Burghley, an energetic administrator, especially in the campaign against recusancy (he claimed to have 'filled a little study with copes and mass-books' within two months of taking office), was given an earldom by James and retired to his country house in Surrey, where he died in 1622, aged eighty.

SECRETARIES AND KEEPERS OF THE SIGNET (from 1525)
1525–50   John Uvedale. Uvedale served as secretary in Richmond's household and remained with the Council in the North after its reorganisation in 1530.

1550–78   Thomas Eynns. At the time of Eynns' appointment, the fruits of the office were increased to £33 6s 8d from £20.

1578–81	George Blythe
1581–6	Henry Cheeke
1586–1601	Robert Beale (jointly with Ralph Rokeby, 1589–95)
1601–4	Sir John Herbert

DEPUTY-SECRETARIES

1527–42	John Bretton	1587–9	Ralph Rokeby
1542–50	Thomas Eynns	1595–1601	John Ferne
1574–8	George Blythe		

ATTORNEYS-GENERAL (from 1556)

1556–8	Thomas Sutton	1570–89	Martin Birkett
1558–9	William Woodroffe	1589–98	William Payler
1559–61	Richard Whalley	1598–1603	Sir Cuthbert Pepper
1561–70	Sir Anthony Thorold		

OFFICERS OF THE COUNCIL IN THE MARCHES OF WALES

PRESIDENTS OF THE COUNCIL

1501–12 *William Smith.* A protege of Margaret Beaufort (in whose household he had been educated), Smith, as chief councillor to Prince Arthur, was probably carrying out presidential duties from c.1490. He continued to do so after Arthur's death (1502). A member of the Privy Council from 1485, Smith was Bishop of Coventry and Lichfield from 1493 to 1496, Bishop of Lincoln from 1496, Chancellor of Oxford University (1500–3) and co-founder of Brasenose College. He died in 1514.

1512–25 *Geoffrey Blythe.* Brother to Bishop John Blythe of Salisbury, Blythe was Treasurer of Salisbury Cathedral from 1494, Dean of York (1496), and Archdeacon of Salisbury (1499). He became Bishop of Coventry and Lichfield in 1503 and died in 1530.

1525–34 *John Veysey.* Born at Sutton Coldfield (Warwicks.), where he spent much of his life, Veysey was a successful lawyer. He became Dean of Exeter in 1509 and Bishop of Exeter ten years later (he held the see until deprived in 1551 and was briefly restored by Mary). Veysey died in 1554.

1534–43 *Rowland Lee.* Lee was the greatest of the Council's Presidents – 'stowte of nature, readie witted, roughe in speeche, not affable to anye of the walshrie, an extreme severe ponisher of offenders', as a member of the Council later described him. His tough policy and his incredible energy (he travelled frequently around Wales and the Marches) made him the ideal man to hold office during these crucial years. Lee was Bishop of Coventry and Lichfield from 1534 and died in 1543.

1543–8 *Richard Sampson.* Sampson was an able lawyer and civil servant who had served Wolsey and Henry VIII in embassies and other duties. A good conservative Henrician – he supported the Divorce but opposed Protestant innovations in worship – Sampson was Bishop of Chichester, 1536–43, and of Coventry and Lichfield from 1543. By 1548 he was forced to succumb to the Protestant pressure emanating from the Council.

1548–50 *John Dudley, Earl of Warwick* (see p. 211). Warwick, the first layman to hold the Presidency, had every intention of playing an active role in Wales but does not seem to have succeeded in meeting his Council. He was soon preoccupied with national affairs, and gave the Presidency to his supporter William Herbert.

1550–3 *Sir William Herbert (1st Earl of Pembroke, 1551).* Born in 1501, Herbert was the son of Sir Richard Herbert, a bastard son of William Herbert, Earl of Pembroke. His marriage to a sister of Queen Catherine Parr brought him the favour of Henry VIII and he obtained extensive monastic lands in Wiltshire, including Wilton Abbey, which became his seat. Herbert's position at Court ensured that he would be a considerable influence in the circle surrounding the young Edward VI. His alliance with the Earl of Warwick against Somerset led to his appointment to the Presidency of the Marches and, soon after, to a Lord-Lieutenancy embracing all Wales. He was given the lordship of Cardiff and extensive Welsh lands. A loyal servant of Mary, despite his Protestantism, Herbert was favoured by Elizabeth, who made him Lord Steward of the Household in 1568. He died in 1570.

1553–5 *Nicholas Heath.* Educated at Cambridge, Heath entered the Royal service and was ambassador to the German Protestants in 1535. In 1539, he was given the bishopric of Rochester and was translated to Worcester to replace Hugh Latimer in 1543. In 1551, he was deprived of his see and gaoled. Mary restored Heath to Worcester, promoted him to York and made him Lord Chancellor, but he was deprived in 1559 and died in obscurity twenty years later.

1555–8 *William Herbert, Earl of Pembroke.* Little is known of the Earl's second term of office – he resigned when criticised by the Queen for laxity in administering the affairs of the Council.

1558–9 *Gilbert Bourne.* A fervent Romanist, sometime Fellow of All Souls and chaplain to Bishop Bonner, Bourne was made Bishop of Bath and Wells in 1554 and was among the judges of the 'Oxford martyrs' – Cranmer, Latimer and Ridley. Bourne's appointment came only weeks before Mary's death and he was soon after deprived by Elizabeth.

1559 *John Williams, Lord Williams of Thame.* Williams was an astute politician who had risen in the service of Thomas Cromwell and amassed a large personal fortune during his tenure of the treasurership of the Court of Augmentations (1544–54). Williams' espousal of Mary's cause in 1553 and his Catholic beliefs brought him a barony in 1554 and he was given charge of the Queen's younger sister Elizabeth. He arrived at Ludlow in June 1559, but died in October.

1560–86 *Sir Henry Sidney.* Sidney, born c.1529, was knighted in 1550 and married a daughter of the Duke of Northumberland. Despite his close links with the Protestant establishment, he succeeded in making his peace with Mary and was sent to Ireland as deputy to his brother in law Lord Sussex. His connections with the Elizabethan court were close: his wife was the sister of Robert Dudley, whose follower Sidney became. Sidney's long period of office was generally a beneficial one for the Council, despite the bitter factional divisions which plagued it during the years after 1575. Sidney died at Ludlow in 1586.

1586–1602 *Henry Herbert, 2nd Earl of Pembroke.* Henry Herbert was the son of a former President and married the daughter of another – Henry

Sidney. In 1570 he succeeded to a rich inheritance of lands in Wiltshire (where he was Lord Lieutenant) and in Wales. (His Welsh connections and the fact that he could speak Welsh made him popular – he was described as *llygad holl Cymru*, 'the eye of all Wales'.) Pembroke was an active and honest administrator, who immediately set out to reform the Council's corruption and inefficiency in a manner which antagonised many. The fall of Essex removed his chief enemy from the scene, but he went on to clash with the legal element in the Council to such an extent that he lost effective control of its workings and gravely reduced its ability to act.

1602–15 *Edward Zouche, 11th Lord Zouche.* Under Zouche factionalism continued to blight the Council – Zouche himself engaged in a bitter quarrel over precedence with Sir Richard Lewkenor, Chief Justice of Chester. A well-educated man (he was a friend of Ben Johnson) with a sound knowledge of political matters, he nevertheless made some success of his commission and the rot which had set in during the 1590s was to some extent halted. Zouche resigned the Presidency in 1615 and was made Warden of the Cinque Ports, a financially rewarding office, in recognition of his services.

VICE-PRESIDENTS
This office was created because of the long absences of Sir Henry Sidney but on account of the expense involved (the Vice-president received £33 6s 8d per annum) was allowed to lapse after 1580 and thereafter the Chief Justice of Chester acted when needed.

1562–? *Sir William Gerard.* A prominent lawyer and protégé of the Earl of Leicester, Gerard was Chancellor of Ireland, Master of Requests, Recorder and M.P. for Chester. His work in Wales was highly praised by Sidney and he was for some years a major influence on the Council.

1565–9 *Sir John Throckmorton.* Throckmorton's successful career (he sat in the Parliaments of 1552/3, 1553, 1554, 1555, 1557/8 and was Recorder of Ludlow, Shrewsbury and Worcester) culminated in his appointment as Chief Justice of Chester in 1558 and he shared power in the Council with Sidney and Gerard. Accusations of fraud and forgery made against him in 1579 ruined him and he died soon after.

1569–71 *Sir Hugh Cholmondeley.* Cholmondeley was from a leading Cheshire family and had distinguished himself as a soldier. He made no significant contribution to the history of the Council.

1575–7 *Sir Andrew Corbet.* Lord Lieutenant of Shropshire, Corbet had little interest in his office and achieved little of value.

1577–80 *John Whitgift* (see p. 220). Whitgift was at this time Bishop of Worcester and most interested in the suppression of recusancy.

JUSTICES OF CHESHIRE

Until 1542, the Justice of Chester had jurisdiction only in Cheshire and Flint; in that year his powers were extended to Denbigh and Montgomery and he became chief Welsh judge. The justices were usually members of the Council. After 1578, the Justice became known as Chief Justice and was assisted by a deputy. It became usual for Chief Justices to assist at the Council as *de facto* Vice-president.

1542–5	Sir Nicholas Hare.
1545–57	Sir Robert Townshend.
1557–8	Sir John Pollard.
1558	George Wood.
1558–80	Sir John Throckmorton, Vice-president of the Council.
1580–9	Sir George Bromley.
1589–1600	Sir Richard Shuttleworth.
1600	Sir Richard Lewkenor.

CLERKS OF THE COUNCIL

This office (dating back at least until 1525) was concerned with the keeping of records and registering of decrees.

1565–90   Charles Fox.

1590–1628   Fulke Greville. Greville was a member of the Council from 1583 and thereafter its secretary and clerk.

SECRETARIES OF THE COUNCIL

This office was originally separate but was later combined with the clerkship. The secretary was the key official.

1558–90 Charles Fox	1590–1628 Fulke Greville

CLERKS OF THE SIGNET

This again, originally a separate office, came to be combined with the other two main administrative posts (the duties of the clerk of the signet were chiefly related to the sealing of orders and decrees).

1540–65	Charles Fox	1581–90	Charles Fox
1540–65	Edmund Fox	1581–90	Fulke Greville
1565–81	Charles Fox	1590–1628	Fulke Greville
1565–81	John Dudley		

QUEEN'S ATTORNEYS IN THE MARCHES

The attorney was chief prosecutor for the Council.

1554–9   William Gerard. (See above.)

1559–62   John Price; suspended from office 1570–1 and 1579–91.

1591–9   Roger Seis.
1599–1609 John Fleet.

QUEEN'S SOLICITORS IN THE MARCHES
The solicitor prepared evidence for judicial hearings.

1560–5   Richard Smith   1580–9   John Amyas
1565–80   Richard Vaughan   1591–1609   Thomas Medlicott

CLERK EXAMINERS
Responsible for the examination of evidence in cases brought before the
Council.

1567–98   Thomas Sherer   1598–1603   Arthur Massinger

ASSIZES

The development of the office of Justice of the Peace during the Tudor period
exemplified the successful partnership between Crown and ruling classes
which made possible a resumption of social and political stability after an
era of breakdown. This partnership was the foundation of conservative Tudor
society. The Crown had no paid civil service and gradually loaded the local
justices with a growing range of responsibilities and duties, both administrative and judicial. Elizabeth's reign saw this process continuing at as fast a
rate as ever, yet the political and religious tensions of the Elizabethan period
were beginning to drive a wedge between the monarchy and the élite on whom
it depended. In 1587 the Archbishop of York, alarmed by the growth of
papistry and puritanism in his diocese, declared that, although there were
'many gentlemen' in Yorkshire, there was 'yet very hard choise of fit men for
that purpose' (that is, to serve as J.P.s).[1] Apart from the incompetence,
laziness and corruption of many J.P.s, there was very obviously a serious
possibility that a substantial proportion of justices might come to question
the ideological basis of the monarchy. The Crown needed a means of monitor-
ing the work of the justices and this was to some extent provided by the system
of assizes.

The origins of assizes have to be sought before the Norman Conquest in
the community law of Saxon England. But the concrete beginnings of a
system of itinerant justices travelling the kingdom to hear cases lie in the
twelfth century. The right of justice lay ultimately with the King and his
Council but was delegated to the law courts. The Assize[2] of Clarendon (1166)
authorised justices to go and try prisoners throughout the realm. By the reign
of Edward I professional judges were visiting groups of shires to hear cases,
which began to include civil as well as criminal business. By the late thirteenth
century a system of thrice-yearly sessions in each shire had become established.

But the establishment of the assize circuits to 'deliver' gaols (that is, try prisoners) was a development of the reign of Edward III. The 'grand' assizes involved a group of judges, drawn from King's Bench, Common Pleas and Exchequer, visiting the principal towns of England to try cases. The Tudors confirmed the continued importance of this system, which represented the chief and final source of justice in the shires. There were six circuits – Midland, Home, Western, Norfolk, Oxford and Northern – and twice a year the justices began itineraries which covered in all fifty towns. In each town the assizes lasted a few days, so the Oxford Circuit, for instance, took twenty-eight days to complete. Civil cases were heard, but the bulk of the business of the assize courts was criminal justice, the trying of felonies, which was increasingly taken out of the hands of the J.P.s.

Tudor government can be seen in terms of interconnecting and overlapping jurisdictions, often with ill-established boundaries. Assizes represented the judicial power of the Crown, the fount of all justice, but the King's Council was represented in some regions by special bodies such as the King's Council in the North, the latter deriving its jurisdiction direct from the Council. So in the North the assize judges worked with that body and its President sat on the bench. The most crucial factor in the development of assizes was their relationship to the justices of the peace. From the 1550s onwards the judicial powers of the J.P.s were becoming increasingly circumscribed, even as their administrative duties were increasing. The division between cases properly heard at quarter sessions and those to be reserved for assizes was blurred and only in 1842 was it laid down in precise terms. Broadly quarter sessions could not try felonies like theft, murder and treason. While a prisoner might suffer long detention awaiting the biannual assizes there is no reason to suppose that the justice they administered was especially harsh – relatively few felons were hanged.[3] In theory the detachment of justices from local interests made their judgements less prone to bias or corruption. From 1573 the judges were allowed an 'expense account' for boarding in the shires – this was intended to deter bribery – but they continued to be lavishly entertained in the towns they visited. The attendance of county justices at the assizes in the county town expressed the alliance of county interests with central government. Throughout England government in practice was represented by the quarter sessions and the assizes. Ideally the two systems were intended to work in harmony. Assizes were occasions when local administrative problems could be discussed, when there could be a dialogue between local and central government. But beneath the periodic judicial and social rituals of the assizes lay the potential rift between the Crown and its local agents. Before setting out for the shires the assize judges were 'charged' by the government and on their return they reported on the state of the kingdom. The reign of Elizabeth saw a determined attempt by central government to reduce the number of justices and to enforce the strict conformity of those who remained to the religious settlement. In both these matters the Crown largely failed to get its way but governmental use of the assize judges demonstrates the way in which they brought government policy to the far corners of England. On occasions they could be a powerful counterweight to the justices, as when judges on the Norfolk Circuit backed the Bishop of Norwich against local Puritan justices.[4] In 1587 a general purge of J.P.s was attempted and the judges were asked to list those who were inefficient, ignorant or whose religious orthodoxy was dubious. Their reliance, as outsiders, on often biased local sources of information resulted in the dismissal of many sound men, while known recusants and men of corrupt character remained on the bench.[5] The Tudor state went to great lengths to secure an efficient and responsive legal profession, recognising that law and politics were inevitably closely intertwined. The training of judges at the Inns of Court was government-regulated. When they went to the shires they received their charges in Star Chamber itself. Although assizes were infrequent and judges could be ignorant of local conditions, the degree of impartiality and professional knowledge they brought to the far corners of England was undeniably beneficial to the cause of justice. But beyond this they provided the government's only direct knowledge of the state of the nation.

NOTES

1. J. T. Cliffe, *The Yorkshire Gentry from the Reformation to the Civil War* (London, 1969) p. 246.
2. 'Assize' means simply a sitting of a court, when the various members joined with the judge to issue a verdict or edict. The term could be applied to the deliberations of the King and his Council, as in this case.
3. J. S. Cockburn, *A History of English Assizes, 1558–1714* (Cambridge, 1972) p. 131.
4. A. Hassell Smith, *County and Court: Government and Politics in Norfolk 1558–1603* (Oxford, 1974) p. 224.
5. Ibid., p. 84.

ASSIZE CIRCUITS AFTER 1558

Home: Essex, Hertfordshire, Kent, Surrey, Sussex.

Midland: Derbyshire, Leicestershire, Nottinghamshire, Lincolnshire, Northamptonshire, Rutland, Warwickshire.

Norfolk: Bedfordshire, Buckinghamshire, Cambridgeshire, Huntingdonshire, Norfolk, Suffolk.

Oxford: Gloucestershire, Herefordshire, Shropshire, Oxfordshire, Staffordshire, Worcestershire.

Northern: Cumberland, Lancashire, Northumberland, Durham, Westmorland, Yorkshire.

Western: Berkshire, Cornwall, Devon, Dorset, Hampshire, Somerset, Wiltshire.

CLERKS OF ASSIZE: 1558–1603

Clerks of assize were the key officials who organised the circuits and managed a staff who kept the records of the courts.

Home

1558	John Lindsell.
1558–94	John Glascock (joint clerk, 1585–94)
1585–99	John Meade (joint clerk, 1585–94)
1595–1603	Henry Glascock (joint clerk, 1595–99)

Midland

1570s	John Forde	c.1590–1603	William Combe

Norfolk

1559–72	Humphrey Bedingfield	c.1600–3	Nicholas Hyde
1573–98	John Woolner		

Oxford

1559–77	William Fowler	1597–1603	Richard Fowler
1578–97	? Fowler		

Northern

1583–5	Richard Franklin	1592–1602	William Watkinson

Western

1560–9	Thomas Andrewes	1597–1603	Edward Hancock
1591–6	Barnabas Lewys		

SOURCE   J. S. Cockburn.

MINOR COURTS

The ancient baronial and popular courts (based on the hundreds) had by Tudor times ceased to possess much significance. As judicial forces, they were almost dead, the victim of Tudor civilisation. However, they were still important in the administration at local level of the land-holding system which still revolved to some extent around the manor.

COURTS BARON

The Court Baron existed in every manor and possessed two main functions. Firstly, it was the customary court of the copy-holders, where transactions relating to land-holding were performed. Secondly, it was the common law court of freeholders (a 'baron' was a freeholder) held to determine all disputes about land-holding and other minor matters. For this purpose, Courts Baron generally met every few weeks.

COURTS LEET

The Court Leet was held twice-yearly and was essentially a court of record at which a 'view of frankpledge' was taken. Frankpledge equalled 'free pledge' and so the Court Leet was a gathering of free men. It formerly possessed powers to deal with minor offences but most of these were annulled by an act of 1461. A nineteenth-century writer, however, reported that 'The Court Leet . . . still exists in some manors as a criminal side of the Court Baron. It is held before the Steward of the manor with reference to trivial offences.' [A. M. White, *Outlines of Legal History* (London, 1895) p. 63.] Here was a medieval institution which long survived the 'Tudor Revolution'.

LORDS LIEUTENANT

Know ye that for the great and singular trust and confidence we have in your approved fidelity, wisdom and circumspection, we have assigned . . . you to be our lieutenant.'[1] Thus ran a typical commission of lieutenancy from Queen Elizabeth to one of her most trusted subjects. The commission, issued under the Great Seal of the realm, was a mandate to that subject to exercise massive powers within the area of the shire to which he was appointed. Like the itinerant assize judges, the Lord Lieutenant was the representative of the central government at local level but, unlike the judges, his supervision was constant. In common with most of the other governmental institutions of Tudor England, the Lord Lieutenancy was not a sixteenth-century innovation, although it was transformed by the Tudor monarchy, and especially by Elizabeth, into a far more significant feature of government than ever it had been previously. Henry VIII had merely followed established precedents in appointing various magnates to supervise defensive arrangements in the shires and in 1549 a similar course was taken as rioting and open revolt alarmed the government of Edward VI. The Duke of Northumberland may have planned to establish the lieutenancy on a permanent basis and to augment its powers but under Mary its chief role remained military and in 1558 most of the existing commissions were terminated. Only under Elizabeth, and especially from 1585 onwards, did the Lords Lieutenant become a permanent institution.

The Lord Lieutenant was one part of a complex series of links between the 'government' (that is the monarch in Council) and the people. In previous centuries the sheriff had been the Crown's chief local agent but in Tudor England sheriffs were reduced to supervising parliamentary elections, executing writs and superintending the county gaols. More and more routine administrative work devolved on the justices of the peace. The justices were local gentlemen and there were frequent complaints about their inadequacy, corruption, excessive numbers and the fact that many were papists or puritans. But by and large the J.P.s served the nation well and were indispensable to the Tudor state. What was absolutely necessary was a means of supervising their work – this was provided by the Lords Lieutenant. Most Lords Lieutenants were always peers and a high proportion were members of the Privy Council – of sixteen members of that body in 1587 eight held lieutenancies.[2] Some privy councillors held a number. In 1579 the Earl of Leicester was Lord Lieutenant in twelve counties.[3] Thus the principal *personae* of central government were themselves closely involved in local government and in touch with the mood of the country. The pressure of work which this situation imposed on these great officers of state made it necessary for them to have deputies in the shires. The deputy lieutenants in practice wielded the powers of the Lords Lieutenant and were the nominees of the Council – by the end of Elizabeth's reign they were being increasingly appointed by individual lieutenants.

Only after 1585 were lieutenants appointed to almost all shires and thereafter the appointment was usually for life. In Norfolk, for instance, there was, previous to this date, no effective lieutenancy during Elizabeth's reign.[4] In Sussex the factionalism of the county and proliferation of great families resulted in two or three lieutenants serving simultaneously.[5] In his county the lieutenant controlled a great deal of patronage and his increasing dominance over the landed gentry who constituted the commission of the peace was a cause of increasing annoyance to the gentry class – in 1642 the lieutenancy was abolished. The establishment of Lords Lieutenant in most counties on a permanent basis was obviously crucial. They were increasingly called on to supervise the J.P.s and recommend men who were suitable for the office, to enforce the economic laws and generally regulate economic life (as when the government forbade grain exports in times of dearth), to punish vagabonds, to collect the Crown's loans and other financial impositions, and to control the enforcement of religious conformity. Mary had been obliged to use the Lords Lieutenant to suppress heresy and her successor employed them to hunt seminary priests and punish recusants. The Lord Lieutenant, usually *custos rotulorum* and head of the local justices, was in an unrivalled position to supervise the day to day administration of the law in his area.

The office of Lord Lieutenant had originally been concerned purely with defence, and it was the Spanish war of the 1580s which was a turning-point in its evolution. For many centuries all Englishmen above a certain economic level had been obliged to keep arms for the defence of the country, the number and type of weapons depending on their wealth. This obligation had been formally enacted in the Assize of Arms (1181) and the Statute of Winchester (1285) and continued to be the basis of national defence during the Tudor period, despite attempts by Henry VIII to maintain during his French wars a form of standing army. The Lords Lieutenant were obliged to call out the militia for inspection and training at regular musters, which were held once in three years for most of Elizabeth's reign but took place yearly or even twice a year in times of war. Only the towns, which held their own musters, were exempt from the Lords Lieutenants' musters, which were always held outside the busiest periods of the agricultural year. The government, which

78

to the Tudor state. What was absolutely necessary was a means of supervising their work – this was provided by the Lords Lieutenants. Most Lords Lieutenant always feared large assemblies of people, ordered in 1559 that no gathering was to exceed three hundred persons. The deputy lieutenants, assisted by officers known as provist-marshals and by the J.P.s serving as commissioners of musters, were responsible for calling out the musters and for recording attendances on muster-rolls. Fines were imposed on those who failed to attend or to supply substitutes. Corruption and inefficiency, which beset Tudor government generally to some degree, resulted in rolls being in-adequately kept and fines not paid. In 1587–88 the Council appointed special agents to supervise the arming of the shires. Even the emergence of a perma-nent lieutenancy did not entirely solve the problems and in 1601 the govern-ment tried to give the lieutenants statutory powers to impress soldiers for military service. The Commons threw out the bill. The potential of the Lords Lieutenant as agents of a despotic Crown was obvious.

NOTES

1. G. Scott Thomson, *Lords lieutenants in the sixteenth century* (London, 1923) p. 73.
2. C. G. Cruickshank, *Elizabeth's Army* (2nd ed., Oxford, 1966) p. 20.
3. M. B. Pulman, *The Elizabethan Privy Council in the Fifteen-Seventies* (Berkeley, U.S.A., 1971) p. 22.
4. A. Hassell Smith, *County and Court: Government and Politics in Norfolk 1558–1603* (Oxford, 1974) p. 313.
5. R. B. Manning, *Religion and Society in Elizabethan Sussex* (Leicester, 1969) pp. 9, 222–3.

LORDS LIEUTENANT 1585–1603

SOURCE J. C. Sainty, *Lieutenants of Counties 1585–1642* (*Bulletin of the Institute of Historical Research*, Special Supplement, *8*, 1970).

Bedfordshire
1586–1613   Henry Grey, 6th Earl of Kent

Berkshire
1586–1601   Henry Norreys, 1st Lord Norreys ⎫
1586–96   Sir Francis Knollys   ⎬ jointly
                                           ⎭
1596–1632   Sir William Knollys (jointly with Lord Norreys, 1596–1601)

Buckinghamshire
1586–93   Arthur Grey, 14th Lord Grey of Wilton

Cambridgeshire
1588–1600   Roger North, 2nd Lord North
1602–6   Thomas Howard, 1st Lord Howard of Walden

Cheshire and Lancashire (associated)
1585–93   Henry Stanley, 4th Earl of Derby

Cornwall
1585   Francis Russell, 2nd Earl of Bedford

1586–7   Sir Francis Godolphin ⎫
          Sir William Mohun   ⎪
          Peter Edgcumbe   ⎬ jointly
          Richard Carew   ⎭
1587–1603 Sir Walter Raleigh (see p. 217)

Cumberland, Westmorland, Northumberland (associated)
1586–95   Henry Hastings, 3rd Earl of Huntingdon

Derbyshire
1585–90   George Talbot, 6th Earl of Shrewsbury
1590?–1616 Gilbert Talbot, 7th Earl of Shrewsbury

Devon
1585   Francis Russell, 2nd Earl of Bedford
1586–1623 William Bourchier, 3rd Earl of Bath

Dorset
1585   Francis Russell, 2nd Earl of Bedford
1586–98   William Paulet, 3rd Marquess of Winchester
1601–11   Thomas Howard, 3rd Viscount Howard of Bindon

Durham
1586–95   Henry Hastings, 3rd Earl of Huntingdon

Essex
1585–8   Robert Dudley, 1st Earl of Leicester (see p. 211)
1588–98   William Cecil, 1st Lord Burghley (see p. 209)

Glamorgan and Monmouthshire (detached from Wales 1602)
1602–28   Edward Somerset, 4th Earl of Worcester

Gloucestershire
1586–94   Giles Brydges, 3rd Lord Chandos
1595–1602 William Brydges, 4th Lord Chandos

Hampshire
1585–98   William Paulet, 3rd Marquess of Winchester
1585–93   Henry Radcliffe, 4th Earl of Sussex (jointly with Lord Winchester)
1595–1606 Charles Blount, 8th Lord Mountjoy (jointly with Lord Winchester, 1595–8)

Hertfordshire
1585–8   Robert Dudley, 1st Earl of Leicester
1588–98   William Cecil, 1st Lord Burghley

Huntingdonshire
1588–96   John St John, 2nd Lord St John of Bletso
1597–1618 Oliver St John, 3rd Lord St John of Bletso

Kent
1585–97   William Brooke, 10th Lord Cobham
1597–1603 Henry Brooke, 11th Lord Cobham

Leicestershire
1587–95   Henry Hastings, 3rd Earl of Huntingdon
1596–1604 George Hastings, 4th Earl of Huntingdon

Lincolnshire
1585–7   Edward Manners, 3rd Earl of Rutland
1587–98   William Cecil, 1st Lord Burghley

Middlesex
1590–1   Sir Christopher Hatton (see p. 214)

Norfolk
1585–96   Henry Carey, 1st Lord Hunsdon

Northamptonshire
1586–91   Sir Christopher Hatton

Nottinghamshire
1587–8 . John Manners, 4th Earl of Rutland
1588–90   George Talbot, 6th Earl of Shrewsbury

Oxfordshire
1586–1601 Henry Norreys, 1st Lord Norreys ⎱ jointly
1586–96   Sir Francis Knollys   ⎰
1596–1632 Sir William Knollys (jointly with Lord Norreys, 1596–1601)

Rutland: as Leicestershire

Somerset
1585–1601 Henry Herbert, 2nd Earl of Pembroke
1601–21   Edward Seymour, 1st Earl of Hertford

Staffordshire
1585–90   George Talbot, 6th Earl of Shrewsbury

Suffolk
1585–96   Henry Carey, 1st Lord Hunsdon

Surrey
1585–1624 Charles Howard, 2nd Lord Howard of Effingham (Earl of
           Nottingham, 1597)

Sussex
1585–1624 Charles Howard, 2nd Lord Howard of Effingham
1586–1608 Thomas Sackville, 1st Lord Buckhurst (jointly with Lord
           Howard)

Warwickshire
?–1590   Ambrose Dudley, 1st Earl of Warwick

Wiltshire
1585–1601   Henry Herbert, 2nd Earl of Pembroke
1601–21   Edward Seymour, 1st Earl of Hertford

Yorkshire
1586–95   Henry Hastings, 3rd Earl of Huntingdon
1599–1603   Thomas Cecil, 2nd Lord Burghley

Wales (one unit for lieutenancy purposes)
1587–1601   Henry Herbert, 2nd Earl of Pembroke
1602–7   Edward Zouche, 11th Lord Zouche

5 THE CHURCH

INTRODUCTION

The history of English religion in the Tudor period centres inevitably on the events of the English Reformation. In England, as in other European countries, the Catholic Church came under fierce attack from critics of its organisation, powers and doctrines. The great English radical William Cobbett, writing in the 1820s, declared that 'the "Reformation", as it is called was engendered in lust, brought forth in hypocrisy and perfidy, and cherished and fed by plunder, devastation and by rivers of innocent English and Irish blood . . .'[1] Cobbett's *History of the Protestant Reformation* was neither the first nor the last in a long series of polemical and partisan accounts of the events of the period. But the cooling of religious passions in the present century has permitted an objective analysis of the causes of the Reformation.

The concentration of this account (and of many others) on the English Reformation – a term conveniently embracing a vast complex of religious, political and cultural changes – should not blind the student of religion in the Tudor period to the fact that religious and spiritual phenomena were never wholly contained within the fold of an established Church or even within the compass of Christianity itself. 'Superstitions' denounced by the Church, often pre-Christian in origin, ranged from a simple faith in charms and potions to malicious attempts to bring afflictions on enemies by the use of tokens and spells. The Church condemned these popularly-held notions as 'sorcery' or 'witchcraft'.[2] They were nonetheless held by many simple people alongside a conventional Catholic faith. Late fifteenth-century England seemed to foreigners a pious land where the people were much given to public demonstrations of their faith. When Henry VII died in 1509, the English Church was still an arm of the international Church which looked to Rome for its fountainhead. To this extent, the reign of the first Tudor king saw no great turning-point between 'medieval' and 'modern' history. Henry Tudor died a pious and conventional Catholic, a faithful son of the Church. His reign had seen no assault on the doctrines of the Church but a number of measures had been enacted which limited the special privileges and immunities so zealously guarded by the clergy. The clerical class had derived its favoured position from its unique involvement in the maintenance of government, education and culture in a violent and semi-literate lay society. Anti-clericalism grew alongside a more civilised and educated social order. Since the corporate wealth and legal protection of the priests did not decline with their general prestige, many laymen viewed the Church as then constituted as a hindrance to the further development of stable monarchical government. Most European rulers sought a redefinition of the place of the Church in society.

By the late fourteenth century, the long tradition in England that the King's chief officers were to be drawn from the ranks of the clergy was being broken. Nevertheless, English Kings continued to recruit large numbers of clerics for their administrative machinery and rewarded them with preferments in the Church. This process, in theory abhorrent to the Church, was freely sanctioned by the Papacy. Canon Law – the Church's own system of jurisdiction – could be bent to allow a complete divorce of cure (the obligation on a priest to serve the parish or church whence he derived his income) from benefice (the right he possessed to that income). In this manner, many clergy accumulated numerous livings and visited few if any of them. While still a child, Cardinal Wolsey's illegitimate son drew an annual income of over £2700 from the Church. He was Dean of Wells, was rector of several parishes and held canonries in half a dozen major churches![3] This was the type of abuse which could be turned easily into a weapon to beat the Church; yet many contemporaries viewed such practices as convenient and even essential to society.

The *modus vivendi* arrived at by the English monarchy and the Papacy was thus in the long term a development full of potential dangers for the ecclesiastical and even the political establishment. Its continuance depended on the goodwill of both sides and ultimately the King held a superior bargaining position. While the partnership of King and Pope ran smoothly, benefiting each partner, no King could see much appeal in the views of radical thinkers who called for a complete Royal domination of Church matters. (The best-known of these was Marsiglio of Padua who, in his *Defensor Pacis* (1324), denied the right of the Church to hold property or to make laws. Significantly, Marsiglio was not much read in England until the early 1530s.) But Anglo-Papal relations did not lack an occasional injection of tension and drama into their placid course. During the Hundred Years War between England and France, the Popes resided for a time at Avignon under the domination of the French Crown. For more than three decades after 1378, the Papacy was divided and its prestige sank lower than ever. While few Englishmen were deeply interested in the affairs of the Pope (or Popes) and even fewer denied the need for a Papal primacy, many resented paying taxes to Rome. Exactions such as Peter's Pence were more irksome than oppressive but latent nationalism lent support to demands for curbs on Papal action. As early as 1307, these demands were loudly voiced in the

Commons and they led eventually to the passage of a group of measures known collectively as Provisors and *Praemunire*.

These were defensive and conservative rather than revolutionary measures. The Provisors Acts (the first was passed in 1351) were purportedly designed to protect English patrons (that is, those laymen who owned the 'advowsons', or rights of appointment, to Church livings) from Papal 'provisions' (or deeds of appointment) to those livings. The Popes had never in fact claimed in practice a right to appoint to all benefices in England any more than they had denied the right of English Kings to nominate men for bishoprics. But laymen felt threatened by Roman pretensions and demanded Royal action. The Provisors Acts were not much used but demonstrated the potential defiance of the English people. The *Praemunire* Acts were similarly potentially valuable weapons against the Papacy. Their definition of the rights of the Crown was useful when Anglo–Papal relations were strained. The so-called 'Great Statute' of *Praemunire* of 1393 was foreshadowed by earlier Acts of 1353 and 1365. The 1393 measure emerged after the attempts of Pope Boniface IX to extend his control over ecclesiastical appointments and banned the import of the relevant Bulls (or edicts) from Rome. A penalty of loss of all possessions was attached. When Boniface's quarrel with Richard II was brought to an amicable conclusion, the statute fell into abeyance. But it remained unrepealed, as did the Provisors legislation – both were to be activated during Henry VIII's breach with Rome. In the early fifteenth century, Pope Martin V declared: 'It is not the Pope but the King of England who governs the Church in his dominions.' The age of Lancastrian and Yorkist Kings saw an easy and tolerant relationship between King and Pope. Henry VII's restoration of Royal power brought with it stringent financial policies which naturally affected the Church. Despite a decline in the flow of Papal taxation, the Papacy acquiesced in Royal policies. It was symptomatic of the traditional approach to government manifested by Henry that Cardinal Morton was among the King's chief ministers as well as Archbishop of Canterbury.

Henry VII's seizure of the Crown and his struggle to retain it in the face of insurrection and invasion brought the issue of law and order to the forefront. The rights of the Church presented an obstacle to Royal policies: the clergy maintained sanctuaries where offenders against the King's law might claim refuge and recognised themselves as subject to no law but the Canon Law. In 1487, a traitor to the Crown, Humphrey Stafford, took refuge in a church, claiming right of sanctuary. Legal opinion subsequently decreed that this right did not apply in cases of high treason. The fact that any man possessing a tonsure (the sign of a first step towards ordination) could claim immunity from Royal justice also presented a problem for an energetic monarch. Measures implemented after 1485 were designed to deal with abuses of the system without removing the special and sacred position of the priesthood. The Church continued as a distinct estate within the realm. In the same way that King and laity largely controlled the financial and institutional aspects of the Church, so the Church made massive incursions into the field of 'secular' life. It maintained a national system of law courts administering its own law and controlling most aspects of morality, marital law and the probate of wills. These courts were resented and even hated by laymen because of what was seen as their autocratic and interfering approach and especially by their financial exactions. Common lawyers (of whom Thomas More was a prominent example) served the cause of the Reformation by defining new limits to Royal power. (More was unable to follow fellow-lawyers such as Christopher St German and Simon Fish in their radical conclusions.) Attempts to secure a thorough reform of Canon Law in the mid-sixteenth century failed (although Thomas Cranmer worked on an unpublished scheme) and Church courts continued to function much as before.

During the Elizabethan and early Stuart period the volume of business passing through these courts increased vastly and they came to be an even more central institution in English life than they had been prior to the Reformation. During the years preceding the outbreak of the Civil War in the 1640s, the issue of the Church courts and their exactions again became one on which bitter dispute raged.[4] Neither did the Reformation remove other aspects of the Church's dominance of lay life. Education and cultural life only gradually emerged from ecclesiastical control. Colleges and schools continued to be staffed by priests, although laymen were emerging as founders. Tithes were paid by all laymen (although many resisted the obligation) and the parish priest continued as a central figure in English life. The Protestant Reformation allowed the priests to take wives and their possession of wives and children enabled the clergy to farm their land more efficiently. Family life was a contributory factor to the process whereby the clergy increasingly aped the life-style of the gentry.

The bitter feelings held by many Londoners towards the clergy were clearly demonstrated over the Hunne case in 1514. Richard Hunne had fallen into dispute with the Church authorities over the issue of mortuary fees (that is, the payments due to priests for conducting funerals). Hunne's parish priest had seized a winding-sheet in lieu of the fee due for burial of Hunne's young son and Hunne charged the priest with *Praemunire*. His arrest and mysterious death followed.[5] While the reaction in London was largely anti-clerical in tone, the charges of heresy against Hunne may not have been unfounded. London contained many heretical groups and London merchants were to be staunch supporters of Tyndale and other reformers. England had been free of any serious doctrinal opposition to Catholicism prior to the late fourteenth century. The Lollard heresy had originated with John Wyclif (d.1384), an Oxford academic who had challenged the philosophical and doctrinal basis of the Church.[6] Wyclif enjoyed the support of many influential laymen for his strictures on the excessive wealth and pretensions of the Church but this support shrank rapidly when he proceeded to deny basic doctrines such as purgatory and transubstantiation. Nevertheless, Wyclif died a natural death at his Leicestershire rectory and only in the fifteenth century did serious persecution of his followers begin. Lollardy was not identified with social revolution (as was the Hussite heresy in Czechoslovakia) but it rapidly became the religion of a minority of the lower orders.

Lollardy continued as an underground religion throughout the fifteenth century and was quite strong in many areas of southern England. In the early sixteenth century, proletarian heresy provided an audience for and was itself stimulated by the influx of Protestant ideas from Europe. John Foxe, the Elizabethan martyrologist, presented the Lollards as the natural ancestors of English Protestantism, opposing Rome on the issues of pilgrimage, the adoration of saints, the vernacular Bible and the Eucharistic presence.[7] Lollardy was the basis of most of the heresy so vigorously persecuted by the Church in the reign of Mary. In many areas, the Lollard tradition was a stimulus to the birth of a local Puritan movement. Certainly, many aspects of religious legislation mirrored old Lollard themes, but Henry VIII's Royal Injunctions (and the general trend of legislation during that reign) have been claimed as examples of Erasmian influence in the English Reformation.[8] While Henry lived, England retained most of the apparatus of Catholicism, although progress towards a Protestant liturgy was accelerated during Henry's later years. As head of the new national Church, Henry VIII took seriously his position as the nation's principal theologian. A recent biographer sums up Henry's mentality as that of 'a rather enthusiastic pedant'.[9] The Royal Supremacy was foreshadowed by Thomas Wolsey's remarkable domination of Church and State after 1518. Wolsey's pre-eminence was a cause of resentment to laymen and clergy alike: the episcopate were as satisfied at his fall as any group in the realm. Their temporary subservience to Wolsey did not, however, necessarily predispose them to accept the novel claims of the King in the early 1530s. The Royal Supremacy was genuinely new: an original concept forged by Thomas Cromwell (significantly a disciple of Marsiglio of Padua).

Wolsey's most serious failing has been adjudged as his total neglect of the pressing need for thorough reform of the Church. Wolsey, a great pluralist himself, was in no position to correct the faults of others. Cromwell emerged from Wolsey's household and from an international training in law and finance equipped with revolutionary ideas on the permanent reconstitution of the Tudor state. His successful conduct of the Royal divorce brought him rapidly to supreme power. Cromwell's brief period of office saw the constitution of a national Church (with Cromwell himself as 'vicegerent' or deputy to the King in all spiritual matters), the reform of doctrine and

87

ceremonial on Erasmian lines, the total destruction of the religious houses, and the massive enrichment of the Royal treasury in consequence. (Henry subsequently squandered the financial benefits in fruitless foreign warfare.) Resistance to this tremendous programme of reform was sporadic but deep-rooted. Acknowledgement of Cromwell's numerous beneficial and progressive actions (Foxe praises him as a patron of the English Bible) should not be allowed to obscure the fact that his policies were implemented with a systematic brutality hitherto unknown in England. Had his schemes for the future of the monarchy come to fruition, England would have acquired a despotism of unshakeable strength.[10] Cromwell's defenders often ignore these aspects of his policies. Cromwell's fall ushered in a period of governmental and religious confusion.

Among the vast majority of the leading men in Church and State who had defended the Henrician Reformation were many who opposed the spread of Protestantism. Prominent among them were Stephen Gardiner, Bishop of Winchester, and Thomas Howard, Duke of Norfolk. Norfolk was discredited by the failure of the marriage between the King and his niece, Catherine Howard. But Gardiner continued as a leading personality in the government of the realm. (Deprived and gaoled in the reign of Edward VI, Gardiner was restored to favour by Mary, who ignored his role as competent defender of the Royal Supremacy under her father.) In the years 1539–40, the English Church lost the leadership it had possessed while Cromwell lived. The passage of the Act of Six Articles signified a major retreat from the advances of the mid-1530s and resulted in the resignation of Latimer and other Protestant bishops. (Latimer, an underregarded figure amongst the reformers, was recognised as the leading personality among English Protestants.) While some Protestants found themselves in trouble for their views, no large-scale persecution ensued (the execution of Barnes was due to the personal hatred of Gardiner for Henry's German emissary). In practice, the Act ('the whip with six strings' as critics called it) was too fierce to be implemented. Had it been enforced, a slaughter of men and women far greater than that which was to occur in the reign of Mary would have followed.

In fact, it is fairly clear that Henry was by no means determined on a policy of total reaction. His continued support for Archbishop Cranmer enabled the latter to proceed with his work on liturgical reform. Henry had no liking for the disorder and strife which had emerged from religious controversy, but there is evidence that in his last years he was moving to a further radical transformation of English religion. A measure proposing the destruction of the chantries passed through Parliament and Henry may even have contemplated the abandonment of the Mass itself.[11] Moreover, his last Queen was a woman known for her moderate but determined Protestant beliefs. Conservative attempts to destroy Catherine Parr by, for instance, associating her with the Lincolnshire gentlewoman Anne Askew, burnt for heresy in 1546, failed miserably. Catherine survived, the much-respected patron of Hugh Latimer, Miles Coverdale, Edmund Grindal, John Cheke and other Protestant scholars. By the time of Henry's death, it was inevitable that the control of government would pass to committed Protestants and it is clear that Henry himself was fully aware of this development. While allowing considerable freedom of action to the conservative faction in his Council, the King acquiesced in the rise to dominance at Court of the party surrounding Edward Seymour, Earl of Hertford. Hertford, a Protestant, was able by the time of the King's death to secure the total discredit of the Howard clan – the Duke of Norfolk was saved from execution only by the death of the King.

The accession of the nine-year-old Edward VI to the throne in 1547 was followed soon after by the appointment of Hertford as Lord Protector. The new government rapidly moved in the direction of Protestantism; the abolition of the heresy legislation inaugurated a period of fierce religious controversy. The King was himself a pious and opinionated Protestant (his father had permitted an education under the tutorship of Sir John Cheke and other reformers). Protestantism had made many converts among the more influential sectors of society – the aristocracy and gentry, the clergy, and the University scholars – and had made good progress among the merchants, craftsmen and artisans in many towns. It was no longer confined to the capital and South-east England – Protestant preachers were as well received in Oldham, Halifax and Leeds as in Ipswich or Chelmsford. While Protestants constituted only a minority of the nation, conservative opinion was divided and lacking in leadership. As in other periods, most of the population probably lacked any real involvement in the religious disputes. The authorities were able to crush the chantries with ease, although prayers for the dead had long been considered essential by most people. It was evident that Cranmer would at last receive approval for the introduction of a new service-book, a development viewed with disapproval by many bishops. The Book of Common Prayer issued in 1549 was, in fact, a conservative document in many ways. Its retention of the form of the Mass, of vestments and of many traditional ceremonies aroused the objections of advanced Protestants. These objections received the support of the much respected Strasbourg reformer, Martin Bucer, who had fled to England in company with other eminent Protestant leaders to escape Imperial persecution. Bucer and other Continental reformers were increasingly influential in intellectual and governmental circles in England. For many years, the doctrines of Huldreich Zwingli of Zurich had been influential in the country and John Calvin of Geneva was much respected by those now in command of the English state. Cranmer himself had abandoned Lutheran views of the sacrament of the Eucharist for a more radical doctrine akin to that of Zwingli, and argument increasingly centred on the issue of the Eucharistic presence. (Zwingli had argued that the Eucharist or Communion should be considered as a mere commemoration of Christ's death and that Luther's notion of a vague 'presence' of Christ in the bread and wine should be repudiated.) Writing to King Edward, Calvin urged the abolition of the 'frivolities' and 'manifest abuses' which still riddled the English Prayer Book.[12]

The new Prayer Book issued by Cranmer in 1552 was a product of these criticisms and of the Archbishop's own changing ideas. The fall of Hertford (now Duke of Somerset) had been seen by conservatives as the prerequisite of a return to Catholicism. However their hopes were dashed when his successor, John Dudley, Earl of Warwick, showed his determination to proceed with an even more thorough Reformation. His reasons for doing so were probably more financial than religious: the completion of the dissolution of the chantries and the seizure of Church treasures brought some relief to a growing cash crisis. (Warwick, by then Duke of Northumberland, resorted to a debasement of the currency in 1551.) But this unscrupulous politician received adulatory support from many Protestants: among his clients were John Knox and John Hooper. Hooper, an idealist who had spent many years in exile during Henry VIII's reign, was given the see of Gloucester but caused a minor crisis by his persistent refusal to be consecrated as a bishop in the usual vestments. He eventually capitulated on the issue after strong resistance by Nicholas Ridley and Cranmer to any relaxation of the usual ordinances for Hooper's benefit. The new bishop thereafter turned his attention to his diocese, administering it (and the diocese of Worcester, which he acquired in 1552) with remarkable energy and devotion. This 'violent and erratic partisan' may be seen as a major founder of English Puritanism, while his opponents amongst the Edwardian bishops have been characterised as 'Anglicans'. It is significant that Ridley sought to discredit Hooper with charges of near-Anabaptism. Many radical sects had emerged on the Continent during the early decades of the sixteenth century and the Forty-two Articles of 1552 were aimed as much at the sectarians as at the Catholics. (The notion that 'Christian men's goods were common' was condemned alongside the doctrines of adult baptism and the denial of Christ's incarnation.) The Edwardian regime had no scruples about executing Joan Bocher and other stubborn radicals, while Hooper condemned Anabaptist doctrine as totally as other bishops.

Northumberland's attempts to block Mary's accession to the throne in 1553 by the substitution as monarch of his daughter-in-law foundered on the rock of popular devotion to the Tudor line. Few Protestants were prepared to deny the right of Mary to succeed, although all must have feared the fate of the Protestant Church under her rule. Similarly, the various attempts to remove Mary from the throne were political rather than religious in motivation. During the years 1553–4 Mary reintroduced the Catholic religion and the Roman Supremacy as it had existed before 1529. There is no reason to suppose that this policy was unpopular with more than a minority of the nation. The fears of the gentry about a possible restoration of monastic lands to the Church were calmed after assurances from the government. Parliament was not willing to countenance any attack on the benefits which the landed classes had gained from the Henrician Reformation – in 1555 it rejected calls for a measure confiscating the property of persons who had fled the country for religious reasons. But the propertied classes put up no resistance to the introduction of a conservative reign of terror promulgated by bishop Gardiner and Cardinal Pole with the Queen's firm support. The burning of over three hundred people further diminished the Queen's popularity, already severely dented by her unpopular marriage to Philip of Spain. Although a number of eminent men (notably Cranmer, Latimer and Ridley) suffered death for their beliefs, most of the victims were of humble rank and most came from the industrial areas of southern England. Few of them were educated Protestants and the beliefs for which they died can often be traced back to the Wycliffite doctrines of the Lollards. While most of the martyrs celebrated by Foxe in his influential *Acts and Monuments* were artisans and craftsmen, it is probably an exaggeration to suggest that 'the English upper class contained little of the stuff of martyrs'.[13] Over eight hundred wealthy Protestants, gentry, merchants and clergy, had fled the realm for the sanctuaries of Protestant Europe.

The sum effect of Mary's reign was to seriously damage the Catholic cause in England permanently. Protestantism had been suppressed (or at least driven underground) and Catholic worship revived. But no attempt had been made to revitalise the English Church with the best influences of the Continental Counter-Reformation. When Elizabeth came to the throne, there was little evidence of any rigid division of the English into Catholics and Protestants. Elizabeth was viewed long before the death of her sister as the potential saviour of English Protestantism and, as daughter of Anne Boleyn, she had a personal interest in the revival of the Henrician Statutes. The Pope and Mary Tudor had declared Elizabeth a bastard and it was obvious that Elizabeth would repudiate the Roman obedience. Nevertheless, she moved with caution, retaining for a time the Catholic rites in her own chapel and forbidding preaching. At the same time, she was under strong pressure to adopt the Protestant religion. Her chief minister, William Cecil, was a Protestant, hosts of Protestant exiles were returning from Geneva and other Continental cities, London was the centre of popular unrest and Catholic services had been made all but impossible there by the attentions of Protestant mobs. Elizabeth's personal views are a mystery. She lacked fanatical devotion to any religious formulary and seems to have favoured a restoration of a modified Henrician settlement, retaining some aspects of Catholic worship and Church order while renouncing the Papal supremacy. The fact that the Papacy initially adopted a moderate policy towards Elizabeth was

91

due in large part to the influence of Philip of Spain, who saw clearly that the alternative to Elizabeth was Mary of Scotland (whose accession would mean French domination of England). Philip seems even to have seriously contemplated marriage to Elizabeth for a time and the dalliance with Spain benefited from the Queen's cautious policy.

A return to the 1549 Prayer Book might well have been the Queen's objective, but her hand was forced by the pressure of Protestant opinion in the Commons. She had already given some signs of her disapproval of the Mass, which continued as the legal form of worship, and the advocates of reform were determined to press Elizabeth for a full reformation of the Church. The reform party in the Commons was led by men who had been exiles under Mary, Sir Anthony Cooke and Sir Francis Knollys being especially prominent. The Queen had at first determined to secure the passage of an Act of Supremacy during this Parliament but to defer any alteration of public worship until a further session. Parliamentary pressure led to the issue of a proclamation legalising Communion in both kinds but this was no final solution of the impasse. At some point during March 1559, Elizabeth seems to have changed her tactics. It was probably evident to her by then that the Marian bishops would refuse to conform to any settlement on which the Queen and Parliament might agree. The Queen's choice of a new leadership for the Church lay amongst committed Protestants, mostly former exiles – her chosen primate, Matthew Parker, was, significantly, a moderate who had lived in obscurity in England during Mary's reign. These men could not be induced to accept office in a Church with a rite as conservative as that of 1549 and the subsequent 1559 Prayer Book was basically that of 1552, with a few modifications made at the Queen's insistence. Elizabeth's acceptance of this Protestant settlement made possible the rapid passage of the Acts of Uniformity and Supremacy. Both contained provisions prophetic of the religious history of Elizabethan England. The quite severe penalties appended to the Uniformity Act demonstrated that the government took seriously the threat of determined resistance to the regime, while its provision for the future revision of the prescribed rites suggested to some that the 1559 settlement was not final.

The Act of Supremacy declared that the Queen was 'Supreme Governor' of the Church rather than 'Supreme Head'. While this title might please Calvinists (who denied the right of monarchs to rule in the Church) and moderate Catholics (who sought a way to accept the Elizabethan Settlement), its real significance lay in its tacit acceptance that Elizabeth was to govern the Church rather as an overseer than as a pseudo-Pope. This recognition, and the very manner in which the settlement of 1559 had been achieved, suggested that Parliament would have an increased role to play in the spiritual affairs of the nation. The events of 1559 had produced a truly Protestant Church of England whose doctrine was basically Calvinist. But

92

Eliz. accomp. her goals w/ patience and control over the Pa

the organisation and externals of the Church were so far from the respected model of Geneva as to leave many zealous radicals unsatisfied. The concept of 'Anglicanism' possessed little significance in the first decade or so of the reign, since 'Puritanism' itself remained an essential constituent element in the mentality of the Church. The emergence of the Puritan attitude as a separatist and divisive force marked a revolutionary turning-point. Puritanism was the faith of 'precisians', those who sought perfection in the Church and based their struggle to achieve it on an inner conviction about their role in God's plan for the English Church. The persecution of Protestants, which culminated in the Marian Reaction, as given a vivid reality by Foxe, was a major contributory factor to this deeply held conviction. Puritanism was novel, subversive, and idealistic: a crusading movement seeking a total redefinition of the Protestant faith in England.

It was basically an individualistic system but at the same time retained traditional Christian attitudes to the social order. Puritans for long sought to capture control of the Church by law established in preference to any secession into nonconformity. But the 'other-worldliness' of the Puritans and their stubborn determination on what seemed to others minor issues, notably that of ecclesiastical vestments, doomed their attempt to failure. 'Paradise is our native country and we in this world be as exiles and strangers', wrote Richard Greenham, summing up a good deal of the Puritan mind.[14] During the 1560s, bitter controversy raged over the externals of worship, notably the prescribed vestments. In 1566 the Queen pressed Parker into a decisive demonstration of strength and it was Robert Crowley, a much-respected writer and Marian exile, who denounced the archbishop's policy and stated clearly the right of the godly to resist ungodly laws. The subsequent disillusionment of the Puritans with the episcopate and their frustration at the ways in which their many Parliamentary bills were blocked by the Queen and her ministers opened the way to the foundation of a Church within a Church. The Puritan 'classical' movement did not mark any retreat from the grand design of reforming the Church: in 1584, 1586 and 1587 serious attempts were made in Parliament to impose on the Church of England a Genevan system of Church government by synods of elders and a Calvinist service-book. The issue of the Marprelate tracts marked the beginning of a new bitterness in the controversy between the authorities and the Puritans. The reign ended in an atmosphere of general persecution for a party which had seen itself as the conscience of the English Protestant movement. The rejection of the Puritans' arguments by James I at Hampton Court in 1604 finally decided the future pattern of English religion. James declared: 'No bishop, no King'; and it remained for a succeeding generation of Puritans to bring his ironic prophecy to pass.

The same problem of divided loyalties which engaged the minds of many Puritans troubled the consciences of most English Catholics in the

Elizabethan period. The staunch Catholic minority which existed in England in 1559 was deprived of clerical leadership by the conformity of the great majority of the clergy to the new regime and the flight abroad of others. English Catholicism was recreated by the efforts of the latter – the seminary priests and Jesuits who entered the country in increasing numbers from the mid-1570s. The Papal Bull of excommunication issued against Elizabeth in 1570 ushered in a period of conflict between Rome and the English govern-ment. It was a war in which many ordinary Catholics sought to be neutral, wishing to sacrifice neither their loyalty to their sovereign nor their faith. The 'church papist' was prepared to attend the services of the Protestant Church to secure freedom from harassment and did not deny the right of the monarch to ordain the form of those services. The new priests urged Catholics to defy the authorities and risk ever-increasing penalties. Wavering sympa-thisers either fell away from the faith and into conformity or became recusants proper. The identification of Catholicism with the Spanish menace did not improve the situation of the faithful in England and Robert Parsons and William Allen both published inflammatory works which did not meet with much approval in English Catholic circles. Anti-Jesuit feelings grew to be-come a serious menace to Catholic unity during the last decade of the reign and in 1603 English Catholics were divided and disorganised.

Catholicism had largely ceased to be a popular faith, despite the efforts of the missionary priests, because its survival came to depend on the very con-servative Catholic gentry. The latter, who desired to enjoy their estates and privileges (while keeping their faith) rejected the clerical revolution born in the seminaries. Social order, family position, and class prestige meant more to them than did wild calls for sacrifice in a religious crusade. Moreover, this crusade was to be led by priests and clerical leadership was unacceptable to men of the gentry class. Most Catholics, like the majority of Puritans, sought a religion which satisfied their consciences but which was untainted with sub-version and fanaticism. Devotion to the Tudor monarchy as opposed to any Catholic candidate the Pope might select implied a belief in the stable social order and the natural obligations which bound men's lives. Catholicism retreated into the homes of the Catholic aristocracy and squirearchy as 'loyalty supplanted enterprise'.[15]

NOTES
1. W. Cobbett, *A History of the Protestant Reformation* (ed. F. Gasquet, n.d.) pp. 2–3.
2. K. V. Thomas's *Religion and the Decline of Magic* (1971) deals thoroughly with these themes.
3. A. G. Dickens, *The English Reformation* (Fontana ed., 1967), pp. 64–5.
4. C. Hill, *Society and Puritanism in Pre-Revolutionary England* (Panther ed., 1969) pp. 288–332.
5. The Hunne affair is fully dealt with in A. Ogle, *The Tragedy of the Lollards' Tower* (1949).
6. For a short account of Wyclif's life and ideas, see K. B. Macfarlane, *John Wycliffe and the Beginnings of English Nonconformity* (1952).

7. Cited by E. G. Rupp, *Studies in the Making of the English Protestant Tradition* (1947) p. 3.

8. Notably by J. K. McConica in his *English Humanists and Reformation Politics* (1965).

9. J. J. Scarisbrick, *Henry VIII* (1968) p. 405.

10. See, for example, Lawrence Stone's review of G. R. Elton's *Policy and Police* in *New York Review of Books.*

11. Scarisbrick, *Henry VIII*, pp. 470–7.

12. Cited by H. C. Porter, *Puritanism in Tudor England* (1970) p. 69.

13. S. T. Bindoff, *Tudor England* (1950) p. 177.

14. Cited by M. M. Knappen, *Tudor Puritanism* (Phoenix ed , 1966) p. 350.

15. J. Bossy, 'The Character of Elizabethan Catholicism', in *Crisis in Europe 1560–1660* (ed. T. Aston, 1965) p. 246.

THE ENGLISH DIOCESES

ADMINISTRATION

On the eve of the Reformation, the English Church possessed an administrative and organisational structure unchanged for many centuries. England was divided into only two provinces, those of Canterbury and York, each under the authority of an archbishop. (The French Church was divided into five times as many, with a correspondingly larger number of dioceses.) Within the province of Canterbury were fourteen English sees and four in Wales. Of these jurisdictions, the Welsh sees of St David's, St Asaph, Bangor, and Llandaff were the most ancient, each dating back to the middle of the sixth century and the heroic days of the Celtic Church. In England, the diocese of Canterbury rested its claim to supremacy on its foundation by Augustine in 597. Of the other dioceses within the province, Winchester was the richest prize by far for ecclesiastical careerists – even in 1559, its nominal value was £3700 per annum. By 1587, Bishop Cooper claimed that it was worth only £398. 'The plunder of the Church' carried out by the Tudor sovereigns was accompanied inevitably by a reduction in the power of bishops. The diocese of Lincoln stretched from the Humber to the Cotswolds but the counties of Northamptonshire and Oxfordshire were abstracted from this vast territory by Henry VIII and the bishop's net income fell from £1962 in 1535 to £894 in 1575. Another large and populous diocese, Coventry and Lichfield, was reduced in size at this period, as were Worcester and Salisbury. Rochester (with an annual episcopal income of about £300) was among the poorest and smallest of the English sees, although it was a wealthy living in comparison with that offered to Welsh bishops (few of whom resided in any case). St David's, the premier Welsh see, was worth £458 in 1535 and but £263 in 1583. In the early seventeenth century, Llandaff was valued at only £130.

The pre-Reformation province of York consisted of three dioceses. York itself was the largest in area of any in England, although much of the territory under the nominal authority of the archbishops was wild and uninhabited moorland and forest. A large piece of the remote western part of the diocese was placed within the new diocese of Chester in 1541. Durham was an especially important see to the English state. The bishops had been given massive secular powers by the Crown in return for their involvement in the government of the far North and the defence of the Scottish border. The Reformation did not remove these powers. Bishop Pilkington was an important regional administrator, as his predecessors had been. In the seventeenth century, his successors were responsible for the provision of considerable armed forces for the defence of the realm. Nevertheless, the income of the bishops of Durham fell from £2821 to £1800 in the four decades after the compilation of *Valor Ecclesiasticus*. The third of the Northern jurisdictions, Carlisle, was a remote and poor diocese of comparatively late foundation.

Henry VIII seems to have had a genuine interest in reforming the structure of the Church. Bishops, whatever their good intentions, were remote from their flocks, incapable of true spiritual leadership. Only zealots of the order of John Hooper (Bishop of Worcester and Gloucester under Edward VI) could manage any personal involvement with their people. Moreover, cathedral towns, as centres of administration, were often remote from the far corners of the dioceses. Henry's enthusiasm for reform made possible the appointment of many suffragan bishops after 1534. In the late 1530s, he planned to establish no fewer than thirteen new sees based on former monastic churches. This scheme was reduced in scale after fuller consideration and six former religious houses with a total income of between £5000 and £6000 per annum were selected for conversion to cathedral establishments. Of these six, one (Westminster) survived less than a decade but the others (Gloucester, Chester, Peterborough, Oxford and Bristol) survived. New dioceses were carved out from the larger of the established dioceses.

Had Henry VIII carried the Dissolution of the Monasteries to its logical conclusion, a number of cathedrals would have disappeared. Canterbury, Rochester, Winchester, Ely, Norwich, Worcester, Durham and Carlisle were all staffed by monks. These cathedrals could not be dispensed with, and new secular chapters were established. In the case of the dioceses of Coventry and Lichfield and of Bath and Wells, each of which possessed both a monastic cathedral and a cathedral staffed by secular clergy, the authorities dispensed with the churches at Coventry and Bath. Henry's efforts, however curtailed by the desire for economy, were the only major attempt at a jurisdictional reform of the English Church attempted between the medieval period and the nineteenth century.

THE BISHOPS

Lists are given of the bishops of seven sees for the Tudor period. The archbishops and bishops of the English Church in the early sixteenth century were great men, substantial landlords and administrators, although within the hierarchy the gulf between the Bishop of Winchester and the Bishop of

96

Rochester was a wide one. All the bishops lost revenue and some status in the Reformation period, although episcopacy (as was to be clearly realised in the mid-seventeenth century) was a major buttress of the English state. In the medieval Church, bishoprics had become the preserve of the King, a reward to be given (with the approval of the Papacy) to his most deserving servants. After their appointment, it was expected that these men, among the nations's most able, would continue to serve their monarch. Thus, most were absent for much of their episcopates from their dioceses. The latter were administered by chancellors, principals, commissaries and bailiffs, while suffragan bishops carried out spiritual functions such as ordination and confirmation. The hierarchy was an economic and administrative hierarchy as much as a spiritual one. Its interests coincided with the interests of the Crown, despite the fact that the Crown was not slow to impoverish the bishops for its own profit. On the eve of the Reformation, most diocesans were lawyers by training, administrators by profession. Most were civil lawyers rather than canonists; few were theologians. In the decisive years of the 1530s, the English episcopate emerged as a strong support of Henry VIII in his quarrel with Rome. Men who owed their position to the King were loyal to him rather than to a remote and suspect authority in Rome. In spite of this, few were sympathetic to the ideas of Continental Protestantism or to notions of a thorough reform of the Church. Many bishops pursued a policy of accommodation to the dictates of the Crown, while disapproving of much that was done. Fervent Protestants called for a return to the apostolic ideal of a bishop as a pastor, the chief minister among other ministers. The ideal bishop, they proclaimed, would be a man sound in doctrine and pure in morals, a learned man and a preacher, who was prepared to eschew the rewards of office in order to serve Christ and His flock. To this end bishops should cease to have large incomes and to possess secular jurisdiction. Church courts should be abolished totally while the Church should ensure that the law of the King was based on sound and godly principles.

While the Reformation did reduce the wealth of the bishops, they remained at the top of English society, men still largely remote from the laity. Church courts became more prominent in the lives of ordinary people. Episcopacy became a suspect notion to extreme Protestants despite the admirable character of many bishops. In the 1530s, many reformers had obtained sees and, in contrast to their conservative colleagues, these men were theologians and, at a later stage, ex-monks or friars. Edward VI's reign saw the promotion to office of a large group of reformers, but after the accession of Mary, these were removed in favour of conservatives, some of them survivors of the Henrician Church but others theologians. Elizabeth I was fortunate that no fewer than ten bishoprics were vacant by the death of their occupants by the beginning of 1559. These were filled by known reformers who had been in exile during Mary's reign, but Elizabeth chose as primate the moderate

Matthew Parker, her former tutor and a non-exile. John Jewel, who became Bishop of Salisbury, emerged as a redoubtable defender of Elizabethan Anglicanism. Other bishops, notably Edmund Grindal, primate from 1575 to 1583, were deeply influenced by Genevan ideas, although they were loyal to episcopacy and to the Royal Supremacy. Under the benevolent authority of Grindal and other Puritans, an uneasy truce continued between the religious radicals and the State Church. Grindal's successor, John Whitgift, initiated a determined assault on the Puritan party, an assault which aroused the fury of Martin Marprelate. The gradual demise of the exiles who had formed the core of the episcopate at the beginning of the reign made room for a new generation of bishops, men of the order of Richard Bancroft. Elizabeth remained convinced that episcopacy was an essential prop of the state, while Puritans felt increasingly that bishops were impediments to the 'further reformation' of the Church. The bishops lost prestige, respect and influence, although the first Stuart sovereign remained committed to the doctrine summed up in the aphorism 'No bishop, no King'. The reaction against Calvinism amongst the hierarchy and the theorists coincided with the spread of Puritanism both among the clergy and the intelligent laity. The stage was set for conflict.

NOTE

Lists of bishops are given below for the principal English sees and for one Welsh see. Complete lists of bishops for all sees are given in *Handbook of British Chronology*, ed. F. M. Powicke and E. B. Fryde (London, 1961).

Biographical notes on bishops marked * are to be found in Chapter 10 (pp. 206–20).

THE ENGLISH DIOCESES TO 1603

Diocese	Date of foundation	Area of jurisdiction
Bath and Wells	909 (Wells), 1218 (Bath and Wells)	Somerset
Bristol	1542	Bristol and part of Gloucestershire (from diocese of Worcester), Dorset (from diocese of Salisbury).
Canterbury	597	Part of Kent
Carlisle	1133	Cumberland
Chester	1541	Cheshire, Lancashire (from diocese of Coventry and Lichfield)
Chichester	1075	Sussex
Coventry and Lichfield	669 (Lichfield), 1148 (Coventry and Lichfield)	Cheshire, Lancashire (to 1541), Staffordshire, Derbyshire, Warwickshire

Durham	997	Co. Durham, Northumberland
Ely	1109	Cambridgeshire
Exeter	1049	Devon and Cornwall
Gloucester	1541	Gloucestershire (from diocese of Worcester)
Hereford	676	Herefordshire, Shropshire
Lincoln	1073	Lincolnshire, Leicestershire, Rutland, Northamptonshire (to 1541), Oxfordshire (to 1541), Buckinghamshire, Bedfordshire
London	604	London, Middlesex, Hertfordshire, Essex
Norwich	1094	Norfolk and Suffolk
Oxford	1542	Oxfordshire (from diocese of Lincoln)
Peterborough	1541	Northamptonshire (from diocese of Lincoln)
Rochester	604	Part of Kent
Salisbury	1075	Dorset (to 1542), Berkshire, Wiltshire
Winchester	679	Hampshire and Surrey
Worcester	680	Gloucestershire (to 1541), Worcestershire
York	625	Westmorland (to 1541), Yorkshire, Nottinghamshire

PRINCIPAL DIOCESES AND THEIR BISHOPS

PROVINCE OF CANTERBURY

Canterbury

1454–86	Thomas Bourchier	1533–55	Thomas Cranmer*
1486–1500	John Morton, Cardinal*	1556–8	Reginald Pole, Cardinal*
		1559–75	Matthew Parker*
1501–3	Henry Deane	1576–83	Edmund Grindal*
1503–32	William Warham*	1583–1604	John Whitgift*

Lincoln

1480–94	John Russell	1514	Thomas Wolsey, Cardinal*
1495–1514	William Smith		

1514–21	William Atwater	1557–9	Thomas Watson
1521–47	John Longland	1559–71	Nicholas Bullingham
1547–51	Henry Holbeach	1571–84	Thomas Cooper
1552–4	John Taylor	1584–95	William Wickham
1554–6	John White	1595–1608	William Chaderton

London

1448–89	Thomas Kempe	1539–49	Edmund Bonner*
1489–96	Richard Hill	1550–3	Nicholas Ridley*
1496–1501	Thomas Savage	1553–9	Edmund Bonner*
1501–3	William Warham*	1559–70	Edmund Grindal*
1504–5	William Barons	1570–7	Edwin Sandys*
1506–22	Richard FitzJames	1577–94	John Aylmer
1522–30	Cuthbert Tunstal*	1594–6	Richard Fletcher
1530–9	John Stokesley	1597–1604	Richard Bancroft*

Winchester

1447–86	William Waynflete	1553–5	Stephen Gardiner*
1487–1492	Peter Courtenay	1556–9	John White
1493–1501	Thomas Langton	1560–80	Robert Horne
1501–1528	Richard Fox*	1580–4	John Watson
1529–30	Thomas Wolsey, Cardinal*	1584–94	Thomas Cooper
		1594–5	William Wickham
1531–51	Stephen Gardiner*	1596	William Day
1551–3	John Ponet	1597–1616	Thomas Bilson

St David's

1485–96	Hugh Pavy	1548–53	Robert Ferrar
1496–1504	John Morgan	1554–9	Henry Morgan
1505–8	Robert Sherborn	1560–1	Thomas Young
1509–22	Edward Vaughan	1561–81	Richard Davies
1523–36	Richard Rawlins	1582–93	Marmaduke Middleton
1536–48	William Barlow*	1594–1615	Anthony Rudd

PROVINCE OF YORK

Durham

1484–94	John Shirwood	1523–9	Thomas Wolsey, Cardinal*
1494–1501	Richard Fox		
1502–5	William Senhouse	1530–59	Cuthbert Tunstal*
1507–8	Christopher Bainbridge, Cardinal	1560–76	James Pilkington
		1577–87	Richard Barnes
1509–23	Thomas Ruthall	1589–95	Matthew Hutton
		1595–1606	Tobias Matthew

York

1480–1500	Thomas Rotherham	1545–54	Robert Holgate
1501–7	Thomas Savage	1555–9	Nicholas Heath
1508–14	Christopher Bainbridge,	1561–8	Thomas Young
	Cardinal	1570–6	Edmund Grindal*
1514–30	Thomas Wolsey,	1577–88	Edwin Sandys
	Cardinal*	1589–94	John Piers
1531–44	Edward Lee	1595–1606	Matthew Hutton

THE RELIGIOUS ORDERS

INTRODUCTION

The advent of the Tudor monarchy in 1485 had no special significance for the English Church or for the religious orders in particular. Henry VII was a pious man, of conventional views, a patron to the monasteries, who was interred in his chapel in the abbey at Westminster with full traditional rites. At the beginning of the sixteenth century, his realm contained around 12,000 monks, nuns and friars. Many houses were as full as they had been since the Black Death of 1349. In the mid-1530s, the total income of the religious houses was estimated at anything between £130,000 and £200,000, one half of the total revenue of the Church of England. The monasteries seemed in 1500 to be a secure and permanent part of English life. They had ceased to be great spiritual centres, except for a few houses, mainly in South-eastern England. Many criticised the luxury prevailing in some houses: in certain foundations, there were four or five servants for every one inmate. Ascetism was not to be found in very many monasteries, neither were intellectual achievement or fervent piety. The friars remained popular with a large section of the population and were to emerge as an important group in the controversies of the Reformation. Popular esteem for them is manifest in the frequent mention of friars in the wills of early Tudor Englishmen and women. Many monks, especially Austin Canons, served in parochial cures. If piety and saintly living were not common, neither were immorality and abuse of the vows. Mediocrity in all things was the keynote of the English religious life at the accession of Henry VIII. The fifteenth century saw the extinction of a few small houses; among the established orders there were no new foundations. Many existing houses had ceased to serve any useful purpose; a few were corrupt enough to deserve complete suppression. Visitations revealed that the population of the monasteries was even rising in some areas, but some houses were reduced to a handful of inmates. In some of these, discipline was bad, the religious having abandoned the rigours of their chosen vocation completely. Cardinal Wolsey made half-hearted attempts to correct abuses in the religious orders but was more enthusiastic about the suppression at random of a group of monasteries whose revenues he wanted for his new college at Oxford. In the years 1524–9, Wolsey secured the dissolution of twenty-nine houses – a good precedent for his royal master in the next decade. The foremost modern historian of the religious orders sums up the state of the English monasteries in the reign of Henry VIII: 'a harmless and contented group of men or women living a regular and devout, if neither zealous nor austere, life'.

If the latter description may well serve as the epitaph for the great majority of monasteries, nunneries and friaries, it should not be forgotten that, even on the eve of their destruction, the orders produced many notable individuals, a few saints, a handful of houses where piety and learning matched those of any previous century of monachism. The first house of the fervent order of Franciscan Observants was founded at Greenwich in 1482. Henry VIII's regard for the order resulted in the foundation of further convents at Canterbury, Newcastle, Richmond (Surrey) and Newark. The house of Bridgettines (which contained both nuns and brethren) at Syon, Middlesex, continued to be a major centre of piety and learning, as did the houses of Carthusian monks. The Yorkshire house of Mount Grace produced a considerable mystical writer in Richard Methley (d. 1528), while the London Charterhouse, near Smithfield, possessed as its last prior the saintly John Houghton. Houghton, along with many of his brethren, faced execution rather than submit to the Royal Supremacy. It is scarcely surprising to recall that it was the London Charterhouse where Thomas More spent four years debating whether to take religious vows.

The Carthusians were the only religious order to remain unscathed in the face of Erasmus's biting criticism of the religious life. Erasmus saw little merit in the observance of the rule of any order – deeply influenced by the *devotio moderna* of the Netherlands, he castigated outward observances in favour of inward repentance and adherence to the Gospel. Erasmus helped to create a mental climate favourable to the elimination of all religious houses. But humanism was not necessarily incompatible with membership of an order. At Winchcombe, abbot Richard Kidderminster, head of that house from 1488, to c.1510, actively revived the state of learning there with a system of regular instruction for his monks. William Selling, prior of Canterbury, and the Dominican Richard Brinckley were merely the most eminent among a vast number of monks and friars interested in the 'new learning'. The friars continued to play an important role in the life of the two Universities and from their ranks emerged an important group of Protestant reformers, among them Barnes, Coverdale, John Bale, John Hilsey and William Roye, Tyndale's assistant. Throughout England, friars were at the very centre of controversy throughout the Reformation period. Many a monastery ended its existence deeply divided over religious issues: at Winchcombe, young monks fresh from Oxford came to despise everything their order represented.

Culturally, the great achievements of the monks and friars lay in the past, although the physical evidence of this achievement, a magnificent series of libraries, suffered grievously at the Dissolution. Although a few houses acquired printing presses, none produced much. In the field of architecture, only minor works were commissioned by most houses (the new church at Bath is a notable exception). In the field of music, the monks could claim to have nourished a few major talents: Thomas Tallis, Robert Fairfax, John Taverner. But none of this adds up to cultural vitality. Neither were the monks great educators. Reformers hoped that a large portion of the wealth of the monasteries would be devoted to education by the King. In this they were to be disappointed, although some monastic wealth did find its way into new school and college foundations through the enthusiasm for learning of laymen who had profited from the destruction of the monasteries.

The ground was prepared for the end of the religious life in England by these factors: the indifferent state of the majority of houses, their irrelevance to the religious life of the people, their lack of any role that could not be fulfilled better by new, lay institutions, and their weakness in the face of criticism from reformers, both Catholic and Protestant. In 1534, Thomas Cromwell, desperate for revenue, 'turned to the Church'. Shortly, the monasteries were the object of his attack. By and large, their inmates were eager to conform in anything the King commanded. The continual process of visitation carried out from 1534 onwards (beginning with the friaries in that year) gradually wore down the will of the religious to persevere. The abbots were, like the bishops, staunch loyalists to the Crown and most hoped for a comfortable pension. Compliance was often well rewarded, several heads of houses receiving country estates and being permitted to remove furnishings and books from their former residences. A number attained to bishoprics, while hordes of humbler monks and friars obtained parochial cures, often within a few miles of their house. Reasonable pensions, paid with remarkable efficiency, supported those unable or unwilling to seek employment. The Court of Augmentations, set up to deal with the wealth of the monasteries, continued to pay out pensions for decades, the last recipient dying as late as 1608. The indifference of the religious to the fate of their houses explains their readiness to succumb to pressure, sometimes of an unpleasant sort. The savage execution of a number of abbots, in addition to memories of the fate of the recalcitrant Carthusians, served to encourage prompt surrender. The last abbey, Waltham (Essex), surrendered in March of 1540.

Mary's eagerness to refound the religious houses was reinforced by guilt at her own possession of monastic revenues. Even before the death of her father, the greater part of these revenues had passed out of the hands of the Crown and into the possession of the gentry and aristocracy. Many of the recipients were themselves staunch Catholics, although none were prepared to hand over their newly-acquired monastic lands. The Queen, mindful of the fact that there were a number of men and women ready to resume the religious

103

life, established six houses, among them the notable communities at Sheen and Syon. A tiny proportion of the ex-religious responded to this move by entering the newly-revived monasteries and a few new postulants were admitted. For the rest, the Queen lacked the power to compel them to resume their regulated lives, even had this been practicable. Nevertheless, bishops were ordered to ensure that those who had ventured to marry, in defiance of their vows (now again declared to be binding for life), were punished and divorced from their partners. Soon after the accession of Elizabeth, the houses were dissolved by Act of Parliament. Many of their inmates crossed the English Channel where they set up communities in exile.

PRINCIPAL EVENTS

1488	Richard Kidderminster becomes abbot of Winchcombe.
1498	Foundation of new houses of Franciscan Observants by Henry VII licensed by Pope Alexander VI.
1499	Creation of the English province of the Observants; convents established at Canterbury and Newcastle-upon-Tyne.
1500	Observant house founded at Richmond.
1515	Richard Kidderminster, abbot of Winchcombe and Dr Henry Standish debate the independence of the Church.
1525	Robert Barnes, Cambridge Austin Friar, attacks ceremonies. Wolsey completes the suppression of twenty-nine religious houses: their revenues transferred to Cardinal College, Oxford.
1530	Twenty-two abbots sign petition to the Pope in support of the Royal Divorce.
1534	The Oath of Supremacy administered to all houses. Houses of Observant Friars closed. Visitation of all friaries by John Hilsey and George Browne.
1535	Compilation of *Valor Ecclesiasticus*. Execution of Prior Houghton and other Carthusian monks. Visitation of all religious houses commenced.
1536	Visitation continued under Dr Richard Layton (later Dean of York), Dr Thomas Legh, John Price, Dr John Tregonwell and Thomas Bedyll, archdeacon of London. Act for the Dissolution of the Lesser Monasteries (27 Hen. VIII, cap. 28): all houses with an annual income of under £200 to become the King's, on account of the 'manifest sin, vicious, carnal and abominable living' they have produced.
1537	Execution of further Carthusians.
1538	Surrender of the friaries under the supervision of Richard Ingworth, suffragan bishop of Dover, and Dr John London, Warden of New College, Oxford (the latter now a prominent Royal agent).
1538–9	Surrender of many great houses under official pressure.

1539   Act for the Dissolution of the Greater Monasteries (31 Hen. VIII, cap. 13).

Closure of remaining houses.

Execution of Thomas Beche, abbot of Colchester, Hugh Cook, abbot of Reading and Richard Whiting, abbot of Glastonbury on charges of treason.

1539–42   Foundation of six new episcopal sees based on former monastic churches: Peterborough, Gloucester, Oxford, Chester, Bristol, Westminster.

1555   Appointment of a committee by Mary to consider re-foundation of certain religious houses.

Reopening of monasteries at Greenwich (Observant Friars), Smithfield (Dominican Friars), Sheen (Carthusians), Syon (Bridgettine Nuns) and King's Langley (Dominicanesses).

1556   Re-foundation of Benedictine house at Westminster under John Feckenham, Dean of St Paul's.

1559   Suppression of re-founded houses by Elizabeth I.

STATISTICS

Numbers

Number of monks in 1500   c.12,000
in 1530   c.11,000

Number of nuns in 1500   c. 2,000
in 1530   c. 1,600

Number of religious houses in 1530   825 (of which 650 were houses of monks or nuns, the rest friaries or hospitals).

Income

Gross income in 1535   c.£165,000

The same, including Welsh houses and friaries   c.£200,000

Classification of houses by income:

Very small (under £20 p.a.)	9%
Small (£20–£100 p.a.)	35%
Medium (£100–£300 p.a.)	35%
Large (£300–£1000 p.a.)	16%
Very large (more than £1000 p.a.)	5%

Disposal of monastic lands

Number of sales of land, formerly monastic, to 1547:   1,552

Number of gifts of land   41

Number of gifts in exchange for other lands, etc.   28

Percentage of monastic lands alienated from Crown by 1547   c.66%

CHRONOLOGY

1487   Growing unease about the legal privileges of the clergy (including men in minor orders) and alarm at the perilous state of the realm led to an assault on rights of sanctuary, which were declared null and void in cases of high treason.

1489   Clerical privileges were now somewhat limited: all guilty felons were to be branded on the thumb when claiming immunity from normal process of law. If they committed a second indictable offence, only full proof of orders could save them from the full legal penalties.

1497   'Petty treasons' were now included in the categories of offence for which clerical immunity could not be claimed.

1503   William Warham became Archbishop of Canterbury.

1512   An Act was passed removing benefit of clergy for many serious crimes. (Henry VIII's government was merely consolidating the changes in the law made under Henry VII in the interests of a more powerful system of monarchy and no general assault on the Church was contemplated.)

1514   Thomas Wolsey, Bishop of Lincoln, became Archbishop of York.

In May, the Pope became involved in the dispute over the rights of the clergy by declaring that no layman might possess authority over a cleric.

In December, bitter anticlerical feelings in London and lay dislike of Church courts and their powers were strongly manifested in the case of Richard Hunne. Hunne had been involved in a dispute with the authorities of London diocese over mortuary fees. He was arrested on heresy charges and murdered in gaol, the Bishop of London's Chancellor being deeply implicated. Hunne's corpse was subsequently burned. Lay indignation at the proceedings was intense and it was claimed publicly that Hunne had been 'made a heretic for suing a *Praemunire*' (see above, Introduction).

1515   Parliament met in February in the aftermath of the Hunne affair and sought to pass bills abolishing mortuary fees and further limiting clerical immunity from arrest.

A formal debate on the issue of clerical privilege took place before the King, the protagonists being Richard Kidderminster, Abbot of Winchcombe (Glos.), for the clergy and Dr Henry Standish, a Franciscan, who argued for further limitations on immunity. Subsequently, the radical Parliamentary measures were abandoned. But the Hunne case was still unsettled and there was further agitation in the Commons. Dr Standish was called before Convocation (see above, Introduction) on account of his criticisms of the Church. The King soon brought about his release (he was later given the see of St Asaph in Wales) and all anticlerical bills were dropped. The guilty parties in the Hunne affair were severely fined.

Thomas Wolsey became Lord Chancellor of England in December and, in the same month, Cardinal. He was now chief Royal minister and virtual ruler of England.

1518   In June, Wolsey was appointed Papal legate *a latere* in England. In practice, his ecclesiastical authority now exceeded that of Warham.

1520   A religious discussion group broadly sympathetic to Church reform was by this year meeting regularly in the White Horse tavern in Cambridge. Its members included Thomas Cranmer, Hugh Latimer, John Frith, Robert Barnes and Miles Coverdale.

Lutheran books were being sold in Oxford by a local bookseller, John Dorne.

1521   The Church authorities gave renewed attention to the Lollard heresy – this year saw a massive persecution in London diocese with many burnings. Wolsey sought to stem the flood of Lutheran books into England and in May many of these were solemnly burned in London before the Cardinal.

Henry VIII published his *Assertio Septem Sacramentorum* (a confutation of Luther) and in October a copy was presented to Pope Leo X. The latter granted Henry the title of *Fidei Defensor*.

1527   Henry VIII's disillusionment with his marriage to Catherine of Aragon and his sincere doubts about its legality (Catherine being the widow of his brother Arthur) preoccupied the King's servants, especially Wolsey. In May, the latter held a court to which Henry was cited for illicit cohabitation. Wolsey hoped to secure Papal support for an annulment but his hopes were dashed in June with the Sack of Rome. The Emperor Charles V, nephew to the Queen, now controlled Rome and Clement VII's freedom of action was much curtailed.

1527–32   Further persecution of Lollard groups, especially in Essex and Buckinghamshire, led to many hundreds of abjurations.

1529   Wolsey had been unable to solve the King's marital problems and in September he was forced to surrender his office of Lord Chancellor. Thomas More, a friend and disciple of Erasmus (see above, Introduction), accepted the office in October. He made clear to Henry his disapproval of the proposed Divorce. Wolsey, who lost most of his ecclesiastical benefices, retired to his diocese of York.

In November, the Reformation Parliament met for the first time and there were renewed calls for Church reform. These now commanded some support from the King and Acts were passed to:

1. regulate fees charged for burial and the probate of wills;
2. abolish rights of immunity for clergy charged with murder or robbery;
3. limit the holding of benefices in plurality by priests and their involvement in commerce.

It was enacted that no Papal dispensation against the terms of the Act could be allowed. Priests offending against the new law might suffer fines of £20.

1530   Royal agents toured European Universities seeking scholarly support for the illegality of the King's marriage.

Pressure on the Church involved *Praemunire* charges against a number of leading Churchmen. These related to their financial dealings with Wolsey (who died at Leicester in November).

1531   Praemunire charges were now extended to all the clergy but an Act for the Pardon of the Clergy was passed on the payments of fines by the clergy (£100,000 from the Convocation of Canterbury, £19,000 from that of York). The clergy were forced to admit a limited measure of Royal Supremacy in their submission.

Thomas Cromwell, a former agent of Wolsey, joined the Privy Council.

Thomas Bilney, a young Cambridge graduate, was burned for heresy at Norwich.

1532   The King's frustration over the divorce and the unyielding attitude of Rome led to the withholding of taxes paid to the Papacy by bishops (annates). The Act authorising this action forbade the payment by any bishop of more than 5% of his income to Rome. Papal refusal to supply Bulls of Consecration for bishops was to be ignored – consecration could be authorised by the King. (This Act was intended to demonstrate the King's determination to obtain satisfaction in his suit – it was not to come into force for one year.)

Cromwell now sponsored the revival of a 'Supplication' from the Commons directed against the bishops (this had been drawn up in 1529). This document brought to the King's notice the oppressions and excessive fees of Church courts, the excessive number of holy-days, the extortions of priests, and the unrepresentative nature of Convocation (which made laws without the consent of the laity).

Convocation, which had already discussed a number of practical reforms, replied with the 'Answer of the Ordinaries', a document largely written by Stephen Gardiner, Bishop of Winchester. Reforming elements amongst the clergy suffered the displeasure of the conservative majority – in March, Warham excommunicated Hugh Latimer whom the King favoured and now defended.

The King now gave his support to a determined assault on the Church. In May, Convocation was forbidden to pass further laws and a searching examination of the whole system of Canon Law was proposed. Warham and seven other bishops signed the Submission of the Clergy, acknowledging Henry as Supreme Head of the Church in spiritual matters and superior to the Pope. More now resigned the Chancellorship.

In August, Archbishop Warham died.

The position of Anne Boleyn, the King's mistress, was recognised with her creation as Marquess of Pembroke.

1533 Thomas Cromwell was now chief minister to the Crown. In January, Henry was married to Anne Boleyn (who was already pregnant) by Thomas Cranmer, the King's choice for the see of Canterbury. In February the Act in Restraint of Appeals was passed. It was declared that "this realm of England is an empire", subject to the King alone, and in future all appeals in ecclesiastical cases should go to the King and not to Rome.

In March, Cranmer was consecrated Archbishop of Canterbury by Papal Bull. In July, the King activated the Annates Act by Letters Patent and was threatened with excommunication by the Pope.

1534 In the Parliament of January–March the following measures were passed:

Act in Restraint of Annates. The temporary measure of 1532 was made permanent. The King was authorised to appoint bishops and abbots.

Dispensations Act. All requests for a waiving of the Canon Law (for example, requests for permission to hold more than one living) should proceed to the Archbishop of Canterbury and not the Pope. A fixed scale of fees was established. Peter's Pence and other Papal taxes were abolished.

Act for the Submission of the Clergy. This gave statutory form to the document of 1532. All measures of Convocation were to be submitted to the Crown for approval and ultimate appeal in ecclesiastical disputes was to lie with the Crown.

Act of Succession. The succession to the throne was to lie with the heirs of Henry and Queen Anne. It was declared treason to dispute that succession and subjects were to swear an oath admitting its validity.

Cromwell's legislative programme was continued in the Parliamentary session of November–December 1534. The following measures were approved:

Act of Supremacy. The King, already head of the Church in practice, was declared by this Act Supreme Head on Earth of the Church of England. He was authorised to conduct visitations of the clergy, supervise preachers, try heretics and pronounce on doctrine.

Treason Act. By this measure, treason was extended to include verbal attacks on the King.

Act concerning First Fruits and Tenths. These taxes, formerly paid to Rome, were to pass to the Crown. (In subsequent years, the Church was to pay far more to the King than ever it had paid to the Pope.)

The King authorised negotiations on doctrinal matters with the German Lutherans. Robert Barnes, a Lutheran friar, was Henry's chief agent.

1535 Thomas Cromwell was appointed viceregent and vicar-general in spiritual matters to the Supreme Head. He immediately began to put into effect his strategy for the seizure of Church wealth. Work was begun on the compilation of *Valor Ecclesiasticus* (a survey of the possessions of the clergy) and this was completed within months. Agents were appointed to visit the monasteries: suppression was definitely planned.

In May, a number of Carthusian monks were executed for denial of the succession and (in June and July respectively) John Fisher, Bishop of Rochester, and Thomas More also suffered death.

A number of leading reformers were promoted to bishoprics: Hugh Latimer became Bishop of Worcester.

1536 The Act for the Dissolution of the Lesser Monasteries was passed; see p. 104.

The dissolution was one cause of the 'Pilgrimage of Grace', a general rising which embroiled the North in the last quarter of the year.

In May, the King's marriage to Anne Boleyn was dissolved by Cranmer. Anne was executed for treason and Henry subsequently married Jane Seymour.

The 'Ten Articles' appeared – a doctrinal formulary showing a measure of compromise with Lutheran theology. The principal points dealt with included:

Penance: it was asserted that auricular confession was necessary.

The Eucharist: the Real Presence was stressed but the definition given was vague and near to that of Luther.

Images: these were to remain in churches but were not to be worshipped. The number of sacraments: there were to be only three – penance, baptism and the Mass.

The saints: praying to the saints was to be permitted, but their supposed role in salvation was firmly denied.

Ceremonies: these were to continue as before.

Purgatory: its existence was denied as a Roman abuse, but prayers for the dead might continue.

Cromwell issued the first set of Royal Injunctions (practical evidence of the King's new role as ecclesiastical head). The clergy were ordered to preach in an approved manner at least once a quarter, to discourage superstitious devotion to shrines and images, to teach the young the faith in English, and to sustain the poor.

1537 A committee of bishops, ordered by the King to consider doctrinal issues, reported and their report appeared in July as *The Institution of a Christian Man* or 'Bishops' Book'. This document did not receive the King's approval but contained some important statements, notably on the issue of the Church. The Church was defined as an inclusive body (the Protestant notion that it was the congregation of the faithful was denied). But the novel idea that national Churches were equal marked the beginnings of the concept of an 'Anglican' Church. The Church of Rome was declared equal to but not superior to the Church of England.

The 'Bishops' Book' asserted that there were but three major sacraments (that is, those defined as such in the 'Ten Articles'). Matrimony, confirmation, holy orders and unction were minor sacraments. Popular devotion to images ('error and rudeness') was condemned but the existence of images was defended.

1538   During the summer months, negotiations with the German Lutherans continued. Success eluded the negotiators, despite the visit of a group of German emissaries to London.

The second set of Royal Injunctions now appeared, a radical document with strong Erasmian influences. The main provisions were:

1. an English Bible was to be set up in every parish church and was to be freely available to all;
2. the clergy were to teach and catechise in English and preach regularly;
3. the clergy were to denounce 'superstitions', including pilgrimages to saints' shrines;
4. abused images were to be destroyed and candles were not to be lit in churches except in front of the Rood and Reserved Sacrament;
5. any persons defending papal authority were to be reported to the authorities;
6. a register of all births, marriages and deaths was to be kept by the parson of every parish;
7. minor alterations were to be made to church services and these chiefly related to the diminished emphasis on saints.

Cromwell now encouraged the initiation of a campaign against shrines and images. The shrine of St Thomas at Canterbury was broken up and its ornaments seized by the Crown.

1539   An Act was passed to dissolve the greater monasteries. See p. 105.

Conservative pressure from Convocation met with a favourable response from the King and in May Parliament approved the Act of Six Articles, a reactionary measure reimposing strict Catholic orthodoxy and stipulating severe penalties for heretics. The Six Articles were:

1. that the Mass contained the true Body and Blood of Christ;
2. that Communion in both kinds was neither desirable nor necessary for lay-people;
3. that priests might not marry;

4. that ex-religious persons might not marry;
5. that private Masses should continue;
6. that auricular confession should continue.

Bishop Gardiner and the Duke of Norfolk were prominent in securing the passage of this Act with its vicious punishments for offenders. Persons denying the Eucharistic presence were to die as heretics (that is, by burning at the stake) and were not to be allowed to recant. Denial of the other five articles was to carry the penalty of death by hanging, drawing and quartering if the denial was public. If it were in private, loss of all possessions was substituted (death was the penalty for a second offence). Any person refusing to receive Holy Communion was to suffer death. Priests who kept concubines were to die, as were their concubines. Commissions were to be appointed to seek and destroy heretical books.

The practical effects of the Act of Six Articles were limited, especially while Cromwell lived. Some Protestant clergy were harried. Latimer and other reformers resigned their sees, while Cranmer sent his wife to Germany. Miles Coverdale was among a number of Protestants who left England.

1540 Despite the events of 1539, Cromwell still hoped for a Protestant alliance for England and secured a Protestant wife for Henry in the person of Anne of Cleves (whom Henry quickly came to detest).

The King's anger over the match increased the influence of conservatives, especially Gardiner, in the Council. Norfolk brought to the King's notice his niece Catherine Howard (whom Henry was to marry in July).

Cromwell's position was by no means hopeless and, in May, he showed his power by gaoling Richard Sampson, the conservative Bishop of Chichester. His fall came in June and he was executed in July.

Cromwell's execution was followed by the arrest of Robert Barnes, who had attacked Gardiner in a London sermon. Barnes was burned for heresy at Smithfield with two other Protestants, William Jerome and Thomas Garrett.

The King was determined not to advance too far in his approval of a conservative reaction. The burnings at Smithfield were accompanied by the execution of three Catholics for treason: Edward Powell, Richard Fetherston and Thomas Abel. Henry pardoned all heresies committed before July of this year, thus mitigating the effects of the Six Articles Act. Debating the sacraments with his bishops, he showed himself by no means a conventional Catholic.

1541 The continuing reaction in the country left moderate Protestants unscathed. Moreover, a Papal plot was uncovered in Yorkshire.

In July, a Royal proclamation abolished various ancient customs associated with holy-days (for example, the sermons by boy-bishops on St Nicholas's Day). In October, all shrines were ordered to be destroyed.

1542 The position of the Norfolk–Gardiner party had been seriously damaged by the discovery of Catherine Howard's adultery. In January, she was executed.

1543 The King continued to show an avid interest in theological matters and permitted Archbishop Cranmer to work on the revision of church services, knowing that the Primate favoured radical changes. Henry supported Cranmer in the face of numerous attempts to charge him with heresy.

No significant changes in worship were approved. A conservative formulary favoured by most of the bishops, the *Rationale of Ceremonial*, was not approved, while Convocation rejected Cranmer's vernacular *Book of Homilies*.

In July, the King married Catherine Parr, a pious widow with moderately Protestant views. But in the same month, a number of Protestant courtiers were burnt by Gardiner at Windsor.

The Act for the Advancement of True Religion sought to curtail massive popular interest in the Bible (which, the King believed, had led to disputing and unrest). The labouring classes were not to read the Scriptures, which were denied to all women below the rank of gentlewomen.

The King instructed three bishops (Salcot of Salisbury, Heath of Worcester and Thirlby of Westminster) to revise the 'Bishops' Book' of 1537. Archbishop Cranmer supervised the project but can hardly have approved of the resulting document: *The Necessary Doctrine and Erudition of a Christian Man* or 'King's Book'. This contained important statements on two issues:

1. The Eucharist: transubstantiation was defended and lay communion in bread alone was to continue.
2. Justification: the role of works in salvation was reasserted and Lutheran doctrine denied. However, it was stressed that 'spiritual' works were more pleasing to God than 'carnal' works.

1544 In May, a Litany in English was introduced in churches. It contained virtually no prayers to the saints.

In July, Sir John Cheke, a Protestant scholar, was appointed tutor to Prince Edward.

1545 The *Kyng's Prymer* was issued. This devotional manual, probably Cranmer's work, replaced earlier, Catholic primers.

A Chantries Act was passed allowing the King to seize these institutions (see above, Introduction). It was not implemented.

1546 Many Protestants suffered harassment and, in July, Anne Askew (Ayscough), a Lincolnshire gentlewoman, was burned for heresy. Attempts to secure the trial of the Queen on similar charges failed. The King, fearing his imminent death, nominated a Council of Regency for his heir and the majority of its members were Protestants.

1547 In January, Henry VIII died and Edward Seymour, Earl of Hertford,

113

later Duke of Somerset, was chosen as Protector of England. Seymour was an idealistic Protestant.

Protestant feelings now erupted in England and there was widespread iconoclasm, especially in London. The religious situation received further stimulation from the arrival of a number of foreign reformers, most notably Peter Martyr and Martin Bucer.

English services were now being used experimentally at Court. In the summer, the Privy Council suspended the powers of the bishops and sent commissioners to tour the dioceses. All clergy were ordered to use Erasmus's *Paraphrases* (in the translation of Nicholas Udall).

Cranmer issued Injunctions (based on those of 1538) and also published the *Book of Homilies*. Gardiner's opposition to these measures led to his arrest and imprisonment. (The Injunctions authorised the use of English in parts of the Mass.)

During the months of October to December, Parliament approved a radical programme of religious legislation which abolished the Catholicism of Henry VIII. The most important measures were:

Act against Revilers and for Receiving in Both Kinds: mild penalties were imposed on persons mocking the Mass; more significant was the extension of communion in both kinds (that is, in bread and wine) to the laity.

Act dissolving the Chantries: all chantries, collegiate churches, hospitals, guilds, fraternities, and other endowments implying prayers for the dead were forfeited to the Crown. (Over 2,500 institutions were involved.)

Other measures enacted during this session implemented freedom of speech, reading and publication, the abolition of the Act of Six Articles and previous heresy acts, and the direct appointment of bishops by the Crown without reference to Cathedral chapters.

1548   In January, Cranmer issued the *Order of the Communion* in English. This was subsequently used in many London churches, including St Paul's.

Between January and March, the Council ordered the abolition of many ceremonies (including those of holy water and holy bread) and encouraged the destruction of remaining images. Many stone altars were demolished.

By early summer, some London clergy had abolished all Latin services. An English Prayer Book had been drawn up by Cranmer and was debated in Convocation. A number of bishops opposed its introduction, prominent among them Edmund Bonner of London and Cuthbert Tunstal of Durham.

1549   In January, the Prayer Book was approved by Parliament and was to come into use on 9 June. All Latin services were to be abolished, but the Book was conservative in tone, providing for an English Mass, vestments, prayers for the dead, private confession, extreme unction and commemorations of the saints.

The First Act of Uniformity was passed to enforce the Prayer Book, which became the only legal service book. Penalties were imposed on those using or advocating other forms. Priests using the Mass in Latin or other services were to forfeit one year's income and to go to prison for six months. A second offence involved deprivation of benefice and one year's imprisonment. A third offence carried the penalty of life imprisonment. Persons attacking the Book could be fined £10 for a first offence, £20 for a second offence, and could be gaoled for life for a third offence.

In June, the introduction of the new services in the West Country led to an outbreak of rebellion. This was crushed, as were lesser risings in Oxfordshire and Yorkshire.

In September, Edmund Bonner, Bishop of London, was deprived of his see for opposition to the new services (Nicholas Ridley replaced him in 1550).

The fall of Somerset in October led to his imprisonment and John Dudley, Earl of Warwick, became the greatest power in the realm.

1550   Warwick (created Duke of Northumberland in 1551) supported the extreme Protestant party and John Hooper, a disciple of Zwingli, became prominent at Court.

An English Ordinal was introduced in March: the rite was much simplified and minor orders were abolished.

John Ponet, a radical Protestant, replaced Ridley as Bishop of Rochester. In June, Bishop Heath was gaoled and Gardiner was put on trial. One month later, John Hooper was appointed to the see of Gloucester.

During this year, Ridley, Hooper and other bishops ordered the removal of altars and screens from parish churches. The government sought to restrain extreme radicals and Joan Bocher and other Anabaptists were burned in London.

The Act for the abolition of divers books and images enjoined the destruction of all images, including roods.

1551   The bishops now discussed a new draft of the Prayer Book, providing for a more Protestant liturgy.

In February, Stephen Gardiner was deprived of the see of Winchester and replaced by Ponet. In October, Heath lost Worcester and Hooper was permitted to combine the see with that of Gloucester.

1552   By April, a second Act of Uniformity had passed through Parliament. This measure repeated the terms of the 1549 Act (adding penalties for persons attending illegal services) and ordered the use of the revised Book of Common Prayer from November. The new Prayer Book reflected the influence of English radicals (notably Hooper) and of Continental reformers, especially Bucer. The Mass was totally abolished, plain bread, surplices, Communion tables replacing hosts, chasubles and altars. Prayers for the dead and private confession were abolished. The Canon (or central portion) of the Mass, which had been left intact in 1549, was split up to demonstrate clearly that no veneration of the sacrament was involved. Kneeling at Communion was still ordered but a 'Black Rubric' issued by the Council denied that this sign of respect implied any 'Real Presence'. Many ceremonies preserved in the first Prayer Book were to cease.

The government decided to issue a set of articles defining the Protestant faith of the Church of England and discussions were held between various divines, including John Knox.

1553   In January, the government began the seizure of all church goods. In June, the Forty-two Articles were finally issued. Many of these were directed against the Anabaptists but the two principal issues related to:

1. The Eucharist: the definition of the Eucharistic presence was Zwinglian in tone. Only true believers truly communicated and then by faith alone.
2. Justification: this could be achieved, it was argued, by faith alone. Purgatory was denied.

In July, King Edward died and Northumberland's attempt to install Jane Grey as Queen failed. On the accession of Mary Tudor, many foreign reformers and English Protestants fled from England.

The deprivation of Protestant bishops was accompanied by the release of Gardiner and Bonner from detention. Cranmer, Latimer, Hooper, Ridley and others were gaoled.

Mary issued a proclamation stating her attachment to the Catholic faith. During the autumn, Parliament met. While refusing to repeal the Royal Supremacy, it approved an Act of Repeal, revoking the following Acts:

Act against Revilers (1547)
Act for the election of bishops (1547)
Act of Uniformity (1549)
Act taking away divers laws against the marriage of priests (1549)
Act for abolishing divers books and images (1550)
Act for ordering ecclesiastical ministers (1550)
Act of Uniformity (1552)
Act for the keeping of holy-days and fasting-days (1550)
Act for the marriage of priests and legitimation of their children (1550)

The Edwardian Reformation was now undone and the Mass, images, holy-days and a celibate clergy all revived.

1554   In January, against a background of Protestant unrest, the Queen announced her marriage to Philip of Spain. Several rebellions were prompted by anti-Spanish feeling, notably that led by Sir Thomas Wyatt in Kent. Wyatt's rebellion did not receive wide support from Protestants and was suppressed by the authorities.

In March, the Queen issued Injunctions to the bishops, ordering them to:
1. suppress heresy and remove heretical priests and schoolmasters;
2. remove married clerics and put them to penance;
3. divorce ex-religious persons who had married;
4. re-ordain any priests ordained under Edward VI's Ordinal;
5. restore all ceremonies, processions and holy-days.

As a result of these Injunctions, between 10 per cent and 25 per cent of the parish clergy were deprived of their livings for marriage. Some were given other benefices after showing their conformity to the new regime.

The Parliament of April–May rejected calls for the reintroduction of the heresy laws but later approved this measure in return for assurances that no attempt would be made to restore monastic lands to the Church.

Cardinal Reginald Pole, Mary's choice as Archbishop of Canterbury, arrived in London in November and absolved the realm from excommunication.

Parliament passed (in November) a second Act of Repeal removing all anti-Papal measures passed since 1529 and undoing the religious revolution enacted under Henry VIII. The following Acts were revoked:

Dispensations Act (1529)
Act in restraint of citations (1531)
Act in conditional restraint of annates (1533)
Act for the submission of the clergy (1534)
Act in restraint of annates (1534)
Act concerning Papal dispensations (1534)
Act of Supremacy (1534)
Suffragans Act (1535)
Act appointing an ecclesiastical commission (1536)
Act extinguishing the authority of the Bishop of Rome (1536)
Acts of Succession
Act authorising new bishoprics (1539)

1555   In February, the newly-revived heresy laws were used to condemn the first Protestant martyr, John Rogers, who was executed this month. Other martyrdoms followed, the victims including Hooper, Ridley, Latimer and Cranmer.

Many ordinary men and women suffered death for their opposition to the revived Catholic faith: three hundred were executed by the end of 1558.

In November, Bishop Gardiner died.

1556   Religious unrest continued in many areas and many more persons were burned for heresy.

The government's position was further damaged by Pole's quarrel with Pope Paul IV (a Neapolitan opposed to the Spanish interest). The Pope deprived Pole of his legacy.

1558 Mary's piety moved her to fill vacant bishoprics and make attempts to improve the financial position of the bishops.

Mary died in November and Pole a day after the Queen.

1559 In January, Elizabeth I's first Parliament assembled.

By April, two Acts establishing a new religious settlement had been approved.

The Act of Supremacy declared that the Queen was 'Supreme Governor' of the Church of England and empowered to visit the Church with Royal commissions. Thus the Caesaro-Papal powers of Henry VIII were revived in a modified form. All Acts repealed by the Marian regime were revived and the Acts of Repeal repealed. The heresy Acts were revoked and the Papal supremacy abolished.

The Oath of Supremacy was to be taken by all clergy, justices, officers and Royal servants. Graduates at Universities and ordinands were to swear the oath. Any person refusing to subscribe was to suffer loss of office and maintainers of foreign authority were to suffer loss of all possessions and life imprisonment. For a second offence of this nature, the penalties of *praemunire* could be invoked and a third offence involved charges of high treason.

Persons assisting offenders could be charged with *praemunire*.

The Act of Uniformity enacted that the Book of Common Prayer was to be used by all clergy on pain of prosecution. A first offence by a cleric entailed loss of income for one year plus six months imprisonment. A second offence carried the penalty of deprivation and one year's imprisonment. A further offence could be punished by deprivation and life imprisonment.

Attacks on the Prayer Book in 'plays, songs, rhymes' were also to carry penalties: a fine of one hundred marks or six months imprisonment for a first offence, a fine of four hundred marks or one year's imprisonment for a second offence, and a penalty of loss of all goods and life imprisonment for a third.

It was ordered that all persons should attend church regularly or pay a fine of 12*d*.

All parishes were to buy a Prayer Book.

The ornaments of the churches were to continue as in 'the second year of the reign of King Edward VI', although further alterations to rites and ceremonies could be ordered.

These measures were followed by the issue of the Royal Injunctions. The most important provisions of these Injunctions were:

1. The clergy were to preach the Royal Supremacy.
2. Images were not to be extolled.
3. Frequent sermons were to be preached.
4. The English Bible was to be freely available to all.
5. Recusants were to be reported to the authorities.
6. 'All shrines, coverings of shrines, all tables, candlesticks, trindals, and

rolls of wax, pictures, paintings, and all other monuments of feigned miracles, pilgrimages, idolatry, and superstition' were to be destroyed.

7. Priests were free to marry.

8. No images were to be kept by private persons.

9. Kneeling at the Communion was to continue.

Gradual return of the Protestants who had been in exile during Mary's reign brought back to England a number of committed reformers imbued with Calvinist ideas (see above, Introduction).

Matthew Parker was appointed Archbishop of Canterbury. Parker was a moderate man, a committed Protestant but not an exile. Among other new bishops was John Jewel, now Bishop of Salisbury. A number of Marian bishops and a small handful of parish clergy were deprived for their un-repentant papalism.

1560   The Geneva Bible in an English translation by William Whittingham (later Dean of Durham) was published in England. This was to become the most popular Biblical version in Elizabethan England.

1561   An English translation of the Genevan *Forme of Prayer* was published in Geneva. This service book came to be seen by radicals as far superior to the English Prayer Book. The *Institutes of the Christian Religion* of John Calvin also appeared in an English translation. The Genevan model was readily available to English Puritans (see above, Introduction) as a standing reproach to the half-hearted Protestantism of Elizabeth.

1562   John Jewel's *Apology of the Church of England* was published. This able defence of the Elizabethan Settlement of religion was aimed chiefly at Catholic critics and its author sympathised with many Puritan criticisms of the Church.

1563   John Foxe's *Acts and Monuments* appeared – a vastly influential and much-read account of the triumph of the true (Protestant) Church over persecution.

In January, Parliament met. An Act was passed extending the obligation to take the Oath of Supremacy to all graduates, schoolmasters and Members of Parliament.

In the same month, the assembly of Convocation saw Puritan attempts to pass measures modifying the Prayer Book. The sponsors sought the abolition of holy-days, the sign of the Cross at baptism, kneeling at Holy Communion, the compulsory use of the surplice, and the use of organs in churches.

These proposals were narrowly defeated.

1564   Many Puritan clergy were deprived during this year for refusal to wear the surplice, which had become a major cause of contention.

1565   Puritan discontent grew more vociferous and the determination of the

Queen and of Parker to defend the *status quo* all the more unyielding. Thomas Sampson, Dean of Christ Church, Oxford, and Laurence Humphrey, President of Magdalen College, were both suspended for nonconformity. Sampson was subsequently deprived of his position.

In the same year, pressure on Catholics at Oxford sent William Allen, a distinguished scholar, into exile.

1566   The disagreement between the authorities and the Puritans, especially over vestments, continued. Many London clergy were suspended from office.

In March, the Queen urged Parker to act severely against those who would not conform. The Bishop of Durham (James Pilkington) was among a number of leading Churchmen in sympathy with the rebels but Parker had the assistance of the Bishops of London (Edmund Grindal), Winchester (Richard Horne), Ely (Richard Cox) and Lincoln (Nicholas Bullingham) in drawing up a set of strict Injunctions for the Queen's use.

Presented with these, the Queen refused to give them any statutory power and they were therefore issued unofficially by Parker as 'Advertisements'. Parker aimed to enforce a more strict control over the clergy on the following issues:

1. Preaching: all preachers were to be 'diligently examined' before receiving licences to preach. They were to extol the doctrines of the Church. All men licensed before 1564 were to renew their licences.
2. Prayers and Sacraments: the Prayer Book was to be used as ordered. Holy Communion was to be celebrated regularly, a surplice being worn by the ministers (a cope in Cathedrals and college chapels). The Communion table was to be properly vested. Kneeling at Communion was to continue and other services were to remain unaltered.
3. Holy Orders: there was to be henceforth a much closer control over ordination. Non-graduates were only to be ordained in a diocese where they had been born or had resided for a long period. All candidates were to be examined and were to provide testimonials if they left their own diocese.
4. Clerical discipline: all clergy were to wear clerical dress (a long gown and a cap) and ex-clergy (those deprived for nonconformity) were to dress as laymen.

Parker's 'Advertisements' did not end the controversy over vestments. Robert Crowley, vicar of St Giles, Cripplegate, London, and a noted writer, published his *Briefe Discourse against the Outwarde Apparell and Ministering Garmentes of the Popishe Church*. This was the first of many published Puritan manifestos.

In Parliament, bills aimed at the reform of ecclesiastical abuses such as simony, non-residence and ignorance were introduced. The Queen acted to prevent further discussion on religious matters.

1567   In February, Theodore Beza and Heinrich Bullinger disappointed English Puritans by stating their moderate approval of the Elizabethan Church.

The existence of a Separatist movement in London was brought to light in July, when a group was discovered in the city.

1568   Mary, Queen of Scots, fled to England. As a danger to the Crown (being both a Catholic and Elizabeth's heir) she was put into custody.

William Allen secured the foundation of a college to train English Catholic priests at Douay in Flanders.

1569   In October and November, the North was embroiled in a revolt led by the Earls of Westmorland and Northumberland. The unsuccessful rebellion sought the restoration of Catholic worship.

1570   The Catholic menace came to the fore with the issue by Pope Pius V of a Bull, 'Regnans in Excelsis', excommunicating the Queen and calling on all Catholics to assist in her deposition. Most Catholics were loyal to Elizabeth in preference to a foreign Catholic ruler but in August one John Felton was executed as a traitor for fixing up a copy of the Bull in London.

Thomas Cartwright lectured on the early Church at Cambridge and compared it favourably with the Elizabethan Church, whose organisation he criticised (especially its bishops). He was subsequently deprived of his Lady Margaret Chair of Divinity.

1571   Parliament met and Puritan Members planned a strong campaign of Church reform. William Strickland introduced a bill to amend the Prayer Book and abolish many usages, including the wedding-ring, surplice and kneeling at Communion. The bill was quashed by the Privy Council.

Other Puritan bills intended to reform the clergy and deal with non-residence, pluralism and other abuses, and to extend the availability of good preaching also failed to pass.

A Subscription Act was approved by Parliament. This embodied in statute the Thirty-nine Articles and enacted that all clergy ordained under Henry VIII or Mary should swear their obedience to the Articles. Any persons taking possession of benefices or receiving orders should also be compelled to swear likewise.

Any man seeking ordination was to supply testimonials and show his ability by rendering an account of his beliefs in Latin. Only Bachelors of Divinity and licensed preachers were to occupy livings worth more than £30 a year.

At the meeting of Convocation, Canons were approved dealing with abuses in Church courts, pluralism and simony. (These were intended to meet some Puritan criticisms.)

In the summer, many more Puritan clerics were deprived or suspended Among them was John Field, a leading preacher and organiser.

Parliament was eager to pass harsh anti-Catholic measures but these were vetoed by the Queen. In the event, three severe Acts were passed:

Treasons Act: it was declared high treason to deny the Queen's supremacy or accuse her of heresy.

Act prohibiting the bringing in and execution of Papal Bulls and other instruments from the see of Rome: those publicising the Bull of 1570 or defending it were to be deemed guilty of high treason. Persons importing crosses, images, rosaries, or other 'vain and superstitious things' from Rome were subject to the penalties of *Praemunire*.

Act against fugitives over the sea: this was designed to deal with the menace of Catholic seminaries. Any persons who had left the country without licence were to lose all their possessions unless they returned within six months. Those motivated by 'blind zeal and conscience onely' were differentiated from traitors. The former might retain one-third of their goods for the use of their families. Offenders who reconciled themselves to the Crown might regain their possessions within a year.

Alarm at the Catholic threat was increased by the discovery of a plot to kill Elizabeth. Roberto Ridolfi, an Italian banker, had acted as intermediary between the Pope and the Spanish King and the Duke of Norfolk and Mary of Scotland.

1572   In May, a Puritan bill was put before Parliament intended to enable congregations to amend the Prayer Book for their own use and thus avoid 'divers orders of rites, ceremonies, and observations' of which Puritans disapproved. The Act of Uniformity was to be employed only against Papists. This bill was abandoned in the face of Royal disapproval.

Puritan anger and frustration led to the issue of *An Admonition to the Parliament* (by Thomas Wilcox) bound with John Field's *A View of Popishe Abuses yet remaining in the Englishe Churche*.

The *Admonition* set the example of 'the best reformed churches' against that of an English Church dominated by 'lordly lordes'. It attacked the Church on the following grounds:

1. Men were not selected as ministers by congregations but ordained by bishops and set loose to seek a living. Thus many unsuitable and immoral men were obtaining orders.

2. Sufficient emphasis was not placed on preaching.

3. Popish vestments, titles and ceremonies survived.

4. The Church was ruled by prelates and their officials and not by congregations as in the ancient Church.

Field's *View of Popishe Abuses* ... continued these criticisms, declaring that the Prayer Book was 'an unperfecte booke, culled & picked out of that popishe dunghil, the Masse booke . . .' The author condemned most of the services and derided bishops and other members of the ecclesiastical hierarchy.

Official fury at the tone and content of the manifesto led to the imprisonment of Field and Wilcox for a short period. Soon after their release, *A Second Admonition to the Parliament* appeared. This demanded the replacement of episcopacy by a Presbyterian scheme of Church government.

In August, anti-Catholic feeling was given a new intensity by reports of the St Bartholomew's Day massacre in France.

1573   John Whitgift answered the Puritans with his *Answer to the Admonition*, an attack on Presbyterian ideas and on Puritanism in general. He in turn received a reply from Cartwright and a literary controversy ensued.

In October, a Puritan-inspired madman stabbed John Hawkins (whom he had mistaken for Sir Christopher Hatton, a leading member of the Council and anti-Puritan). This incident reflected discredit on Puritans in general.

1574   Walter Travers, minister to the English merchants of Antwerp, published his *Full and Plain Declaration of Ecclesiastical Discipline*. This important book proposed a system of Church government by elders, deacons and ministers, bishops being reduced to the level of pastors.

A relaxation of anti-Catholic feelings led to the release of several Papist prisoners, including John Feckenham, ex-abbot of Westminster.

The first seminary priests arrived in England.

1575   Death of Archbishop Parker, who was succeeded by the Archbishop of York, Edmund Grindal.

1576   In Parliament, bitter attacks on the failings of the clergy were made by a number of Members led by Peter Wentworth. The Puritans demanded more preaching in the Church.

Convocation approved a set of Canons designed to remedy obvious abuses in the Church. These measures covered the following issues:

1. Ignorant ministers: these were not to be admitted to the priesthood. No man was to be ordained unless he had a living.
2. Preaching: greater emphasis was to be placed on the place of preaching.
3. Baptism by midwives: this was to be banned.
4. Marriages in Lent and other seasons: the ban on this – objected to strongly by Puritans – was to be lifted.
5. Church courts: their proceedings were to be simplified.

Archbishop Grindal sought to encourage the participation of Puritans in the reinvigoration of the Church and encouraged 'prophesyings' (see above, Introduction). He strongly denounced nonconformists.

In December, the Queen instructed Grindal to suppress all prophesyings.

The primate refused, asserting the value of these gatherings, and offered his resignation.

1577 John Aylmer, a fervent opponent of Puritanism, was appointed Bishop of London.

Grindal continued to resist the Queen's policy on prophesying and, in June, was suspended from office. An Ecclesiastical Commission was appointed under the chairmanship of Bishop Aylmer to suppress non-conformity. Many prophesyings continued under the protection of leading magnates and bishops.

The government ordered a return to be made of the numbers of Catholic recusants in each diocese. A determined attempt was made to apprehend seminary priests. Cuthbert Mayne was executed at Launceston (Cornwall) in November.

1578 John Nelson, like Mayne a Douay priest, was executed at Tyburn in February and, a few days later, a Catholic layman Thomas Sherwood was hanged.

'Quarterly synods' (a serious attempt at clerical education) were arranged in the diocese of York by Archbishop Edwin Sandys.

1579 An English College at Rome was founded under the patronage of Pope Gregory XIII and the supervision of the Jesuit order.

1580 In the summer of this year, three Jesuits arrived in England: Robert Parsons, Edmund Campion and Ralph Emerson (a lay-brother). Parsons and Campion visited recusant families in many areas.

1581 Alarm at the prospect of a Jesuit 'invasion' of England ('a rabble of vagrant friars now sprung-up') gave rise to fiercely anti-Catholic bills in Parliament (death sentences were to be passed on priests saying Mass; recusants were to face crippling fines). The Queen intervened to modify these measures but two severe Acts were passed:

Act to retain the Queen's Majesty's subjects in their true obedience, provided that:

1. persons teaching the Roman Supremacy were to die as traitors;
2. persons aiding the same were to be deemed guilty of misprision of treason;
3. priests saying Mass faced a fine of two hundred marks and one year's imprisonment;
4. persons found guilty of hearing Mass faced fines of one hundred marks and a year's imprisonment;
5. those refusing to attend church were to pay a fine of £20 per month;
6. persons absent from church for over a year were to obtain sureties of £200 for their better behaviour in future.

Act against seditious words and rumours uttered against the Queen's most excellent Majesty: a second offence against this measure carried a death penalty.

Edmund Campion's arrest at Lyford Grange (Berkshire) was followed by his appearance before the Queen and Leicester. He refused to conform and accept preferment in the Church of England and was executed in December with two Douay priests, Ralph Sherwin and Alexander Bryant. Parsons was condemned to death in his absence and fled to France.

London Puritanism was strengthened by the appointment of John Field and Walter Travers to preaching posts in the capital.

In Parliament, Peter Wentworth moved a public fast but this was rejected by the Queen (who denied the right of the Commons to initiate religious legislation). A petition was forwarded to the Queen regarding Church reform. This was considered by a group of bishops, who rejected calls for a further reform of the ordination system.

1582 Puritan failure in successive Parliaments led to the gradual formation of a 'classical' movement – a loose federation of Presbyterian 'classes' or synods. Several classes began to meet regularly in East Anglia.

During the course of this year, eleven seminary priests were executed.

1583 A French plot to invade England was uncovered: its chief English agent was Francis Throckmorton, a Catholic squire, and Parsons and other Jesuits were deeply implicated.

In August John Whitgift became Archbishop of Canterbury. He was a known anti-Puritan and issued a set of Articles ordering that:

1. the recusancy laws were to be fully enforced;
2. all unauthorised preaching was to cease;
3. all clergy were to wear approved dress;
4. no layman was to preach;
5. all clergy were to subscribe to the Supremacy, Prayer Book and Articles of Religion;
6. no man was to be ordained without a title to a benefice;
7. all ordinands were to prove their aptitude.

Whitgift drew up a set of twenty-four questions to be put to suspect ministers (a procedure condemned by Burghley and other Privy Councillors) and initiated a new High Commission. Between three and four hundred clerics refused to subscribe under pressure from this body.

1584 Within a year, Whitgift secured the subscription of most clerical rebels to a revised version of his articles. Puritan opposition largely collapsed.

In November, Parliament met and many Puritans criticised Whitgift's policies. Petititions sent from Essex, Warwickshire and Lincolnshire complained about the hindrance of preachers.

Peter Turner sought to introduce a Presbyterian order – 'the bill' – with Genevan worship – 'the book'. Turner's bill was denied a reading.

Parliament petitioned for a more learned clergy, the reform of abuses, the restoration of persecuted ministers and an end to Whitgift's harsh policies. The Queen continued to support the primate strongly.

1585 Elizabeth ordered her bishops to deal firmly with the Puritans ('curious and busy fellows'). The Commons demonstrated their displeasure by obstinately proceeding with a bill relating to the admission of men to the ministry.

Thomas Cartwright returned to England after an exile of eleven years. He received a position from Leicester.

Whitgift combined his continued attack on nonconformity with further reforms. Convocation approved a measure relating to the educational standards of ordinands and it was ordered that no incumbent should be allowed to hold a living he could not serve. Fees in Church courts were to be scrutinised and clerical standards investigated on a national basis.

Parliament passed an Act against Jesuits, seminary priests and other suchlike disobedient persons. This was directed chiefly against the Jesuits – the preamble stated that 'divers persons called or professed Jesuits' had come to England to 'stir up and move sedition, rebellion, and open hostility' to the Queen. The Act provided that:

1. all ordained Catholic priests should leave England within forty days;
2. after this period, it should be illegal for any priest to remain in England;
3. any priest arrested after this period should suffer death as a traitor;
4. any persons assisting priests should die as felons;
5. any persons abroad in seminaries were to return to England or be declared traitors;
6. any persons assisting those in seminaries should be subject to the penalties of *praemunire*;
7. any parent sending his children abroad for education (without Royal permission) should be subject to a fine of £100.
8. persons concealing their knowledge of the whereabouts of priests should be liable to a fine of two hundred marks;
9. no Jesuit who had submitted should be ever allowed to come within ten miles of the Queen's presence.

1586 The authorities discovered the involvement of Anthony Babington, page to Mary, Queen of Scots, and several priests in a plot to murder the Queen. Mary was to have been placed on the throne.

During this year, twelve priests and three lay-people were executed. At York, Margaret Clitheroe was pressed to death for hiding priests.

In June, a Star Chamber decree tightened control of the printing presses.

In October, Parliament pressed for more severe fines on recusants. It was enacted that any convicted recusant was henceforth liable to a regular fine of £20 every month.

Puritan Parliamentary tactics centred on a bid to replace the Book of Common Prayer with the Genevan *Forme of Prayer*. Peter Wentworth was prominent in this unsuccessful move.

1587　In February, Anthony Cope moved the 'bill and book' again in Parliament: a revised Genevan service book was to be imposed in England with a Presbyterian system of Church government. Peter Wentworth argued the right of Parliament to debate religious matters, much to the displeasure of the Queen. Cope, Wentworth and Edward Lewknor were gaoled. Government spokesmen dissuaded the Commons from further discussion of the proposals.

There was widespread discussion of Walter Travers' *Disciplina Ecclesiae* in Puritan circles.

In October, Henry Barrow and John Greenwood, the leaders of the London Separatists, were imprisoned.

The execution of Mary Stuart in February was popular with Parliament but did not remove the very real menace of Catholic invasion of England. Philip of Spain's plans were enthusiastically supported by William Allen, now created Cardinal by Pope Sixtus V. Allen attempted to rouse English Catholics to rebel against Elizabeth by publishing tracts in which he referred to the Queen as 'an incestuous bastard, begotten and borne in sinne of an infamous courtesan'.

1588　The defeat of Philip of Spain's Armada did not lessen the government's determination to crush Catholicism. Thirty-one priests were executed during the year.

In March, the Puritans lost a major personality in the person of John Field, whose death occurred that month. However, Puritanism was still capable of producing effective propaganda. In October, the first of a series of attacks on the bishops ('pettie popes') was made in an anonymous pamphlet published under the pseudonym 'Martin Marprelate'.

1589　Sir Christopher Hatton, opening Parliament in January, condemned both Puritans and Papists, especially Allen. Puritan attempts to hold religious debates were foiled.

Further Marprelate tracts appeared and the authorities issued a proclamation against printers of seditious books. During the summer, the Marprelate publishers were arrested; one of them, the Welsh preacher John Penry, fled to Scotland.

Richard Bancroft now emerged as a powerful aide to Whitgift. Preaching at Paul's Cross, he condemned Puritanism as sedition.

A third English Catholic seminary was founded by Robert Parsons at Valladolid in Spain.

1590　During this year, nine Catholic priests were executed.

The anti-Puritan campaign continued: Thomas Cartwright and other leaders were arrested and brought before High Commission. John Udall, a minister at Kingston-on-Thames, was arrested for publishing seditious books. Udall died in prison.

1591　In May, Cartwright and other Puritans were finally brought before Star Chamber on charges of slandering the bishops, attacking the Prayer Book, and participating in Presbyterian organisations. The charges were not finally proved, but the men spent eighteen months in gaol.

A proclamation was issued against priests and Jesuits. This stated that seminaries were centres of sedition and their inmates traitors ready to aid a Spanish invasion. Commissioners were to be appointed to investigate the menace in every shire.

1592　Robert Parsons founded a new seminary in Seville.

A Jesuit and poet, Robert Southwell, published *An Humble Supplication to her Majestie*, protesting Catholic loyalty to the Crown. Southwell was later arrested and executed.

1593　At the meeting of Parliament in February, the government sought to move severe anti-Catholic legislation, providing that persons keeping recusant servants should pay monthly fines of £10, that no Catholic should be allowed to hold public office, and that children of Catholic parents should be removed from their homes at the age of seven.

The Commons resisted these extreme measures and eventually two Acts emerged from this session.

Act against Popish Recusants: this referred to 'sundry wicked and seditious persons, who, terming themselves Catholics . . . and hiding their most detestable and devilish purposes under a false pretext of religion and conscience, do secretly wander and shift from place to place [in order to stir up] sedition and rebellion'. The Act provided that:

1. all known and convicted recusants should return to their homes within forty days and should thereafter remain within a radius of five miles;
2. any such person failing to return to his home was liable to suffer loss of all his possessions;
3. any recusant without fixed abode should go to his parents home or birthplace (a similar penalty being appended);
4. all recusants should report their names to the parson (who was to send a list to a local justice);
5. recusants lacking home and property should leave the realm for ever or suffer death as felons;
6. any suspected Jesuit or priest might be kept in gaol indefinitely if he failed to confess his crime;

7. any recusant desiring to travel outside a five-mile radius of his home should obtain a licence from a bishop or lord-lieutenant or from two justices.

Act to retain the Queen's subjects in obedience: this measure was directed against 'seditious sectaries and disloyal persons' (that is, Puritans rather than Papists). The Act ordained that:

1. any p rson over the age of sixteen who refused obstinately to attend church, encouraged others to do the same, attacked the established religion, or attended a conventicle should go to prison until he conformed;
2. if a convicted sectary refused to conform within three months of arrest, he should be permanently exiled;
3. sectaries who refused to leave the realm or returned from exile should suffer death as felons;
4. sectaries repeating their offences after submission should also be subject to the death penalty;
5. persons sheltering offenders under this Act should face a fine of £10;
6. Catholic recusants were specifically excluded from the workings of the Act.

The weakness of the Puritans in Parliament simplified the passage of the above Act. Peter Wentworth, who dared to raise the issue of the succession to the Crown in the Commons, was arrested and died in gaol.

Henry Barrow and John Greenwood (who had been held in prison for some time) were executed with John Penry on sedition charges. This act was designed to terrify the Puritan opposition.

Richard Hooker's *On the Laws of Ecclesiastical Polity* was published – a powerful assertion of the moderate Anglican position.

Richard Bancroft published two notable attacks on Presbyterianism: *A Survey of the Pretended Holy Discipline* and *Dangerous Positions and Proceedings*.

1594 Several factors served to weaken the Catholic position:
Cardinal Allen died.

At Wisbech Castle (the official prison for priests and Jesuits) bitter quarrels divided the secular and Jesuit prisoners.

Robert Parsons *A conference about the next succession the Crowne of Ingland* (in which he argued for the candidature of the Infanta of Spain) angered many of his English co-religionists. Many Catholics became fiercely anti-Jesuit.

1595 The University of Cambridge was divided over the issue of predestination (a doctrine which remained the official belief of the Church of England). William Barrett, a chaplain who had attacked the doctrine, was forced to recant his views. Archbishop Whitgift gave qualified support to the University authorities and agreed to the issue of a set of articles (the Lambeth Articles) which reaffirmed Calvinist ideas.

The Queen ordered a halt to discussion of this issue.

1596 Despite the events of the previous year, the debate over predestination continued at Cambridge. Peter Baro was prominent among the assailants of Calvinism.

1597 In Parliament, Puritan bills dealing with excessive fees in Church courts and the issue of subscription to the Articles were abandoned because of lack of support. The Puritan contingent in the Commons had diminished in numbers and in influence.

Archbishop Whitgift drew up a set of constitutions, dealing with abuses in the Church, which were approved by Convocation. These measures ordered changes in the following fields:

1. the selection of ordinands;
2. pluralism;
3. the abuses of excommunication;
4. fees in Church courts;
5. abuses in the issue of marriage licences.

1598 The Pope appointed George Blackwell archpriest of England to control the Catholic clergy. Jesuits were excluded from Blackwell's jurisdiction, and many Catholics saw his appointment as a Jesuit attempt to dominate their Church in England.

Two priests who travelled to Rome to petition the Pope on this issue were imprisoned on the orders of Fr. Parsons and despatched home without an audience.

1599 The divisions of the English Catholics were demonstrated by the negotiations conducted by some priests with Bishop Bancroft. The authorities sought to exploit these divisions.

1602 The new attitude of the authorities towards Catholicism was clear in the tone of a proclamation against priests issued this year. Jesuits were to leave England immediately; other priests were allowed until the beginning of 1603 to make their departure. There was to be a strict search for Jesuits; other priests were to be encouraged to submit. Priests who submitted would receive favourable treatment.

1603 During the course of the year, thirteen secular priests submitted to the government.

THE BIBLE

1495 William Tyndale was born in Gloucestershire, of uncertain parentage.

1496   John Colet, humanist scholar and later Dean of St Paul's, returned from studying in Italy and lectured at Oxford on St Paul's *Epistle to the Romans*. He set the *Epistle* in its proper historical context and used its evidence about the early Church to criticise the Church of his own day.

1509   Erasmus of Rotterdam arrived on his third visit to England (he had visited the country briefly in 1499 and 1506). He received friendly treatment from Bishop Fisher and others and obtained preferment at the University of Cambridge.

1511–14   During this period, Erasmus worked intensively on his Latin translation of the Greek New Testament at Cambridge.

1516   Erasmus's New Testament was published.

1522   Martin Luther published his German New Testament (based on Erasmus's text) at Wittenberg.
   Tyndale, having left University, served for a short period as a tutor in a gentleman's household in Gloucestershire. Here he quarrelled with the local clergy and decided to seek facilities to translate the Bible.

1523   Tyndale was in London, but received no assistance in his project from the Bishop of London, Cuthbert Tunstal, and became involved in Protestant circles.
   The first parts of the Old Testament in German appeared at Wittenberg (the last was not completed until 1533).

1524   Tyndale left England for Germany with the assistance of the London merchant Humphrey Monmouth. He visited Hamburg, Wittenberg and Cologne.

1525   Work began on printing Tyndale's English New Testament at Cologne (he based his translation on Erasmus and Luther). The work was interrupted by the Church authorities and was completed at Worms.

1526   By April, Tyndale's Testament was being sold in England. The authorities moved to prevent its distribution. The Bishop of London banned it in his diocese and a copy was burned at Paul's Cross.
   Christopher Endhoven of Antwerp printed a further edition of the work.

1528   Cardinal Wolsey prosecuted a number of men for distributing the Tyndale Testament, including Thomas Garrett of Oxford.

1530   Tyndale's edition of the Pentateuch (the first five books of the Old Testament) was printed by Hoochstraten at Antwerp.
   A new edition of the New Testament was printed by Endhoven.
   Henry VIII ordered a Commission to examine the need for an English Bible: their report was favourable to the proposition.

George Joye produced an independent translation of the Psalms (based on Martin Bucer's Latin version). Joye, an associate of Tyndale who enjoyed somewhat uneven relations with the great translator, produced other translations: the Books of Isaiah (1531), Jeremiah (1534), Proverbs and Ecclesiastes (1535).

1534   A complete German Bible was published in Wittenberg.

A new edition of Tyndale's New Testament was published in Antwerp.

Miles Coverdale began work on his Biblical translation at Antwerp.

In December, the Convocation of Canterbury petitioned the King for an English Bible. Cranmer asked a number of bishops and other scholars to correct and modify Tyndale's new Testament, but no worthwhile product emerged.

1535   In May, Tyndale was arrested and imprisoned at Vilvorde Castle near Brussels.

The printer James Nicholson sought permission to print Coverdale's complete English Bible in London (an edition had already appeared in Cologne). The King authorised the printing, without granting any formal approval.

1536   Cromwell planned this year to order the English Bible to be set up in churches, but abandoned his injunction on the fall of Anne Boleyn (a firm friend to the vernacular Bible).

In August, Tyndale was executed at Vilvorde.

1537   Two revised editions of Coverdale's Bible were issued by Nicholson. The version now claimed to possess Royal approval.

In August, John Rogers, chaplain to the English merchant community of Antwerp and a friend of Tyndale, issued a Bible, under the pseudonym of 'Thomas Mathew', which was largely based on Tyndale's. The 'Mathew Bible', published by Richard Grafton and Edward Whitchurch, was printed with the permission of the King (persuaded by Cromwell). Rogers' version cost more than Coverdale's and was too Protestant in tone to secure general approval.

1538   In the summer of this year, Grafton and Whitchurch worked at Paris under Coverdale's direction on a new, official Bible. Coverdale used the 'Mathew Bible' and toned down its strongly Protestant emphasis to ensure Royal approval. After the work was stopped by the French ecclesiastical authorities, the press moved to London.

Cromwell's Injunctions of this year ordered that a Bible was to be provided in every church and the vicar-general further instructed the bishops to supervise the introduction of Bibles.

1539   In April, the 'Great Bible' finally appeared.

132

Richard Taverner produced a Bible based on Rogers's version but less extreme in its tone. Taverner, a friend and protégé of Cromwell, was a notable Greek scholar.

1540   In April, a second edition of the Great Bible appeared. This contained a preface by Cranmer.

The first cheap edition of the Great Bible appeared (printed by Berthelet).

John Porter, a young Londoner, was arrested by the officers of the Bishop of London for reading the Bible aloud in St Paul's and commenting on its interpretation.

1541   A fifth edition of the Great Bible was issued.

Despite the increased influence of the conservative faction in the Council, a further order was issued regarding the provision of a Bible in all parish churches.

1542   The ascendant conservative group in Convocation pressed for a revision of the Great Bible which gave greater weight to the Vulgate version. Cranmer appointed fifteen bishops to examine the New Testament. However, the King decided to impose the task on the Universities. The work was never completed and the Great Bible remained available (although no more editions appeared during Henry's reign).

1543   The Act for the advancement of true religion severely curtailed the right to read the Scriptures.

1550   John Cheke, Professor of Greek at Cambridge, worked on a popular version of the New Testament. This was never completed.

1551   William Salesbury published an edition of the Epistles and Gospels in Welsh.

1553–8   During Mary's reign, while Bible-reading was not specifically forbidden, many Bibles were destroyed.

1554   John Standish published his *Discourse . . . whether the Scipture should be in English*. Standish blamed heresy and rebellion on the English Bible.

1556   William Whittingham and William Kethe, exiles at Geneva, produced a new translation of the Psalms.

1557   Whittingham produced a version of the New Testament.

1559   The Royal Injunctions ordered a Bible to be made available in every church.

1560   In April, the 'Geneva Bible' appeared – a massively influential work which was to go through one hundred and forty editions by 1644. It was the work of Whittingham, Anthony Gilby and Richard Sampson. The great popularity of the Geneva edition was based, perhaps, not so much on its Calvinist tone but on its cheapness and the introduction of useful innovations such as the division of chapters into verses, the introduction of figures and maps, and the use of Roman type.

1562   A new edition of the Great Bible was published.

1563   An Act was passed ordering the translation of the Bible into Welsh. The work, to be completed within three years, was entrusted to the Bishops of St David's, Bangor, St Asaph, Llandaff and Hereford.

1566   A further edition of the Great Bible was published.
   Work began on a new translation sponsored by Archbishop Parker. Its aim was 'to follow the common English translation' (the Great Bible) but to correct it where it erred.

1567   A Welsh New Testament, mainly the work of William Salesbury, appeared.

1568   Parker's version (the 'Bishops' Bible') was published.

1572   A revision of the Bishops' Bible was carried out incorporating suggestions by Giles Lawrence, Professor of Greek at Oxford.

1576   The Geneva Bible was first published in England.

1578   Gregory Martin, an English seminary priest, began work on an English Catholic version of the Bible. This Rheims/Douay version, superintended by William Allen, was a translation from the Vulgate and not of high literary merit.

1582   Martin's version of the New Testament was published. (The Old Testament did not appear until 1609.)
   Martin entered into a literary controversy with William Fulke on the issue of Biblical translations.

1588   The first Welsh Bible was published by William Morgan, Bishop of St Asaph.

1596   Hugh Broughton, a noted Hebrew scholar, issued a new translation of the Book of Daniel (he later worked on other sections of the Old Testament). At this time, there were many calls for a new version of the Bible. The Authorised Version finally appeared in 1611.

6 EDUCATION

SCHOOLS

INTRODUCTION

> When faith and learning are combined,
> Then only do we true religion find.[1]

The inscription carved above the door of the Lady Chapel at St Alban's Abbey (after its conversion to a schoolhouse) sums up the attitude of Tudor governments to education in general and to schools in particular. The latter were seen by those in authority as 'an effective means of unifying the religious outlook and consolidating the social order'.[2] They also met the increasing demand from ever wider sections of the community for learning (a means of scaling the social ladder and entering the expanding professions) and it was for this reason that schools grew in size and number during the sixteenth century. The manner in which this growth was channelled and controlled, and the increasing supervision of the content of education, is symptomatic of the efforts of Tudor administrations to control those aspects of the lives of their citizens previously left to the Church or some lesser agency. The Tudor achievement was great, but the extent of the educational provision of medieval England must not be underestimated. Much of this provision was under the direct control of the Church: schools were attached to cathedrals, both those staffed by monks and the secular foundations, monasteries, especially the larger houses, collegiate churches (like those of Southwell (Notts.) and Wimborne (Dorset)) and to chantries. But many schools were already being run by laymen, through guilds, merchant companies and town councils. Ipswich and Hull were among the towns which had borough schools in the fifteenth century. Yorkshire had ten schools by the early fifteenth century and thirty-five by the mid-1520s. There are many difficulties in arriving at any estimate of the number and quality of schools in this (or indeed in any other) period prior to the last century. A. F. Leach estimated that there were over three hundred schools by the 1530s. The same writer proceeded to condemn the destruction wrought in the educational field by the Henrician dissolution of the monastic houses.[3] He had to concede, however, that new foundations more than compensated for any loss of facilities. Undoubtedly, schools were

135

lost and reformers like Hugh Latimer were bitterly disappointed that at least a few of the former monastic buildings were not made available for use as schools. At the same time, due weight must be given to the new cathedral foundations. That at Canterbury, known as the King's School, was designed for fifty pupils, while the foundation at Worcester had a complement of forty. Henrician governments saw the value of expanding the educational system (the latter term can be used only loosely at this time) and bringing it under closer control. England was passing through a period of religious revolution and the desire for religious unity and conformity were to remain prime objectives of education throughout the Tudor period. For this reason, education was a matter firmly kept within the orbit of religious legislation and the desire for uniformity led to the issue of officially approved teaching aids, most notably the series of official Latin grammars.

The expansion of education in Tudor England was in large part due to the desire for education emanating from the middle ranks of society – the gentry, professions and substantial merchant and commercial classes. Children from humbler backgrounds were not excluded – the sons of yeomen and craftsmen are found in many school registers – but, despite the common absence of tuition fees, the expenses of educating a child were by no means inconsiderable. Entrance fees were common, materials had to be bought, and the child attending a school became unavailable for useful work in workshop, field or home. At the same time, increasing numbers of the landed classes were sending their offspring to grammar schools, some of which soon established regular boarding facilities. Academies for gentlemen (of the kind established, for example, in France) did not become a feature of the English educational scene. The favour of great men accorded increasing prestige to some schools – Sir Nicholas Bacon took a great interest in the school at St Albans, the Earl of Huntingdon extended his patronage to that at Leicester.

The reign of Edward VI saw, it has been convincingly argued, the beginnings of a system of schools in England.[4] The Edwardian Chantries Act of 1547 had threatened a high proportion of existing schools but in the event few were lost and many new schools and refoundations on a more impressive scale emerged. Sedbergh School (Yorks.) – subject to the terms of the measure – was kept in existence by a Royal stipend for three years until it was given new endowments.[5] Where schools had not existed before (but were thought now to be desirable) Edward VI's commissioners, given the control of chantry resources, frequently rectified the situation with an entirely new foundation (this happened at Newent (Glos.)). Elsewhere, old schools attached to chantries or guilds were refounded. Many schools went through a whole series of refoundations. At Leeds, Ilminster (Som.) and elsewhere, the townspeople bought the confiscated chantry lands for the use of their schools without waiting for official action.[6] By the end of Edward's reign, most counties possessed several schools of high standard: in Warwickshire, the school at Stratford-on-Avon (a guild school) was re-endowed in 1553 and survived to educate (it is generally supposed) William Shakespeare. In Great Yarmouth and High Wycombe, the religious changes again benefited the cause of education (albeit at the expense of poor relief): ex-hospital lands were put to school use. Elsewhere, earlier foundations like Macclesfield (1502) and Giggleswick (1512) received generous new endowments. Among benefactors, the landed classes were still not a negligible factor but mercantile enterprise was of growing importance. Tonbridge School was founded by Andrew Judd, a skinner, in 1553, while Blundell's School at Tiverton was the result of benefactions made by Peter Blundell, wool merchant. Clerics (for example, Matthew Parker and Alexander Nowell, who both founded Lancashire schools) were still among the ranks of the founders, and piety continued to motivate men like Richard, Lord Rich. Rich refounded a chantry he had set up in Mary's reign as a school – Felsted – in the reign of her sister.

The average age of entry to the lower forms of a Tudor grammar school was six or seven years: new pupils learned not only the ABC and the rudiments of Latin but also the Lord's Prayer, Commandments, Creed and Catechism. They then proceeded to the real business of the schools: the study of grammar, logic and rhetoric, the components of all speaking and writing. Letter-writing was taught and Latin authors (notably Cicero) studied intensively if somewhat mechanically. 'The grammar school gave the linguistic basis of grammar, rhetoric, and logic'; and it has been concluded that 'if William Shakespeare had the grammar school training of his day – or its equivalent – he had as good a formal literary training as had any of his contemporaries'.[7] Education remained the preserve largely of males of the middle to upper classes (although village schools, and informal education, provided in some fashion for the impecunious and sometimes for women. Leicestershire had forty-five such schools by the first half of the seventeenth century).[8] It was undoubtedly for some a means of social mobility, while at the same time it served to define class and status barriers. Tudor people were passionately interested in education and the triumph of the vernacular tongue opened all learning to the growing body of the literate. Not all educational media could be controlled in the way that Tudor rulers thought proper – although all governments sought to control the way people wrote, spoke and even thought. Schools and Universities could be (and were) subjected to official supervision and the drive for uniformity gained momentum in the reign of Elizabeth. It could no longer be assumed that schoolmasters were men loyal to Crown and true (established) religion. Hence, the insistence on oaths, subscriptions and licences which was enforced upon the teaching profession (in so far as such a body existed – many schoolmasters were still clergymen). Erasmus, the inspiration of many Tudor educationalists, had demanded more education as a means of training the child to serve God. Increasingly, the Tudor state came to see it as a way of training its subjects in its own service.

NOTES

1. Quoted by Joan Simon, *Education and Society in Tudor England* (Cambridge, 1966) p. 299.
2. Ibid , p. 196.
3. A. F. Leach, *English Schools at the Reformation* (London, 1896) pp. 5–6.
4. Simon, op. cit., p. 244.
5. Ibid., p. 228.
6. K. Charlton, *Education in Renaissance England* (London, 1965) p. 91.
7. T. W. Baldwin, *William Shakspere's Small Latine & Lesse Greeke* (Urbana, U.S.A., 1944) II, p. 663.
8. Simon, op. cit., p. 376.

MAJOR FOUNDATIONS AND REFOUNDATIONS

Bedfordshire
Bedford   1552, 1566

Buckinghamshire
High Wycombe   1562

Cambridgeshire
King's, Ely   1543

Cheshire
Stockport   1487
Macclesfield   1502
King's, Chester   1541
Wallasey   1590

Derbyshire
Repton   1557
Elizabeth College, Buxton   1563
Derby   1570

Dorset
Sherborne   1550
King Edward's, Poole   1552
Dorchester   1569

Essex
Brentwood   1557
Felsted   1564

Gloucestershire
Bristol   1532
Crypt, Gloucester   1539

Hampshire
Andover   1571

Hertfordshire
Berkhamsted   1541

Kent
Cranbrook   1520
Canterbury   1541
King's, Rochester   1542
Maidstone   1549
Tonbridge   1553

Lancashire
Manchester   1515
Bolton   1524
Rochdale   1565
Blackburn   1567

Leicestershire
Wyggeston, Leicester   1564

London
St Paul's   1509
Christ's Hospital   1552
Merchant Taylors'   1561
St Olave's   1571
Emanuel   1594
Alleyn's   1597

Middlesex
Highgate   1565
Harrow   1571

Norfolk
Gresham's, Holt   1554
Norwich   1574

Northamptonshire
Northampton   1541
Oundle   1556
Wellingborough   1595

Northumberland
Newcastle   1545

Nottinghamshire
Nottingham   1513

Rutland
Oakham   1584
Uppingham   1584

Shropshire
Shrewsbury   1552

Somerset
King's, Bruton   1519
King's College, Taunton   1522
Blundell's, Tiverton   1599

Staffordshire
Wolverhampton   1515
Queen Mary's, Walsall   1554

Suffolk
Bury St Edmund's   1550

Warwickshire
King Edward's, Birmingham   1552
Rugby   1567

Wiltshire
Devizes   1543

Worcestershire
King's, Worcester   1541

Yorkshire
Giggleswick   1512
Pocklington   1519
Sedbergh   1525
Leeds   1552
Wakefield   1591

Wales
Christ's College, Brecon   1541
Wrexham   1580

CHRONOLOGY

1536   The first Royal Injunctions of Henry VIII ordered all clergy to instruct the young. In addition, wealthy clerics were to provide a scholarship to school or University for each £100 of their annual income.

1538   Henry VIII's second Injunctions provided for the availability of the English Bible to all lay-people: priests were to expound it to their parishioners.

1539   Plans were drawn up for the utilisation of monastic wealth and buildings. A considerable proportion (it was proposed) should go to education (e.g. a school with sixty scholars at St Albans). These plans were later abandoned, although schools were attached to the new Henrician cathedral foundations.

1540–2   An official Latin Grammar was issued (a revision by Leonard Cox, schoolmaster of Reading, of a work by William Lily).

1543   The King's Primer was issued. All schoolmasters were ordered to use it.

1547   The Injunctions issued this year restored the use of the English Bible (forbidden to all but gentlemen in 1543). Priests were to buy Erasmus's *Paraphrases* on the Gospels. Chantry priests were to 'exercise themselves in teaching youth to read and write and bring them up in good manners and other virtuous exercises'.

The Act for chantries, colleges and free chapels ceded to the Crown all these institutions plus the possessions of fraternities and guilds. (Oxford and Cambridge colleges and the schools at Winchester and Eton were excluded).

1548   A survey of all the above institutions was made: most educational foundations were awarded stipends for continuation.

Certain schools were protected by private Act of Parliament.

1549   A new Royal Grammar – the *Brevissima Institutio* – was issued.

1550   The Chancellor of the Court of Augmentations was authorised to provide funds for school foundation: many former chantry schools subsequently received new endowments.

1553   A new official Catechism – the work of Bishop Ponet – was issued.

1557   It was ordered that all schoolmasters should obtain licences from bishops.

1559   Two significant measures affecting education were passed. The first provided for the statutory foundation of schools left incomplete at the end of Edward VI's reign. The second dissolved all chantries and monasteries founded under Mary but provided for the preservation of any annexed schools.

1571   Convocation ordered all teachers to subscribe to the Articles of Religion and Prayer Book: a number were subsequently deprived.

A new Catechism – the work of Alexander Nowell and containing 'good lessons to godliness' – was prescribed for general use.

1585   The practice whereby Catholics sent their children abroad for education in their own faith was declared illegal (Act against Jesuits, etc.). Fines of £100 were to be imposed on offenders.

UNIVERSITIES

INTRODUCTION

'Piety, virtue, self-restraint and knowledge' – these qualities (enunciated here in the foundation statutes of Henry VIII's Trinity College at Cambridge) were those which the Tudor University ostensibly sought to stamp upon the minds of the male élite who came to it for instruction.[1] Recent interest in the Tudor Universities has tended to concentrate attention upon the role which these institutions played in society: as agents of modernisation, cultural change and social control. According to one historian, they assumed 'broad responsibilities for the mental and moral cultivation of all influential groups in the community.'[2] In the medieval period, they had produced clerics and divines; in the second half of the sixteenth century most of the important men in government and many of those in the cultural field were products of Oxford and Cambridge. In the 1584 Parliament, almost one third of the members had been at one of the Universities.

The potential of the Universities for expansion, both in size and influence, would not have appeared obvious to an observer of the fifteenth century. Education was divorced from effective power in the realm – the sons of the ruling elite were generally raised in household service and early Tudor magnates were not required to master the studies offered at Oxford and Cambridge (some were virtually illiterate). The two seats of learning were essentially places where priests were produced to form an educated leadership for the Church (and a useful body of servants for the King). This was their principal function and continued to be an important function after the Reformation. The student at medieval Oxford or Cambridge studied grammar, logic and dialectic for four years. After taking his B.A., he was expected to remain in the University another three years, studying philosophy and teaching a new generation of students. Those who had attained the level of M.A. were free to proceed to the higher studies – medicine, law and most prestigious of all, theology. No man might attain the degree of Doctor of Divinity without sixteen years of study. Most graduates entered the priesthood, becoming Fellows of Colleges or residing elsewhere in the towns and moving on to profitable Church livings. The most able gained rapid promotion through a study of law, both Canon and Civil, and entered the Royal service, being rewarded with bishoprics and other well-endowed benefices. (It is noticeable that most of the conservative bishops in the mid-sixteenth century were lawyers by training. Among the most prominent was Stephen Gardiner.) While at University, students boarded in houses which became institutionalised as 'halls'. In 1450, there were close on sixty of these in Oxford. Existing Colleges (for example, Peterhouse and Balliol) tended to be small and penurious communities of priest-scholars to whom students came for instruction. Students did not reside within Colleges (which lacked facilities and finance). The most impressive Colleges at Oxford were those maintained by the religious orders (for example, the Benedictine Gloucester College) for the education of their members. (Cambridge lacked institutions of this type but the friars played an important part in University life there as at Oxford.)[3] The fifteenth century saw much evidence of vitality at both Universities. At Oxford, the Colleges of Lincoln, All Souls and Magdalen were founded and at Cambridge King's, Queen's and St Catharine's. All Souls was to be a typical medieval College and remains to the present day a community of scholars without undergraduate membership (its original function was to act as a chantry for souls). But Magdalen admitted student members within its walls and set a pattern for Tudor foundations.

The acceleration of social, cultural and religious change which permeated English life in the sixteenth century was not and could not be resisted by the

Universities. The most basic fact in their history at this period is that they grew. In 1500, about 150 men were being admitted to each; this figure had trebled by the end of the century.[4] More new foundations were made, some of them extremely ambitious. Later in the century, laymen became prominent as founders but Churchmen led the way. When Bishop Fox of Winchester decided to found his own College at Oxford, he is said to have planned a monastic community until warned by his friend Hugh Oldham that the days of the monastic life might well be limited. Fox's foundation (Corpus Christi), in which he took a deep personal interest, was to consist of a President, twenty Fellows and a like number of scholars or 'disciples'.[5] Henry VIII's Christ Church (plucked from the ruins of Wolsey's grandiose scheme) had in contrast a hundred students from the start and the society numbered 200 by the early seventeenth century. Its revenues were over £2000 a year. The removal of the monks and friars put the Universities under the control of the secular clergy in their Colleges. The Colleges grew at the expense of the halls (only eight of the latter remained in 1559). Students now resided within the Colleges, which provided the bulk of the teaching on their premises (the tutorial system emerged as a characteristic component of the education they offered).

The Henrician Reformation removed Canon Law from the curriculum (although it did not remove the clergy or the role of the Universities as seminaries). New subjects emerged (if taught in an old-fashioned manner) and it has been strongly argued that the Universities emerged as educators of the ruling class and modernisers of society. The fact that the education the ruling class received was superficial and mostly of little practical utility supports the contention that they sought status and social assurance rather than any more tangible benefits. Humanist effort and increased literacy had made learning fashionable and the broadly defined gentry class flocked to the Colleges alongside the sons of magnates and knights. Many became 'commoners' (outside the statutory community of the Colleges) and left without taking degrees. In 1584, fewer than a third of the Crown officials in Parliament had been to University, and only three had degrees. Some influential commentators (for example, Thomas Starkey and, later, Humphrey Gilbert) had argued that the University education was useless to a man destined to exercise authority in the realm. He should receive an education with due emphasis on the practical and the general – there should be an opportunity for the youth to acquire skill in riding and the arts of war and in foreign languages useful in travel and diplomacy. The independent academy suggested by Gilbert never materialised. Young men of gentle birth went to a University and then perhaps on to an Inn of Court. At both, much of their time was spent at 'histories, tables, dice and trifles'. The conclusion that men of this class came in increasing numbers to Oxford and Cambridge does not imply that those of humbler stock were excluded – there is plenty of evidence that the sons of yeomen and merchants and of even poorer men still entered the Colleges (although whether they were treated as equal to their social betters is doubtful). Indeed, a strong 'middle class' element gained increased strength in the second half of the sixteenth century. Charitable funds provided for the needy scholar, and the admission of the wealthy as 'commoners' meant that the places on the foundation remained available to a wide section of the community.[6]

The most noticeable element in the history of the Tudor Universities is the increasing intervention of the State and the ever-stronger emphasis on the control of thought and opinion. This is scarcely surprising in a realm subject to authoritarian supervision at every level. The ruling élite, of which the monarch was the centre and symbol, saw danger in any expression of dissent, yet the Reformation, which had been led by the Crown, had unleashed an avalanche of controversy and criticism of the *status quo*. The authorities needed a supply of orthodox preachers and this need it was the duty of the Universities to meet. After 1559, Catholic elements were driven from Oxford and Cambridge (much to the disadvantage of scholarship) and a series of measures made it impossible for those who opposed the Protestant Church to teach or study at a University. In the reign of Edward VI, the arrival of foreign reformers at Oxford and Cambridge (of whom Martin Bucer was probably the most notable) stimulated religious discussion and activity. Cambridge became a strongly Protestant community, where many men were convinced that the Church of England needed further reformation after the model of Geneva and other Continental churches.[7] (In the reign of Mary, one in five of all those persons who went into exile were ex-Cambridge men, and half of the latter had held Fellowships.)[8] Puritans shattered the calm atmosphere which the government of Elizabeth sought to maintain at both Universities (Oxford Puritanism has been too often underestimated). The measure of freedom allowed by the Elizabethan régime did not preclude the gaoling of academics for teaching unpalatable ideas which seemed to the government to threaten not only Church but civil authority too. The latter rested on calm and the absence of controversy – hence the defence of Calvinism by Whitgift in the 1590s.[9] But by the later Elizabethan period, Protestantism had triumphed in England and reformers could more easily afford to quarrel among themselves. Certainly the Universities had played an important part in the defeat of Catholicism. Emmanuel College (a major training ground for preachers) was built symbolically on the site of a Dominican convent.

The shortcomings of the Tudor Universities were many. The new studies initiated in the early Tudor period lost ground – by the reign of Elizabeth interest in Greek had waned drastically. No formal provision was made for modern languages and literature, little progress was made in science and medicine (John Dee, the great scientist and astrologer, refused to teach at Oxford. Englishmen who wished to pursue their studies in the medical field had ideally to go to Padua.) There were many alarms about the state of the seats of learning: in 1541 Oxford was said to be 'in no small ruin' and ten

143

years later it was said that it had lost 90 per cent of its students.[10] But the recovery in numbers made in Mary's reign continued under Elizabeth. The same was true of Cambridge: the population of that University was 1200 in 1564, had increased by 50 per cent within ten years, and was over 2000 by 1600. By the early seventeenth century there were few (save the opponents of hierarchy in Church and State) who questioned the established place of the Universities in the commonwealth.[11] Over nearly a century, they had risen to a central position in English government, religion and culture.

NOTES

1. Quoted by Joan Simon, *Education and Society in Tudor England* (Cambridge, 1966) p. 214.

2. M. H. Curtis, *Oxford and Cambridge in Transition 1558–1642* (Oxford, 1959) p. 261; among other important discussions are K. Charlton, *Education in Renaissance England* (London, 1965), H. Kearney, *Scholars and Gentlemen* (London, 1970) and Lawrence Stone, 'The educational revolution', in *Past and Present*, July 1964.

3. Friars tended to be a disruptive and heretical element.

4. Kearney, op. cit., p. 22.

5. Fox's interest in the College is evident in many of his letters, edited as *Letters of Richard Fox, 1486–1527* by P. S. and H. M. Allen (Oxford, 1929).

6. Notable among the funds was one established by Robert Nowell, a Lancashire gentleman and brother to the Dean of St Paul's.

7. P. Collinson, *The Elizabethan Puritan Movement* (London, 1967) pp. 122–30.

8. Based on an analysis of C. H. Garrett, *The Marian Exiles* (Cambridge, 1938).

9. Curtis, op. cit., pp. 211–26.

10. *Victoria County History of Oxfordshire*, III, pp. 119–20.

11. Kearney, op. cit., p. 97.

COLLEGE FOUNDATIONS

OXFORD

College	Date of foundations	Founder(s)
Brasenose	1509	William Smith, Bishop of Lincoln, and Sir Richard Sutton
Corpus Christi	1517	Richard Fox, Bishop of Winchester
Christ Church	1526, refounded 1532 and 1546	Cardinal Wolsey; refounded by Henry VIII, first as King's College, then as Christ Church
Trinity	1554/5	Sir Thomas Pope, Treasurer of the Court of Augmentations
St John's	1555	Sir Thomas White, Alderman of London
Jesus	1571	Dr Hugh Price, Chancellor of St David's

No further foundation followed until 1612, when Wadham College was founded.

CAMBRIDGE

College	Year	Founder
Jesus	1496	John Alcock, Bishop of Ely
Christ's	1505 (refounded; had been God's House).	Lady Margaret Beaufort
St John's	1511	Lady Margaret Beaufort
Magdalene	1542	Thomas, Lord Audley
Trinity	1546	Henry VIII
Gonville and Caius	1557 (refounded from Gonville Hall)	John Caius
Emmanuel	1584	Sir Walter Mildmay, Chancellor of the Exchequer
Sidney Sussex	1596	Lady Frances Sidney, Dowager Countess of Sussex

No further foundation followed until Downing (1800).

SOURCES *Oxford University Calendar; Cambridge University Annual Register.*

CHANCELLORS OF OXFORD
1483 John Russell, Bishop of Lincoln
1494 John Morton, Archbishop of Canterbury
1500 William Smyth, Bishop of Lincoln
1503 Richard Mayew, Bishop of Hereford
1506 William Warham, Archbishop of Canterbury
1532 John Longland, Bishop of Lincoln
1547 Richard Cox, Dean of Christ Church
1552 Sir John Mason
1556 Reginald Pole, Archbishop of Canterbury
1559 Henry Fitzalan, Lord Arundel
1559 Sir John Mason
1564 Robert Dudley, Earl of Leicester
1585 Sir Thomas Bromley (deputising for Leicester, absent in the Netherlands)
1588 Sir Christopher Hatton
1591 Thomas Sackville, Lord Buckhurst

CHANCELLORS OF CAMBRIDGE
1485 Thomas Rotherham, Archbishop of York
1490 Thomas Cosyn
1494 John Blythe, Bishop of Salisbury
1496 George FitzHugh
1499 Thomas Rotherham

1500   Richard Fox, Bishop of Durham
1502   George FitzHugh
1503   Thomas Ruthall, later Bishop of Durham
1504   John Fisher, Bishop of Rochester
1535   Thomas Cromwell
1540   Stephen Gardiner, Bishop of Winchester
1547   Edward Seymour, Duke of Somerset
1552   John Dudley, Earl of Northumberland
1553   Stephen Gardiner
1556   Reginald Pole
1559   William Cecil
1598   Robert Devereux, Earl of Essex
1601   Robert Cecil, Earl of Salisbury

CHRONOLOGY

1497   Lady Margaret Beaufort, mother of the King, established Readerships in Divinity at both Universities.
1499   John Dogget, a humanist, was appointed Provost of King's Cambridge.
1500   William Grocyn began to lecture on Greek at Oxford.
1501   John Fisher, an influential educationalist and chaplain to Lady Margaret Beaufort, was made Vice-Chancellor of Cambridge.
1504   Fisher was appointed both Chancellor of Cambridge and Bishop of Rochester. A Lady Margaret preachership (at £10 per annum) was set up.
1505   Fisher was appointed Provost of Queen's College, Cambridge.
1506   Fisher received Erasmus as a visitor. William Warham was appointed Chancellor of Oxford.
1511   Erasmus returned to Cambridge and lectured on Greek. He was subsequently appointed Lady Margaret Professor of Divinity.
1514   Erasmus left Cambridge.
1517   A printing press was established at Oxford. Lectures in Greek, Latin and Divinity began at Corpus Christi, Oxford. Wolsey appointed a number of lecturers at Oxford including Nicholas Kratzer, Thomas Lupset and Ludovicus Vives.
1518   Sir Robert Reade set up lectures in philosophy, logic and rhetoric at Cambridge. Richard Croke lectured in Greek.
1520   Printing began in Cambridge.
1522   Hugh Latimer appointed Chaplain to the University of Cambridge.
1524   Thomas Linacre established medical lectures at Oxford.
1525   Robert Barnes, a friar, attacked Wolsey in a sermon at Cambridge. He was forced to do penance and an attempt was made to suppress Lutheranism in the University.

1530   The Universities debated the Royal Divorce. Committees were established to examine dangerous books.

1531   Thomas Bilney, a Cambridge reformer, was burned at Norwich.

1535   Visitation of the Universities by Royal agents led to the reform of the Statutes and the abolition of Canon Law. Thomas Cromwell became Chancellor of Cambridge.

1536   Dissolution of monasteries at Oxford meant the end of monastic Colleges.

1540   Stephen Gardiner became Chancellor of Cambridge. Regius Professorships were established.

1547   Somerset became Chancellor of Cambridge.

1549   Visitation of the Universities by Royal Commissioners led to the reform of the Statutes and the destruction of 'Popish' books and images. Bucer and other emigré divines arrived in England.

1553   Members of the Universities were ordered to subscribe to the Articles of Religion when proceeding to their M.A. (This order was not implemented because of the death of Edward VI). Mary's government ordered graduands to subscribe to the Catholic faith. Many College heads were deprived.

1556/7 Pole's Visitations reimposed Catholicism.

1559   Royal Visitations recommenced. At Oxford the heads of University, Merton, Balliol, Queen's, Lincoln, Magdalen, Corpus, Christ Church and Trinity were removed for Popery. Edwardian Statutes were revived.

1564   The Queen visited Cambridge.

1565   New Statutes were imposed at Oxford. Many Cambridge academics protested at news of Parker's plans to impose religious conformity.

1566   The Queen visited Oxford.

1569   Thomas Cartwright was appointed Lady Margaret Professor of Divinity at Cambridge. He demanded radical Church reform.

1570   Cartwright was deprived of his chair by the Vice-Chancellor, John Whitgift. New Statutes were promulgated at Cambridge.

1573   Unrest among radical elements at Cambridge led to the expulsion of a Peterhouse Fellow.

1574   Peter Baro, who was to become a controversial opponent of Calvinism, was made Lady Margaret Professor at Cambridge.

1576   It was declared that all graduands should subscribe to the Thirty-nine Articles.

1580   All graduands were to take the Supremacy Oath.

1581   All persons resident at Oxford were to take an oath of subscription.

1583   A University Press was established at Cambridge.

1585   A new press was set up at Oxford.

1589   Two Fellows of Christ's were gaoled for sedition.

1592   The Queen visited Oxford, which still presented a loyal show.

1595   William Barrett attacked Calvinism at Cambridge but was silenced by Whitgift.

1596   Baro, forbidden to press his views, left Cambridge.

1602   At Oxford, the University Library (dismantled under Edward VI) was re-established by Sir Thomas Bodley.

THE INNS OF COURT

The study of Roman and Canon law at the Universities had ceased, long before the Tudor period, to comprehend the whole of legal practice. The growth of a system of Common law courts during the thirteenth century had gone hand in hand with the extension and strengthening of Royal justice. The King's courts at Westminster were the centre of this system, served by a new class of lay professional lawyers. Law became a profitable calling for a young man of gentle birth and lawyers thrived on the ever-growing complexities of the legal code. Those who wished to acquire legal knowledge came to London, to the Courts, and lodged in houses which were the forerunners of the Inns of Court. All four great Inns (Gray's, Lincoln's, Middle Temple and Inner Temple) were established by the end of the fourteenth century and were thriving in the following century, when Sir John Fortescue wrote of them as a great legal academy. By the early seventeenth century, they were described as 'the third University of England' – annual admissions were six times what they had been in 1500 and averaged three hundred a year.[1] The Inns thus participated in the general growth of education that took place in Tudor England and, like the schools and Universities, they adapted themselves to meet the needs of a changing society.

The common law of England gained enormously in influence and prestige during the sixteenth century: with the advent of the Reformation and the assault by statute on the Church it 'came into its own'.[2] Lawyers like Thomas More (a common-lawyer who opposed the Reformation) possessed a prestige, as Fortescue had put it, 'not less eminent or solemn than the degree of doctor . . .' The Inns were essentially the preserve of the wealthy – residence was expensive and there were no endowments (such as the Universities possessed) to finance poor scholars. This does not mean that any status-discrimination applied to admissions – many prosperous yeomen's sons came to London for a legal training. Students resided and studied at the Inns, usually after a period of preparation at a lesser Inn or Inn of Chancery. This at least was the ideal – in practice they were more akin to 'residential clubs or hotels' with both senior and junior members often living elsewhere or residing occasionally.[3] The system of education depended on a balance of legal theory and practice. A man needed seven years study as an 'utter barrister' before admission as an 'inner barrister'. After three more years, he might practise the law and become eligible for a senior position at his Inn. The 'benchers', or senior members, provided the readers who expounded the law to the student community. Exercises and 'moots' then enabled the younger men to acquire skill in pleading and the presentation of cases. (This was made much more difficult by the universal use of legal French, a strange jargon abolished only in 1650.) There is plenty of evidence to suggest that the standard of teaching at the Inns declined seriously in the Tudor period but that, at the same time, students came to them in ever larger numbers. The litigiousness of the Tudor Englishman and the growing volume of business in law courts of every kind meant that barristers might find it tempting to abandon their teaching duties for the more profitable arena of the courts. The Inns had no means to pay their senior members – they remained rather informal associations of lawyers. They derived their income from the fees they levied for admission and the rent of rooms, and the rise in membership in the Elizabethan period meant that they had cash to spare for the erection of impressive new buildings.

While the expanding economy and civil peace of Elizabethan England provided a sound basis for the expansion of the legal profession (and thus for that of the Inns of Court too), not all entrants necessarily desired a lengthy training. The young man of means wanted possibly only an opening to the society of London (which was coming increasingly to dominate English life in every field) together with the smattering of legal expertise necessary to a justice of the peace. Thus the Inns became 'finishing schools' for the gentry.[4] They were a useful training-ground for those who sought to add status as gentlemen to their existing wealth. Despite a decree by James I that only gentlemen 'by discent' should be admitted, the Inns continued to receive men of all sorts (those who could afford the estimated £40 a year needed for maintenance at the end of the sixteenth century). Inns were nevertheless socially exclusive institutions to a much greater extent than the Universities and became increasingly so. A very large number of entrants were heirs to landed wealth.[5] In a hierarchical society these men were the future rulers and their presence at the Inns was more important than their motives in seeking admission or the quality of the education they received during their stay. The governors of the Inns exercised little control over their members, who were generally free to cultivate the pursuits and vices of London at will. But the government was determined that they should not be the prey of seditious elements, especially the Catholic seminary priests who sought converts among the ruling élite. Measures were taken, both by the State and the authorities of the Inns, to exclude Catholics (for example, by means of oaths and compulsory chapel attendance). Puritan preachers not always in favour with the government were introduced at the Inns to counteract Catholic influence. Perhaps the fact that the control exercised was less stringent than that over the Universities reflects official awareness that the Inns were places where intellectual and political activity remained at a limited (and safe) level. Changing fashions meant the rapid decline of the Inns as educational institutions after the Civil War, but their continuance as professional enclaves was ensured by the ever-increasing prosperity and prestige of the lawyers.

The great expansion of what we would today term 'higher' or 'further' education which took place in the Tudor age was confined within an existing framework. No new Universities were founded and the desire of reformers that godly colleges should be founded in abandoned monastic buildings was ignored. From all over England men came to Oxford and Cambridge (and to the Inns of Court in London). Only in the seventeenth century was there a serious suggestion that a University should be founded in Northern England (at York, where this University was not to arise for another three centuries). In London Gresham College was founded in 1596 to provide lectures in 'liberal sciences' (for example, astronomy and geometry) for citizens; but it had no imitators. However, it should be emphasised that, in an age eager for learning and discovery, not all education took place in formal channels. Just as the teaching of children was not merely the preserve of schools, so the 'institution of a gentleman' involved travel, the cultivation of foreign languages, and the consumption of some at least of the ever-increasing tide of printed books flowing from Tudor presses.[6]

NOTES
1. W. R. Prest, *The Inns of Court under Elizabeth I and the Early Stuarts, 1590–1640* (London, 1972) p. 6.
2. Joan Simon, *Education and Society in Tudor England* (Cambridge, 1966) p. 55.
3. Prest, op. cit., p. 16.
4. J. E. Neale, *Essays in Elizabethan History* (London, 1958) pp. 230–1.
5. Prest, op. cit., p. 31.
6. See, for example, Part 3 of K. Charlton's *Education in Renaissance England* (London, 1965) pp. 199–296.

LITERATURE AND LEARNING

INTRODUCTION

'Learning bringeth preferment, yea even to them which are but basely borne.' Writing in 1580, Abraham Fleming effectively summed up the attitude of perhaps the majority of Tudor Englishmen to the benefits of education.[1] Too much emphasis has been placed on the bourgeois, 'middle-class' origins of what has been described as the 'educational revolution' (wealthy townsmen tended to ape the aristocracy); but many members of the mercantile and professional classes did become actively involved in the founding of schools and colleges. At the same time, the spread of literacy provided an increasingly large market for books of every type. Professor L. Stone supposes that 50 per cent of the population of early Stuart England was literate, while dismissing Thomas More's claim that this was the case a century earlier. 'Basic literacy', he claims, 'was common enough even among the poor and ... cultural activity was appreciated and practised by the whole of the rural and urban propertied classes, not merely by a tiny élite of noblemen and higher clergy'.[2]

The 'basic literacy' of the lower classes was the result of widespread if irregular attendance at 'petty schools' (which were attended by girls as well as boys). Grammar schools existed to train men for the Universities and Inns of Court. Few artisans can have been as well read as the Coventry mason, Captain Cox. Cox's collection of books included large numbers of works which indicate the Elizabethan taste for ballads and romances (these include 'By a bank az I lay', 'The fryar & the boy' and 'The churl & the burd'). Cox had few religious books.[3] Yet polemicists of all religious persuasions debated at length the likely outcome of the invention of printing vis-à-vis their respective faiths. John Foxe was convinced that printing had been essential for the spread of reformed doctrines. Yet the Puritan Philip Stubbes saw clearly that most readers rejected a constant diet of improving works: 'bookes and pamflettes of scurrilitie and baudrie [he wrote] are better estemed and more vendible than the godliest and sagest bokes that bee . . .'[4] Many writers and preachers lamented that women, children and servants learned only disrespect and arrogance from the consumption of books.

The inevitable result of the advent of printed books was the availability of knowledge to a wide section of the population – the invention of printing was 'quite literally, an *epoch-making* event . . .'[5] New ideas were disseminated by books, which created a new public for those ideas. Printing coincided with a renaissance in science, topography, geography, history and many other disciplines. The 'scientific renaissance' gained an especial impetus from the new availability of printed illustrations, though scientific ideas which, like those of da Vinci, remained unpublished were increasingly ignored.[6] It is not intended to suggest that the works listed below form a select group of 'key' books of the period, but they do include some of the more influential contributions in certain fields. Literary interest in these areas of thought reflects the contemporary debate over religion, politics and morals and the educational, scientific and social developments of the Tudor age.

NOTES
1. Cited by L. B. Wright, *Middle Class Culture in Elizabethan England* (Chapel Hill, 1935) p. 46.
2. L. Stone, 'The Educational Revolution in England, 1560–1640', *Past and Present*, 28 (1964) *passim* esp. p. 79.
3. Wright, op. cit., pp. 84–5.
4. Ibid., p. 101.
5. E. L. Eisenstein, 'The Advent of printing and the Problem of the Renaissance', *Past and Present*, 45 (1969) p. 19.
6. M. Boas, *The Scientific Renaissance 1450–1630* (1962) pp. 29–30.

CHRONOLOGY OF BOOKS PUBLISHED

RELIGION AND POLITICS
1517 T. More, *Utopia* (Latin version; the first English translation appeared in 1551)

1521   Henry VIII, *Assertio Septem Sacramentorum*
1525   The New Testament, translated by W. Tyndale
1528   W. Tyndale, *The Obedience of a Christian Man*
1535   Marsiglio of Padua, *Defensor Pacis*, translated by W. Marshall. S. Gardiner, *De Vera Obedientia*
        The Bible, translated by W. Coverdale (the first complete English version, based on Tyndale's work)
1539   The Bible (the 'Great Bible', a revision by Coverdale of Mathew's 1537 version)
1547   *The Book of Homilies*
1549   D. Erasmus, *The Praise of Folly*
        J. Cheke, *The Hurt of Sedition* (an attack on the rebellions of that year)
        The Book of Common Prayer
1558   J. Knox, *The Monstrous Regiment of Women*
1559   J. Aylmer, *An Harbour for faithful subjects* (a defence of Elizabeth against Knox's censures of the previous year)
        The Mirror for Magistrates
1560   The Bible (Geneva version, translated by W. Whittingham and others, which became the most popular Biblical version)
1561   J. Calvin, *The Institutes of Christian Religion*
1562   J. Jewel, *Apologia Ecclesiae Anglicanae* (a classic defence of the Elizabethan religious settlement; later translated into English)
1572   J. Field and T. Wilcox, *An Admonition to the Parliament*
1580   T. Rogers (translator), *The Imitation of Christ*
1582   E. Campion, *Rationes Decem*
1583   T. Smith, *De Republica Anglorum* (the only complete contemporary account of Elizabethan government)
        P. Stubbes, *Anatomy of Abuses*
1584   W. Allen, *A True, Sincere and Modest Defence of the English Catholics*
1588   'Martin Marprelate', *The Epistle of Martin Marprelate* (the first of this series of extreme Puritan attacks on the hierarchy)
1593   R. Bancroft, *Dangerous Positions and Proceedings* (an attack on the Puritans)
1594   R. Hooker, *The Laws of Ecclesiastical Polity* (first four books)
1600   W. Perkins, *Works* (the first collected edition of an extremely influential Puritan writer)
1603   J. Dod and R. Cleaver, *A Plain and Familiar Exposition of the Ten Commandments*

EDUCATION AND SELF IMPROVEMENT
1487   J. le Grand, *The Book of Good Manners*
1496   J. Stanbridge, *Vocabula* (an early example of the printed Latin grammar)

1509   J. Colet and W. Lily, *Grammatices rudimenta* (this became a standard school text)

1519   W. Horman, *Vulgaria*

1521   A. Barclay, *The Introductory to Write and to Pronounce French* (the earliest French grammar)

1524   L. Cox, *The Art and Craft of Rhetoric*

1529   R. Whitford, *A Work for Householders*

1531   T. Elyot, *The Governor* (a classic Tudor treatise on education)

1538   T. Elyot, *Dictionary*

1547   W. Baldwin, *A Treatise of Moral Philosophy*

1550   W. Thomas, *Principal Rules of the Italian Grammar*

1561   B. Castiglione, *The Courtier*, translated by T. Hoby

1570   R. Ascham, *The Schoolmaster* (a book on the practice of education by Queen Elizabeth's tutor)

1572   H. Gilbert, *Queen Elizabeth's Academy*

1573   J. Hollyband, *The French Schoolmaster*

1580   J. Calvin, *Catechism* (very widely used in Elizabethan schools)

1581   R. Mulcaster, *Positions* (another influential treatise on educational methods)

1591   R. Percival, *Bibliotheca Hispanica* (a Spanish dictionary)

SCIENCE AND TECHNOLOGY

1523   J. Fitzherbert, *The Book of Husbandry* (the first guide to practical agricultural methods)

1525   Anon., *The Handywork of Surgery* (a translation from German of a work by Jerome of Brunswick)

1539   T. Elyot, *The Castle of Health* (advice on diet)

1551   W. Turner, *A New Herbal*

1552   J. Cains, *A Book against the Sweating-sickness*

1553   T. Geminus, *A Compendious Rehearsal of All Anatomy*

1556   R. Recorde, *The Castle of Knowledge* (the first English exposition of Copernican theory)

1557   T. Tusser, *A Hundred Good Points of Husbandry*

1566   J. Alday, *Theatrum Mundi* (a compilation of natural phenomena)

1574   W. Bourne, *A Regiment for the Sea* (an important navigational treatise)

1585   'I.B.', *The School of Beasts* (an English adaptation of a French work by P. Viret)

1597   J. Gerard, *The Herbal* (a lavishly illustrated production)

HISTORY, TOPOGRAPHY AND TRAVEL

1542   E. Hall, *The Union of the . . . Families of Lancaster and York* (a glorification of the Tudor dynasty)

1549   W. Thomas, *A History of Italy*

1557   T. More, *A History of King Richard the III* (in More's *Works*, edited by J. Rastell)

1563   J. Foxe, *Acts and Monuments* (a vastly influential history of the true [Protestant] Church)

1568   R. Grafton, *Chronicle* (a massive 1400-page compilation by a successful populariser)

1576   W. Lambarde, *A Perambulation of Kent* (a pioneer study in local topography)

1577   R. Holinshed, *Chronicle*

1582   R. Hakluyt, *Divers voyages touching the discovery of America*

1586   W. Camden, *Britannia* (a description of Britain)

1591   J. Browne [?], *The Merchant's Avizo* (a compilation of useful information for merchants in foreign lands)

1592   J. Stow, *Annals of England*
       J. Norden, *Speculum Britanniae . . . a description of Middlesex*

1596   W. Raleigh, *The discovery of the . . . Empire of Guiana*

1598   J. Stow, *A Survey of London*
       J. Norden, *Speculum Britanniae . . . a description of Hertfordshire*

1602   R. Carew, *A Survey of Cornwall*

7 WAR, REBELLION AND DIPLOMACY

The Tudors shared the difficulty of being without standing armed forces, except for a number of small corps such as the Yeomen of the Guard, a body which was formed by Henry VII and reached a peak of six hundred men in 1513. They also had in common the recurring need to have armed forces at their disposal, either for the purposes of internal security – against rebellion or invasion – or for overseas expeditions. Two expedients were available to meet these requirements.

Firstly, though efforts were made to curb retaining throughout the period, forces were still raised by the device of the Signet Letter, which was a personal summons to a magnate to recruit amongst his own dependants and followers. In periods of political uncertainty, such as the reigns of Edward VI and Mary, generous licences to keep retainers were given to royal supporters, but the potential threat to royal authority in the system was obvious.

The alternative was the militia, a force based on the county and summoned by Commissions of Array. The obligation of every able-bodied man between the ages of sixteen and sixty to present himself at a muster was redefined in a statute of 1558 – 'An Act for the having of Horse, Armour and Weapons' – which set out the equipment appropriate to each of ten classes of wealth.

The efficiency of the militia system improved under the administration of the Lords Lieutenant. The Lord Lieutenancy grew up as a temporary institution in mid-century, but became increasingly permanent after the Northern Rebellion in 1569. Two paid officials, the Muster-Master and the Provost-Marshal, assisted the Lord Lieutenant at the musters, which might be held once in three years in peace-time, or once or twice a year in unsettled times. Corruption flourished, despite attempts to curb it, such as the 'Act for the Taking of Muster' of 1558.

The militia system had three great disadvantages. Firstly, in the event of a rebellion, the county levies might share the grievances of the rebels; for instance, in January 1554 an army sent from London under the Duke of Norfolk defected to Sir Thomas Wyatt. Secondly, the militia was deficient in the new elements necessary for sixteenth-century warfare, particularly against a continental enemy – arquebusiers, pikemen and heavy cavalry. Both these first two problems could be overcome by hiring foreign mercenaries, but this was an expense which Tudor rulers could ill afford. The alternative solution which was attempted was the introduction of a degree of specialisation in equipment and training into the militia. The failure of a plan in the 1560s for the formation of an élite corps of 4000 arquebusiers led in 1573 to an order for the creation of 'trained bands', suitable men being selected at the musters for special training. This scheme was implemented, but only in the face of local opposition as training cost money; the Cornish J.P.s, for instance, offered only 400 out of 6800 men on the muster-roll for special training.

The third disadvantage of the militia was that it was essentially a local defence force, which could not legally be sent abroad. The need to recruit men for overseas expeditions had therefore to be met by relying on volunteers and the conscripting of vagabonds. This latter group might be extremely inadequate militarily, and complaints from commanders in Ireland in the 1590s caused the Privy Council to attempt to improve the qualities of the drafts. Despite the difficulties, over 100,000 men were sent to fight abroad in the years 1585–1602.

LEVIES IN ENGLAND AND WALES FOR SERVICE ABROAD 1585–1602

	Men Levied	Principal Destination
1585	7,500	Netherlands
1586	4,870	Netherlands
1587	4,800	Netherlands
1588	6,000	Portugal
1589	4,850	France
1590	4,270	Ireland
1591	8,425	France and Netherlands
1592	2,490	France
1593	3,025	France
1594	4,800	France and Netherlands
1595	1,806	Ireland
1596	8,940	Cadiz and Ireland
1597	8,835	Ireland and the Azores
1598	9,164	Ireland and Netherlands
1599	5,250	Ireland
1600	4,885	Ireland
1601	12,620	Ireland
1602	3,300	Netherlands

SOURCE C. G. Cruickshank, *Elizabeth's Army* (2nd ed., 1966) Appendix I.

WEAPONS AND ARMAMENTS

Throughout the Tudor period bows and arrows were declining in importance compared with firearms. Governments exercised great caution on this issue, attempting to preserve the bow as a popular weapon, whilst recognising the growing importance of firearms and hiring mercenary arquebusiers when necessary. A chronology of some measures connected with the use of the bow shows how slow the transition was:

1509   The use of guns or crossbows was forbidden except under special royal licence.

1511   All men under the age of forty were required to possess and practise with bows and arrows.

1541   All men between the ages of seventeen and sixty were required to have bows and arrows, and boys were to be trained in their use from the age of seven.

1566   The cost of bows was pegged at a price yeomen could afford.

1569   Trained archers were forbidden to learn the use of firearms.

1585   The Earl of Leicester took a company of bowmen with him to the Netherlands, though nothing is known of their performance.

1595   The trained bands were ordered to exchange their bows for calivers and muskets.

From the 1540s there was a considerable debate on the rival merits of bows and guns. The principal issues in the debate were the respective rates of fire, the cost, the effect of weather on their performance, their tactical strength in attack or defence and the amount of training required for their effective use. The complexity of the situation explains why historians have not been able to give a simple explanation of why arquebusiers replaced bowmen at a time when the former were in many respects at a disadvantage. The bow was also regarded as a symbol of the past glories of the English nation, and whilst occupied training with bows, men could not be tempted towards less moral pursuits. The debate reached a peak towards the end of the century with such books as *A Brief Discourse of War* by Sir Roger Williams and *Certain Discourses Military* by Sir John Smythe, both published in 1590, and continued on into the seventeenth century. (For a complete list of military books of the period, see M. J. D. Cockle, *Bibliography of Military Books up to 1642*, (London, 1900; repr. 1957).) Despite their attempts to arrest it, the decline in the use of the bow did work to the benefit of the Tudors in that it lessened the impact of popular revolt, as demonstrated by the decisiveness of the mercenary arquebusiers in putting down Kett's rebellion in 1549.

Efforts were made during the Tudor period to encourage the home munitions industry, and in the 1520s gun foundries in England were placed on a permanent footing. In 1537 Henry VIII granted a patent to the overseers of the Guild of Saint George (now the Honourable Artillery Company), by which they were authorised to establish a perpetual guild to supervise the 'science of artillerie'. However, in times of emergency England still had to rely on the importing of munitions, such as the large quantities shipped over from the Low Countries by Sir Thomas Gresham at the beginning of Elizabeth's reign.

THE TUDOR NAVY

The Tudor period saw significant developments in the scale, administration and role of the royal navy. The union with Brittany in 1491, which gave France valuable ports and skilled sailors, provided an initial stimulus to the growth of a royal navy on this side of the Channel. Henry VII built four important ships – *Regent, Sovereign, Sweepstake* and *Mary Fortune* – and gave bounties for the building of merchant ships fit for war; in 1496 the first dry dock was constructed at Portsmouth. Henry VIII's ambitious involvement in continental affairs led to unprecedented naval expansion, with two major periods of building – in the opening years of the reign and again in the late 1530s. The threat of invasion also led to the construction of a series of royal castles at such places as Walmer, Camber, Pendennis and St Mawes. By the end of 1540 there were twenty-six castles and strong points on the coast between Gravesend and Portland. At Henry's death the fleet consisted of fifty-three seaworthy ships, a total tonnage of 11,268. His reign also saw the growth of royal dockyards at Portsmouth, Woolwich, Deptford and Erith, and a second dry dock was constructed at Deptford in 1517. The design of ships – intended for closing with, and boarding the enemy – remained essentially medieval, though Henry VIII did equip his with heavier ordnance, which tended to accentuate the difference between merchantmen and warships, and make them less interchangeable. The crucial change came in Elizabeth's reign, when the influence of John Hawkins caused the replacement of the clumsy, high-built carracks by galleons – low-built, fast-sailing and heavily-gunned. The first true galleon of the Elizabethan era, the *Foresight*, appeared in 1570, followed by *Revenge* in 1575. Hawkins also created a large force of fast pinnaces, so that by the time of the Armada there were twenty-five modern or modernised fighting ships of over one hundred tons and eighteen ocean-going pinnaces.

Since the thirteenth century the administration of the fleet had been in the hands of the Clerk of the Ships, but the rapid growth of the navy after 1509 necessitated the creation of new officers. The first was the Keeper of Storehouses, who became the Treasurer of the Navy, and the second the Comptroller of the Ships, who took over provisioning. In 1545 three more officers were appointed – the Lieutenant of the Admiralty (discontinued in 1562), the Master of the Ordnance for the Ships and the Surveyor of the Ships. These five officials, along with the Clerk of the Ships, were known as the Principal

Officers of the Navy, and from 1546 they met regularly as the Navy Board, which was responsible for the administration of the fleet under the Lord Admiral. In Edward VI's reign Northumberland created a separate department for victualling, under the Surveyor of the Victuals. Although Northumberland also began the building of the dockyard at Chatham, the period 1547–58 was one of comparative neglect, and the strength of the navy declined to twenty-four seaworthy ships, a total tonnage of 7000. In the first twenty years of Elizabeth's reign, naval affairs were in the hands of the Navy Board dominated by Sir William Winter, the Surveyor of the Ships and Master of the Ordnance, and the administration suffered badly from minor peculation. John Hawkins convinced Burghley where the trouble lay and he was made Treasurer of the Navy in 1577. In 1579 he proposed a contract (the 'first bargain') whereby he undertook the care and maintenance of the Queen's ships in return for a fixed yearly sum, and nearly achieved the annual saving of £4000 which he had promised. In 1585 Burghley agreed to the 'second bargain', by which Hawkins undertook all building, equipping and repairing. Among his reforms, in 1586 Hawkins reduced the size of ships' crews and substantially raised the scale of sailors' pay.

Along with the increased size and expanded administration of the fleet, in Elizabeth's reign there was the realisation of the wider role the navy could fulfil, now that the principal enemy was not France, but Spain. Under the first two Tudors, the functions of the navy were two-fold – to support the army by transporting it to the field of operations, assisting in those operations if possible; and to foil any invasion attempts against England. However, men like Hawkins and Drake saw the potential of the navy as an independent, long-range force, which could attack Spanish trade and her communications with Flanders and the New World, and which could be used for amphibious operations against distant shores. In this way the navy might exert a decisive influence on the outcome of the war with Spain. The attempts to put these ideas into practice met with varying success (see 'Expeditions' pp. 164-7). The Spanish became increasingly well-prepared to meet the threat, and there were never sufficient ships to meet all the requirements in the face of the number of strategic options. Hawkins' plan for a continuous blockade off the Azores was never effectively implemented. In fact, throughout the Tudor period, the royal navy was only the nucleus, though an increasingly important one, round which a larger fleet of private ships could be created. In the attack on Cadiz in 1587, of the twenty-three ships only six belonged to the Queen, and in the 1590s, as more money had to be set aside for the army in the Netherlands, sea operations had increasingly to be left to private enterprise.

LORD ADMIRALS OF ENGLAND*
1485 21 Sep John de Vere, Earl of Oxford
1513 17 Mar Edward Howard, Kt.

1513	4 May	Thomas, Lord Howard (Earl of Surrey, 1514; Duke of Norfolk, 1524)
1525	16 July	Henry Fitzroy (Duke of Richmond, 1525)
1536	16 Aug	William Fitzwilliam (Earl of Southampton, 1537)
1540	28 July	John, Lord Russell (Earl of Bedford, 1550)
1542	Dec	Edward Seymour, Earl of Hertford (Duke of Somerset, 1547)
1543	26 Jan	John Dudley, Viscount Lisle (Earl of Warwick, 1547; Duke of Northumberland, 1551)
1547	17 Feb	Thomas Seymour (Lord Seymour, 1547)
1549	28 Oct	John Dudley, Earl of Warwick
1550	14 May	Edward, Lord Clinton (Earl of Lincoln, 1572)
1554	20 Mar	William Howard (Lord Howard of Effingham, 1554)
1558	10 Feb	Edward, Lord Clinton
1585	8 July	Charles Howard, Lord Howard of Effingham (Earl of Nottingham, 1597)

* The title 'Lord Admiral', as opposed to just 'Admiral', first appeared in 1540.

SOURCE Sir Maurice Powicke and E. B. Fryde (eds), *Handbook of British Chronology*.

ADDITIONS TO THE NAVY 1485-1603

	Built	Rebuilt	Purchased	Prizes	Total
1485-1509	4	–	1	1	6
1509-30	24	2	11	6	43*
1531-47	38	7	8	8	61
1547-53	8	1	–	6	15
1553-8	3	8	–	1	12
1558-88	38	8	5	2	53
1589-1603	22	8	2	4	36

* In addition, one ship was requisitioned and one received as a gift from the Emperor.

SOURCE R. C. Anderson, *List of English Men-of-War 1509-1649* (The Society for Nautical Research, Occasional Publications No. 7, 1959).

INTERNAL REBELLIONS

1486 Yorkist Risings
An attempted rising in March in North Yorkshire led by Lord Lovell collapsed as the King travelled north, and Thomas and Humphrey Stafford failed to raise the West Country. Lovell fled abroad, and the Staffords were removed from sanctuary at Culham, near Oxford; Humphrey was executed.

1489 The Yorkshire Rebellion
The Earl of Northumberland was murdered by an angry mob whilst attempting to collect the subsidy granted by Parliament for military intervention in

Brittany. The rioting which followed led by Sir John Egremont was put down by the Earl of Surrey.

1497   The Cornish Rebellion

Cornwall objected to paying taxes for a war against Scotland, and 15,000 rebels marched on London. They were led by Michael Joseph, a blacksmith, Thomas Flamank, a lawyer, and Lord Audley, a discontented nobleman.

On 16 June 1497 they camped on Blackheath overlooking London, but the following day, their numbers reduced to 9000 by desertions, the rebels were defeated by royal forces. The leaders were executed, and heavy fines imposed on all those involved in the rebellion.

1525   Rebellion against the 'Amicable Grant'

Wolsey's attempt to exact a forced loan to finance a war against France provoked widespread resistance, which was particularly serious in Suffolk. In the face of this, Henry VIII abandoned the grant and the continental campaign.

1536   The Pilgrimage of Grace

A rising in Lincolnshire, which began at Louth on 1 October, collapsed in a fortnight in the face of royal threats and an army under the Duke of Suffolk. However, the rebellion spread to Yorkshire and on 16 October rebels led by Robert Aske captured York. The commander of the royal army, the Duke of Norfolk, was forced to make a truce when confronted by 30,000 rebels at Doncaster.

The rebels then formulated their demands, which showed a general hostility to the Cromwellian regime, to religious innovations and the suppression of the monasteries, and also anxiety about the state of the economy of northern England. Aske took these to Norfolk on 6 December, and the rebels began to disperse when he promised a general pardon and the calling of a free Parliament. However, fresh outbreaks in the North in January and February 1537 gave the King the opportunity to revoke the pardon. 216 executions are recorded; Aske was hanged in July 1537.

1549   The Western Rebellion

In June 1549 the West of England rose, principally against the compulsory adoption of the new Prayer Book and the religious policies of Edward VI's reign. Exeter was besieged for six weeks before Lord Russell, with Italian mercenaries, relieved it on 6 August. The rebellion was finally crushed at Sampford Courtenay on 17 August.

1549   Kett's Rebellion

On 12 July 1549 rebels led by Robert Kett, a prosperous Norfolk tanner and landowner, set up camp on Mousehold Heath overlooking Norwich. The rebellion arose as a protest against enclosures and exploitation by the gentry; there was also an element of anti-clericalism in the rebels' grievances, though in contrast to the Western Rebellion, the new Prayer Book was used on Mousehold Heath. The rebellion was crushed by the Earl of Warwick, using foreign mercenaries, in a battle at Dussindale on 27 August. Kett was hanged on 7 December.

1554   Wyatt's Rebellion
In January 1554 Sir Thomas Wyatt with 4000 men marched from Kent on London. The rebellion, which was particularly serious because of its nearness to the seat of government, was part of a more widespread but abortive conspiracy to prevent the marriage of Mary and Philip of Spain by deposing the Queen. Wyatt crossed the Thames at Kingston, but found Ludgate defended against him and he surrendered on 7 February. He was executed 11 April.

1569   The Rebellion of the Northern Earls
As a result of a conspiracy to marry Mary Queen of Scots, the Duke of Norfolk was sent to the Tower, and the Earls of Northumberland and Westmorland were summoned to Court. Instead they rebelled and on 14 November they entered Durham, and restored Catholic worship in the Cathedral. But in the face of the Earl of Sussex advancing with a royal army, the rebels retreated and dispersed.

A third northern magnate, Leonard Dacre, rebelled in January 1570, but was defeated in a battle between Carlisle and Hexham.

1601   Essex's Rebellion
In November 1599 the Earl of Essex disobeyed the Queen's orders and returned from Ireland. He was confined to his house, deprived of his various offices and of his monopoly of sweet wines. A conspiracy was formed, and on being summoned by the Council, Essex attempted to raise the population of London (8 February 1601). He failed and was executed on 25 February.

INVASIONS AND ATTEMPTED INVASIONS OF ENGLAND

1485   Establishment of the Tudor Dynasty
Henry Tudor, who claimed to inherit the Lancastrian right to the English throne, landed at Milford Haven on 7 August 1485, and reached Shrewsbury unopposed. King Richard was killed at the Battle of Bosworth Field near Leicester on 22 August after treachery in the ranks of his army by the Stanleys and the Earl of Northumberland.

1487   Lambert Simnel

An invasion in the name of the pretender, Lambert Simnel, was planned at the Court of Margaret, widowed duchess of Burgundy and sister of Edward IV. In May 1487 the rebels landed at Dublin, where Simnel, who had been trained by an Oxford priest, Richard Simonds, to impersonate Richard III's nephew, the Earl of Warwick (who was actually in the Tower), was crowned as Edward VI. In June a mixed force, including Irish and 2000 mercenaries provided by Margaret, led by the Earl of Lincoln and Lord Lovell, landed in Lancashire. On 16 June 1487 they were defeated at the Battle of Stoke. Lincoln was killed; Simnel became a kitchen boy and later a falconer.

1495–7   Perkin Warbeck

Warbeck was one of the crew of a Breton merchant ship put in to Cork in 1491, who was persuaded to impersonate Richard, the younger of Edward IV's sons murdered in the Tower. Supported by Margaret of Burgundy, at whose Court he had taken refuge, Warbeck made a half-hearted attempt to land in Kent in July 1495, then sailed off to Ireland and eventually to Scotland. There he remained until July 1497, when he sailed to Cornwall, landing on 7 September. An attack on Exeter failed, and as the King's army closed in, Warbeck fled to sanctuary at Beaulieu and then surrendered. Warbeck was hanged in 1499 after being implicated in a fresh conspiracy, as a result of which the Earl of Warwick was also executed.

1513   Invasion from Scotland

James IV crossed the border on 22 August 1513 in an attempt to take advantage of English involvement in a war with his allies, the French. On 9 September at the Battle of Flodden an English army of 26,000 led by the Earl of Surrey, inflicted a crushing defeat on the Scots, who numbered 30–40,000. James IV himself was killed, along with many of the Scottish nobility.

1545   French Invasion Attempt

On 18 July 1545 the French were seen approaching off the Isle of Wight. They planned to land at Portsmouth, but on 19 July the galleys which Francis I had brought from the Mediterranean were driven off. Some French troops landed on the Isle of Wight itself, but local levies forced them to withdraw. A further attempt was made to land at Seaford, but this was also repulsed. On 15 August a naval battle took place off Shoreham, but with sickness rife in both fleets, the following day it was found that the French had withdrawn to Havre.

1588   The Spanish Armada

The Armada, consisting of 130 ships and 27,000 men, sailed in May 1588 under the command of the Duke of Medina Sidonia, who had orders to link up with Parma in the Netherlands and escort his 17,000 veterans across the

163

Channel. The Spanish were sighted off the Lizard on 19 July, and a running battle developed with the English fleet under Lord Howard. On 28 July fire-ships were sent amongst the Spanish fleet at anchor off Calais, which broke up its defensive formation, and paved the way for the decisive battle of Grave-lines the following day. The Armada fled round the north of the British Isles, and reached Spain with probably half its strength lost in September 1589.

1596-7 Further Spanish Invasion Attempts

In October 1596 the Governor of Castile sailed from Ferrol with over 100 ships and 16,000 men intended for the conquest of England, but the fleet was dispersed by a gale off Finisterre.

A further attempt in the autumn of 1597 with a fleet of 136 ships and 9000 troops was again scattered by a storm off Brittany.

EXPEDITIONS

1488-9 Expeditions to Brittany

In February 1488 a body of volunteers was sent to aid the Bretons, but the English envoy was not well received, and Henry VII renewed the truce with France.

In April 1489 6000 troops, to be paid for by the Bretons, were sent in accordance with the terms of the Treaty of Radon.

1492 Invasion of France

In October Henry VII crossed to Calais and besieged Boulogne. But by the Treaty of Etaples in November he ended the campaign in return for a financial settlement.

1511 Expeditions to Spain and the Netherlands

In May Lord Darcy took 1500 men to join in Ferdinand's attack on the Moors; they found on arrival at Cadiz that they were not wanted and re-turned home within a fortnight. From July to September an army led by Sir Edward Poynings assisted Margaret of the Netherlands against the Duke of Gelders.

1512 Expedition to Northern Spain

In June an army of 10–15,000 led by the Marquis of Dorset was sent to north-ern Spain to invade France in cooperation with Ferdinand. However, Ferdi-nand used the English army as a cover while he conquered Navarre, and the English army sailed home in October in defiance of Dorset's orders. The fleet under Sir Edward Howard, which had escorted the army, defeated the French navy in a running battle off Brest.

1513 Invasion of France

The first of Henry VIII's three invasions. The royal army of 24,000 was joined in France in June 1513 by 6000 mercenaries, and captured the towns of Thérouanne and Tournai. On 16 August a French cavalry detachment was defeated in the Battle of the Spurs. At sea Sir Edward Howard was killed off Brest in April while attempting to attack the force of galleys brought by the French from the Mediterranean. At the peace in 1514 Henry VIII was ceded the two captured towns and given an increased pension.

1522–3 Invasion of France

The campaign planned for 1522 was abandoned when the promised Imperialist cavalry and pikemen did not arrive to reinforce the English army of 13,000. An invasion into Picardy in 1523 ended when the army, demoralised by hunger and frostbite, retreated in December to Calais.

1542–4 Expeditions against Scotland

In August 1542 English troops were defeated at Haddon Rig near Berwick. An attempted English invasion under the Duke of Norfolk was met by a Scottish counter-attack towards Carlisle. This was defeated in the rout of Solway Moss on 23 November 1542, after which James V died of a 'broken heart'.

A fresh attack on Scotland was planned in 1544, with cooperation between the army under the Earl of Hertford and the navy under Lord Lisle. In May 1544, 4000 horsemen invaded from Berwick, while 12,000 foot were transported by the navy into the Forth. Leith and the city of Edinburgh were taken and considerable destruction was done before the army withdrew.

1544 Invasion of France

In February 1544 Henry secretly agreed to a military alliance with the Emperor by which they would join forces on the Marne in August 1544 for the 'Enterprise of Paris'. After landing at Calais on 6 June, the English army of 36,000 was augmented by 6000 Germans and began the siege of Boulogne. This held out until 14 December and a few days later the Emperor signed a separate peace with the French. At the Peace of Ardres in 1546 Henry agreed to surrender Boulogne in return for an indemnity, and it was in fact given up in 1550 after a brief French campaign.

1547 Invasion of Scotland

Somerset crossed the border with an army of 18,000 on 4 September, supported by 60 ships under Lord Clinton. The Scots were defeated at the Battle of Pinkie (10 September 1547), and various strongpoints were occupied, the last of which was evacuated in September 1549. The expedition failed in its purpose of bringing about the marriage of Mary Queen of Scots and Edward VI; in July 1548 the former was sent to France to marry the Dauphin.

1558   The Loss of Calais

In June 1557 England declared war on France and in July 7000 men under the Earl of Pembroke crossed to assist the Spanish besieging St Quentin; a relieving army was routed in August. However, the French attack on Calais began on 1 January 1558, and it was forced to surrender on the 8th.

1560   Intervention in Scotland

Intervention by a naval force under William Winter and an army led by Lord Grey de Wilton to assist the Scottish Lords in expelling the French.

On 6 July the Treaty of Edinburgh was signed, by which the French evacuated Scotland.

There was further intervention in 1571–3 by English troops under Sir William Drury in support of Morton, the Scottish regent.

1559–97   Aid to the Protestants in France

In April 1559 an expedition took supplies to the Huguenots of La Rochelle, though as Elizabeth had withdrawn her official assistance, it went as a private trading venture.

In September 1562 a secret treaty was made with the Huguenots to furnish them with 6000 troops. Half the force went as a garrison for Le Havre, which was not withdrawn until July 1563, although the Huguenots had been defeated and made the Peace of Amboise in March.

In July 1589 the Protestant Henry of Navarre succeeded to the French throne on the assassination of Henry III, and civil war broke out in France with subsequent intervention by Spanish forces. In September 1589 Elizabeth sent £20,000 and 4000 men under Lord Willoughby to the aid of Henry of Navarre. Further English troops were sent, principally to Brittany, under the command of Sir John Norris each year from 1591 to 1594. The last English troops were withdrawn in 1597.

1572–1603   Aid to the Dutch

In 1572 a number of volunteer companies under Sir Humphrey Gilbert went to fight in the Netherlands.

A treaty was signed on 10 August 1585 by which England was to send 5000 foot and 1000 horse to the Netherlands and to garrison Flushing and Brille. The forces crossed the Channel in December under the Earl of Leicester. English troops fought in the Netherlands throughout the 1590s, and assisted the Dutch at the victories of Turnhout (24 January 1597) and Nieuport (2 July 1600) and in the defence of Ostend (1601).

1587   Raid on Cadiz

Drake sailed from Plymouth on 12 April 1587 and in an attack on Cadiz

166

(19–20 April) did much damage to the Spanish Armada preparations, destroying some thirty ships. He cruised off the Spanish coast and captured a rich Portuguese convoy off the Azores, before returning to Plymouth on 26 June.

1589   The Portugal Expedition

The expedition which sailed in April 1589 consisted of 150 ships and 12,000 men commanded by Drake and Sir John Norris. Conflicting views on the correct purpose of the expedition and delays caused by the attack on Corunna, led to the failure of the attempt on Lisbon aimed at restoring Don Antonio to the Portuguese throne. The expedition returned to England at the end of June.

1589–97   Expeditions to the Azores

These naval expeditions were unsuccessful attempts to intercept the Spanish treasure ships. In 1591 a Spanish fleet sailed from Ferrol and attacked Sir Thomas Howard's squadron at Flores; after an heroic struggle Sir Richard Grenville and his ship *Revenge* were captured.

1595   Expedition to the West Indies

Drake and Hawkins sailed from Plymouth in August 1595 with 17 ships and 2500 men under Sir Thomas Baskerville. The expedition was largely a failure, and both Drake and Hawkins died during the voyage. It returned to England in the spring of 1596.

1596   Expedition to Cadiz

A considerable fleet under the Earl of Essex and Lord Charles Howard, along with 6000 troops under Sir Francis Vere, attacked Cadiz on 20 June 1596. They captured the city and held it until 5 July when they left it in flames. Faro and Loulé were burnt on the return journey.

IRELAND

Four major rebellions took place in Ireland during Elizabeth's reign – that of Shane O'Neill (1559–66), the Fitzmaurice confederacy in Munster (1569–72), the Desmond rebellion (1579–83), and Tyrone's rebellion (1594–1603).

The last was the most serious and necessitated the sending of large numbers of English troops to Ireland. In September 1601 a Spanish fleet with 4000 men occupied Kinsale, but the Irish and Spanish were routed on 24 December. Tyrone finally submitted on 30 March 1603. (See also pp. 176–8.)

For biographical details of Elizabethan seamen and soldiers, see chapter II, pp. 206–20.

ENGLISH TREATIES

22 July 1486	Convention with the Duke of Brittany.
2 Jan 1487	Renewal of Edward IV's treaty of 1478 with Burgundy.
10 Feb 1489	Treaty of Radon for military assistance to Brittany.
14 Feb 1489	Treaty with Emperor Maximilian and Philip of Burgundy.
28 Feb 1489	Commercial treaty with Emperor Maximilian and Philip of Burgundy.
27 Mar 1489	Treaty of Medina del Campo with King and Queen of Spain for marriage of Prince Arthur and Katherine the Infanta.
6 Aug 1489	Treaty of peace with the King of Denmark.
18 Aug 1489	Renewal of treaty of 1378 with Portugal.
15 Apr 1490	Commercial agreement with Florence.
11 Sep 1490	Convention with Emperor for waging war on France.
3 Nov 1492	Treaty of Etaples with France.
8 Mar 1493	Treaty with King and Queen of Castille.
24 Feb 1496	Treaty with Philip of Burgundy. Parties: England and the Empire.
18 July 1496	Henry VII adheres to the Holy League.
1 Oct 1496	Treaty with Spain for the marriage of Prince Arthur and Katherine.
24 May 1497	Treaty of peace and commerce with Charles VIII of France.
7 July 1497	Treaty with Burgundy.
30 Sep 1497	Treaty of Ayton with Scotland.
18 July 1498	Treaty with France against piracy.
26 Nov 1498	Treaty with Arch-Prefect and citizens of Riga.
14 Dec 1498	Treaty with Emperor for the mutual surrender of rebels.
25 Apr 1499	Confirmation of commercial relations with Burgundy.
10 July 1499	Treaty for marriage of Prince Arthur and Katherine.
12 Jan 1502	Agreement with Bishop of Liège.
24 Jan 1502	Treaties with Scotland for peace and the marriage of King James IV to Henry VII's daughter, Margaret (renewed 29 June 1509).
19 June 1502	Commercial treaty with Emperor.
20 June 1502	Treaties with the Emperor of peace and friendship, and for not receiving rebels.
23 June 1503	Treaty with Spain for marriage of Prince Henry and Katherine.
30 Dec 1505	Convention with Duke of Saxony.
9 Feb 1506	Treaty with Philip, King of Castille.
20 Mar 1506	Treaty of marriage between Henry VII and Margaret of Savoy.

30 Apr 1506	Commercial treaty with Burgundy.
5 June 1507	Provisional commercial treaty with the Empire.
21 Dec 1507	Treaties of friendship and for marriage of Henry VII's daughter, Mary, and the Archduke Charles. Parties: England and the Empire.
23 Mar 1510	Treaty of friendship with France.
24 May 1510	Treaty with King Ferdinand of Aragon and the Queen of Castille.
17 Nov 1511	League for the rescue of the Pope. Parties: England and Aragon (joined by Castille 13 April 1513).
5 Apr 1513	Agreement with Pope Leo for the defence of the Church. Parties: England, the Pope, the Empire, Aragon and Castille.
15 Oct 1513	Articles of Agreement with the Empire for renewing the war against France, and solemnising the marriage of Charles, the Emperor elect, and Mary, Henry VIII's sister.
7 Aug 1514	Treaties with Louis, King of France, for peace and his marriage to Princess Mary.
5 Apr 1515	Treaty of peace and commerce with Francis I.
19 Oct 1515	Treaty of friendship with Ferdinand, King of Aragon.
24 Jan 1516	Treaty of friendship with the Prince of Spain.
24 Jan 1516	Commercial treaty with Burgundy.
19 Apr 1516	Treaty of peace with Charles, King of Spain.
29 Oct 1516	League for the defence of the Church. Parties: England, the Empire and Spain.
2 Oct 1518	Treaty with France (joined by Spain and the Pope in 1518, the Empire in 1519).
4 Oct 1518	Treaties with France for the marriage of Princess Mary and the Dauphin, for restoring Tournai, and for the suppression of piracy.
8 Oct 1518	Treaty with France for arranging a conference.
14 Jan 1519	League against the Turk. Parties: England, France, the Pope and Emperor Charles V.
12 Mar 1520	Convention with France for arranging a conference.
11 Apr 1520	Treaties with Emperor of commerce, and arranging for his visit to England.
6 June 1520	Treaties with France.
14 July 1520	Treaty with Emperor Charles V to abstain for two years from fresh alliances with France.
25 Aug 1521	Treaty for marriage of Charles V and Princess Mary.
11 Oct 1521	England adheres to treaty between France and the Empire of 2 Oct 1521 for securing the freedom of the Narrow Seas.

24 Nov 1521	Treaty with Charles V against the King of France and the enemies of the church (renewed June 1522).
19 June 1522	Treaty for marriage of Charles V and Princess Mary.
17 Jan 1523	Commercial treaty with Charles V (renewed 10 April 1548 for ten years).
28 May 1524	Treaty with the Emperor for the supplying of troops for an invasion of France by the Duke of Bourbon.
30 Aug 1525	Treaties with France.
8 Aug 1526	Treaty of reciprocal obligation with France.
30 Apr 1527	Treaties with France against the Emperor.
18 Aug 1527	Treaties between Cardinal Wolsey and the King of France.
5 Aug 1529	Peace with the Empire.
18 Feb 1530	Treaties with France.
2 Dec 1530	Treaty with France concerning arrears in financial payments.
23 June 1532	Treaty of friendship with France.
28 Oct 1532	Confederation with France to oppose the advance of the Turk.
4 Oct 1539	Marriage treaty between Henry VIII and Anne, sister of the Duke of Cleves.
1542	Offensive and defensive League with the Emperor against France.
11 Feb 1543	Articles of treaty with the Empire for invading France.
1 July 1543	Treaties of Greenwich with Scotland for peace and the marriage of the Prince of Wales and Queen Mary.
31 Dec 1543	Treaty with the Empire for the invasion of France.
7 June 1546	Peace of Ardres with France (Boulogne to be restored after eight years).
24 Mar 1550	Treaty with France for the immediate restoration of Boulogne in return for 400,000 French crowns.
19 July 1551	Treaty of Angers for marriage of Edward VI and Elizabeth, daughter of the French King.
12 Jan 1554	Treaty for marriage of Queen Mary and the Prince of Spain.
2 Apr 1559	Treaty of Câteau-Cambrésis with the King of France, the Dauphin and his wife, Mary.
27 Feb 1560	Treaty of Berwick for English aid to the Scottish Lords.
6 July 1560	Treaty of Edinburgh for non-interference by France in Scottish affairs.
22 Sep 1562	Treaty of Richmond: agreement between Elizabeth and Louis de Bourbon, Prince of Condé, for English assistance in the defence of Rouen, and occupation of Dieppe and Havre.

Dec 1562	Articles of treaty with Gaspard de Coligny, Admiral of France, upon the imprisonment of the Prince of Condé.
11 Apr 1564	Treaty of Troyes with Charles IX of France.
21 Apr 1572	Treaty of Blois with Charles IX.
28 Aug 1574	Treaty of Bristol with Spain (compensation for shipping confiscations).
7 Jan 1579	Treaty of alliance with the States-General of the Low Countries.
11 June 1581	Treaty for the marriage of the Queen and François, Duke of Anjou and Alençon.
10 Aug 1585	Treaty of Nonsuch for aid to the States of the United Provinces of the Netherlands (supplemented 12 August 1585; renewed 16 August 1598).
5 July 1586	Treaty of Berwick with King James of Scotland.
1592	Treaty for providing aid to the King of France.
14 May 1596	Confederacy and alliance with Henry IV, King of France, against Philip of Spain (joined by the Netherlands, 31 October 1596).

PRINCIPAL SOURCE Clive Parry and Charity Hopkins, *An Index of British Treaties 1101–1968* (London: H.M.S.O., 1970).

8 SCOTLAND AND IRELAND

CHRONOLOGY OF EVENTS IN SCOTLAND

1485   James III recovers Dunbar Castle.

1486   Death of Margaret, wife of James III (14 July).

1488   Defeat and murder of James III after Sauchieburn (11 June); accession of James IV; James IV's first Parliament meets (September).

1489   Rebellions by Lennox in the West (October) and Forbes in the East (April) suppressed by James IV; Spanish embassy arrives in Scotland.

1490   Scottish diplomatic alliance with France renewed. Scotland now bound to attack England in the event of an English-French war.

1491   Truce between England and Scotland at Coldstream (21 December).

1492   See of Glasgow created an Archbishopric (9 January).

1493   Sentence of forfeiture passed by Scottish Parliament on John, Lord of the Isles (May).

1495   Papal Bull of Alexander VI (10 February) institutes Aberdeen University. Perkin Warbeck arrives at Stirling (20 November).

1496   James IV, accompanied by Warbeck, crosses the Border (September). Raid proves a failure.

1497   Perkin Warbeck leaves Scotland (6 July). James IV fails to take Norham Castle; truce negotiated with England.

1498   War with England narrowly averted.

1499   Truce with England renewed at Stirling (July). Epidemic of pestilence rages in Scotland.

1501   Negotiations for marriage of James IV to Margaret Tudor.

1503   Marriage of James IV to Margaret Tudor at Holyrood (7 August); Alexander Stewart appointed Archbishop of Glasgow.

1505   Threat of war against England by James IV (April).

1508   First book printed in Scotland (4 April) – *The Maying and Disport of Chaucer*. James IV declines to give an understanding not to renew the French alliance; aid sent to Denmark on renewal of war with Sweden and Lubeck.

1511   Death of Andrew Barton (sea-captain). Building of the warship *Great Michael* by James IV.

1512   Renewal of alliance with France. Birth of James IV's third son (the future James V) on 10 April.

1513   Battle of Flodden Field (9 September). Death of James IV. Succeeded by James V, with Margaret as his guardian.

1514   Marriage of Margaret, Dowager Queen of Scots, to Earl of Angus (August).

1515   Arrival of John, Duke of Albany, in Scotland (May). Created Lord Governor by the Scottish Parliament; secures possession of James V. Flight of Margaret to England (30 September). Birth, in October, of her daughter Margaret.

1516   Angus makes terms with Albany.

1517   First return of Albany to France (June); return of Margaret to Scotland.

1518   Quarrel between Margaret of Scotland and her husband, Angus.

1519   Margaret in alliance with the Earl of Arran, enemy of her husband Angus.

1520   Return of Albany to Scotland (19 November).

1522   Scottish estates reject Henry VIII's request to expel Albany (January). Angus retires to France (February). Albany, having threatened the English frontier, goes to France (25 October); James Beaton created Archbishop of St Andrews.

1523   Scotland invaded by English army under Dorset (April). Albany returns from France (September) but retires (November).

1524   Albany returns to France (May). Margaret governs Scotland in alliance with Arran.

1527   Margaret divorced from Angus. Concludes secret marriage with Henry Stuart (Lord Methven).

1528   Fall of Angus; flight to England. Five-year truce with England concluded by James V. Patrick Hamilton, Abbot of Ferne, burnt for heresy.

1532   College of Justice founded by James V.

1533   Renewal of the truce between Scotland and England.

1534   Peace Treaty between England and Scotland. Norman Gourlay and David Straiton burned in Edinburgh for heresy (27 August).

1535   Order of the Garter conferred on James V by Henry VIII.

1536   Arrival of James V in France (10 September).

1537   Marriage of James V to Madeleine, daughter of Francis I (1 January). James V returned to Scotland (19 May); Madeleine died (7 July).

1538   Second marriage of James V, to Mary of Guise. David Beaton created Cardinal, succeeding his uncle as Archbishop of St Andrews.

1540   Coronation of Mary of Guise at Holyrood (22 February).

1541   Border friction with England.

1542   Scots defeat Sir Robert Bowes at Hadden Rig in Roxburghshire (24

August). Birth of Mary, Queen of Scots (8 December). Death of James V (14 December). Arran appointed Regent for Mary.

1543 Coronation of Mary (September); reconciliation of Arran and Cardinal Beaton (September); Treaty of Greenwich repudiated by Scottish Parliament (11 December); French alliance renewed.

1544 Flight of Lennox to England; subsequent marriage to Margaret Douglas; Parliament called by Arran (December).

1545 Birth of Henry Stuart (Lord Darnley); defeat of English force at Ancrum Moor (25 February) by Angus and Arran.

1546 Wishart burnt for heresy (2 March) at St Andrews; murder of Cardinal Beaton (29 May).

1547 St Andrews captured by the Regent (July); John Knox shipped to France; Scots defeated by Somerset at Battle of Pinkie (10 September); Kinghorn and the Forth towns raided by English ships.

1548 Arrival of French auxiliaries in Scotland (June). Mary Queen of Scots arrives in France (13 August).

1550 Scotland is included in the Peace signed between England and France (March).

1555 Return of John Knox to Scotland.

1556 Knox goes to Geneva (July).

1557 Knox returns again to Scotland; the First Covenant is signed (3 December).

1558 Walter Milne, last of the Scottish Protestant martyrs, burnt (April); marriage of Mary Queen of Scots, to the Dauphin Francis (24 April); Protestant riot in Edinburgh (1 September); publication of John Knox's *The First Blast of the Trumpet against the Monstrous Regiment of Women*.

1559 Reformation Movement in Scotland advances. Knox in Fife (May); riots in Perth (May–June) against Mary of Guise and Roman Catholicism. Deposition of the Regent in Scotland (21 October).

1560 Treaty of Berwick (27 February) between the Scottish Lords and Elizabeth; English Army enters Scotland (April); death of the Queen Regent of Scotland at Edinburgh Castle (10 June); the Treaty of Edinburgh (6 July) constitutes triumph for the 'Lords of the Congregation'; Scottish Parliament abolishes Papal jurisdiction; (August) Calvinism now adopted.

1561 Mary Queen of Scots lands in Scotland (19 August).

1562 Battle of Corrichie; defeat of George Gordon.

1565 Marriage of Mary Queen of Scots, and Darnley (29 July).

1566 Scottish Parliament meets (March); murder of Rizzio; Birth of James VI (later James I of England), 19 June.

1567 Murder of Darnley (10 February); marriage of Bothwell and Mary

174

Queen of Scots; surrender of Mary to the Lords Associators at Carberry Hill (15 June); Mary a prisoner at Loch Leven Castle (16 June); abdication of Mary in favour of James VI; James Stuart (Earl of Moray) appointed Regent (24 July).

1568   Catholic rising in Scotland; escape of Mary Queen of Scots from Loch Leven (2 May); battle of Langside (13 May); flight of Mary to Carlisle (19 May).

1570   Assassination of the Earl of Moray (23 January); Matthew Stuart, 4th Earl of Lennox, proclaimed Regent (27 January).

1571   Archbishop of St Andrew's hanged (7 April) for complicity in murder of Moray; death of the Regent Lennox (4 September); succeeded as Regent by John Erskine, 6th Earl of Mar.

1572   Death of the Regent (Earl of Mar) in October; James Douglas, 4th Earl of Morton elected Regent (24 November); death of John Knox at Edinburgh (24 November).

1573   Edinburgh Castle surrendered by Sir William Kirkcaldy; virtual end of Mary's party and supporters.

1575   English force defeated at Redswire in Roxburghshire (7 July).

1578   James VI takes over full reins of government; Earl of Morton resigns as Regent (12 March).

1579   Arrival of d'Aubigny in Scotland.

1581   James VI signs second 'Confession of Faith' (28 January); execution of Morton for complicity in Darnley's murder (2 June).

1582   Protestants gain possession of James VI (the Raid of Ruthven, 22 August).

1583   Escape of James VI to St Andrews (27 June).

1584   The Earl of Gowrie (one of the instigators of the Raid of Ruthven) beheaded at Stirling (4 May).

1585   James VI signs pact with England.

1587   Execution of Mary, Queen of Scots (18 February).

1589   James VI's voyage to Denmark (22 October); his marriage to Anna, daughter of Frederick II, King of Denmark.

1590   Return of James VI to Leith (1 May).

1592   Murder of James Stuart, Earl of Moray by the Earl of Huntly (7 February); repeal of the Black Acts by the Scottish Parliament; establishment of Second Book of Discipline; Fraserburgh University founded (1 July).

1593   Presbyterianism strengthened by discovery of Catholic plot; foundation of Marischal College, Aberdeen, by George Keith (2 April).

1594   Defeat of Highlanders under Earl of Argyll by George Gordon, 6th Earl of Huntly (3 October).

1599   James VI writes the Basilicon Doron.

1600   'Commissioners' appointed to the ancient sees by James VI; conspiracy to murder James VI by Gowrie and Ruthven. Both are killed (5 August).

1603 James VI proclaimed King of England, Scotland, France and Ireland in Edinburgh (31 March); James leaves Scotland (5 April) and is crowned at Westminster (25 July).

CHRONOLOGY OF EVENTS IN IRELAND

1487 Landing at Dublin of Lincoln, Lovell and other Yorkists with German troops under Swart (5 May).

1487 Simnel crowned in Dublin (24 May).

1487 Earl of Kildare, together with Anglo-Irish colony in the Pale, declares for Simnel (June).

1491 Arrival of Perkin Warbeck in Cork.

1494 Sir Edward Poynings becomes Lord Deputy of Ireland (13 September); fails to reduce Ulster.

1494 Irish Parliament enacts Poynings' Laws (December).

1495 Warbeck fails to take Waterford (August).

1496 Poynings returns to England; Earl of Kildare appointed Deputy in Ireland.

1497 Warbeck lands at Cork (26 July).

1521 Surrey recalled from Ireland; Ireland now ruled by Sir Piers Butler and Gerald, Earl of Kildare, successively.

1526 Earl of Kildare committed to the Tower. Ireland administered by Sir William Skeffington.

1529 Kildare returns to Ireland.

1532 Kildare succeeds Skeffington as Lord Deputy in Ireland; increase of disorders.

1533 Kildare dies in the Tower. His son succeeds him, and besieges Dublin in a revolt. Forces under Skeffington and Brereton relieve Dublin.

1536 Lord Leonard Grey succeeds Skeffington in Ireland (1 January).

1537 Execution of 'Silken Thomas' and other Irish rebels in London (February).

1540 Sir Antony St Leger appointed Lord Deputy of Ireland.

1541 Henry assumes the titles of King of Ireland and head of the Irish Church (June).

1542 First Jesuit Mission visits Ireland.

1548 Return of St Leger from Ireland; Sir Edward Bellingham succeeds him.

1549 Rebellions in King's and Queen's Counties suppressed by Bellingham.

1550 St Leger returns as Lord Deputy of Ireland.

1557 Recall of St Leger for alleged papist practices.

1552 St Leger acquitted by Privy Council.

1553   St Leger reappointed Lord Deputy.
1556   St Leger recalled on embezzlement charges; dies in England; succeeded in Ireland by Sussex. Shane O'Neill the most powerful man in Ireland.
1560   David Wolfe, Jesuit priest, sent to Ireland (August); Elizabeth orders the subjugation of Shane O'Neill.
1561   Defeat of Sussex in Ireland.
1562   Shane O'Neill arrives in London, making submission to Elizabeth (6 January).
1563   Sussex again fails to restore order in Ireland.
1564   Sussex recalled from Ireland.
1566   Henry Sidney appointed Lord Deputy of Ireland.
1567   Death of Shane O'Neill.
1568   Attempted settlement in Munster by Devon adventurers.
1569   Revolt of the Desmonds in Ireland. Second Irish Parliament of Elizabeth's reign meets.
1573   Revolt of the Desmonds crushed. Attempts to plant Ulster begin.
1576   Imprisonment of deputation from Ireland protesting at collection of 'cess' (purveyance). Recall of Henry Sidney to Ireland.
1579   Outbreak of Desmond revolt in Ireland; Munster laid waste. Six hundred Spanish troops land in July under Fitzmaurice and Saunders.
1580   Lord Grey de Wilton appointed Deputy.
1582   30,000 deaths in Munster, mainly from starvation.
1583   Death of Gerald Fitzmaurice, 15th Earl of Desmond. Plantation of Munster begins.
1584   Perrot appointed Lord Deputy (January). Remains until 1588.
1585   Elizabeth's third Irish Parliament meets (April). Secretary Fenton's visit to Munster (November) plans scheme to repeople the province.
1588   Perrot leaves Ireland pacified. Succeeded by Sir William Fitzwilliam.
1589   Commission appointed to examine progress of Munster plantation.
1591   Sir Henry Bagnal appointed Chief Commissioner for the Government of Ulster; Trinity College, Dublin, founded by Elizabeth.
1594   Hugh O'Neill, Earl of Tyrone, heads rising in Ulster; appeals to Spain for help.
1595   Attempts by Sir John Norris, commander of the English forces in Ireland, fail to crush Tyrone's revolt.
1597   Sir William Russell superseded as Lord Deputy by Lord Burgh. Burgh died on October 1597. Truce in Ireland until June 1598.
1598   Battle of the Yellow Ford (14 August). Defeat of English force under Bagnal. Ascendancy of Hugh O'Neill in Ireland.
1599   Essex made Deputy in Ireland; lands at Dublin (15 April) and concludes treaty with Tyrone (8 September); Essex returns to London (28 September).
1600   Tyrone invades Munster (January); Lord Mountjoy succeeds Essex as

177

ENGLISH HISTORICAL FACTS 1485–1603

Deputy; order restored in the Pale (July–August); Tyrone drives North (September–October); arrival of two Spanish ships (November); Earl of Desmond captured.

1601 Suppression of the O'Byrones in Wicklow (January); landing of 5000 strong Spanish force at Kinsale (September) under Aguilar. Kinsale harbour blockaded by Sir Richard Leveson (December). Second Spanish fleet under Zubiaur destroyed in Castlehaven Harbour. Mountjoy defeats Tyrone's attempt to break the English lines (24 December).

1602 Spaniards under Aguilar capitulate (2 January) in Kinsale; pacification of Munster.

1603 Submission of Tyrone in March.

9 TUDOR ECONOMIC LEGISLATION

INTRODUCTION

The paramount tasks of the Tudor Government were the maintenance of law and order and the defence of national security; it is in the context of these aims that its economic legislation must be seen. Tudor Government was practical government, concerned to maintain stability which meant upholding the traditional social and economic structure.

The sixteenth century saw the extension of government control. In general and in the economic area the picture is one of great activity by the state. There was an enormous amount of economic legislation which had increased for a number of reasons, the most important being the developing complexity of economic life. The rise in population and high inflation, together with the emergence of a national market superseding local markets brought new problems and it was the state which was expected to deal with them. There had long been a tendency to look to the King as the remedy for evil, to protect the welfare of all the King's subjects. As a result of the Reformation the Crown inherited the duty of defending and implementing the social and economic teaching of the Church, and the middle years of the sixteenth century saw a constant appeal to the state to uphold an economic and social morality which the Church could no longer enforce.

The success of the Tudors in enforcing statutes and proclamations is extremely hard to assess. The responsibility for enforcement was increasingly given to the Justices of the Peace and much depended on their willingness and conscientiousness. 'The frequent re-enactment of existing legislation and the evidence of court records point to a wide gap between intention and fulfilment' (P. Ramsey).

AGRICULTURAL LEGISLATION

The Government was concerned with agrarian problems largely as a matter of public order. Agrarian discontent would provide an excellent breeding ground for other grievances and might spark off a general revolt. Depopulation through enclosure and conversion from arable land to pasture would be

179

bound to have a demoralising effect on those peasants turned off their land and without employment. The rise in population meant a greater demand for food and it was expected that the Government would ensure adequate supplies; this too led to a great deal of legislation against the enclosure and conversion of land.

SUMMARY OF THE MAIN LEGISLATION

1488   4 Hen. VII c.16
An Act against engrossing (i.e. the consolidation of several holdings to the detriment of neighbours) in the Isle of Wight. This was an important strategic area, and the military ill-effects of depopulation here were stressed.

1489   4 Hen. VII c.19
A general Act against depopulation which claimed that in certain areas where 200 people had previously been employed, there now remained only two or three herdsmen. The Act ordered all occupants of 20 acres upwards of land which had been tilled in the past three years to maintain that land in tillage on pain of forfeiting half the profits to the lord of the manor.

1515   6 Hen. VIII c.5
An Act specifically ordering the reconversion of pasture land to arable, and the rebuilding of decayed houses.

1516   7 Hen. VIII c.1
An Act applying only to parishes where most of the land used to be tilled and ordering that if such land had been converted it was to be reconverted and the population were to return.

In 1517 the *first enclosure commission* was set up by Wolsey. It was ordered to enquire into what land had been converted to pasture since 1488 and what villages had decayed in consequence. A number of cases of breaches of statutes were brought before the courts and offenders were compelled to enter recognizances to destroy their hedges.

1526   Proclamation ordering that all land enclosed and converted since 1488 be restored to tillage.

1528   Proclamation requiring men to disclose to the Lord Chancellor the names of 'such persons as do enclose any grounds or pastures to the hurt of the commonwealth'.

1529   Proclamation ordering anyone who had enclosed land contrary to government legislation to destroy the hedges and ditches they had made.

1533–4   25 Hen. VIII c.13
An Act forbidding any man to keep more than 2000 sheep or to hold more than two farms unless they were in the parish in which he lived.

1536   27 Hen. VIII c.22

An Act referring to that of 1489 and enacting that the King would be entitled to receive half the profits from those lands not yet reconverted.

1536   27 Hen. VIII c.28

An Act requiring all those to whom monastic lands had been granted to maintain that land which had been tilled in the past 20 years as arable land.

In 1548 a second enclosure commission was appointed but it did not complete its work. It was to inquire into what villages or hamlets had decayed as a result of enclosure, how many persons kept 2000 sheep or more, what common land had been seized into private hands and whether recipients of monastic lands had maintained those lands in cultivation.

1552   5 & 6 Edw. VI c.5

An Act introducing a permanent body of commissioners to search out offenders against the enclosure acts.

1555-6   2 & 3 Ph. and M. c.2

An Act confirming that of 1489 and making it applicable to all houses with 20 acres of land.

1563   5 Eliz. c.2

An Act confirming statutes passed under Henry VII and Henry VIII and enacting that all land which had been farmed for the space of four years since 1528 was to remain in tillage, and that no land currently tilled was to be converted.

1569   Proclamation warning that the statutes concerning enclosure were to be obeyed, and that the government would proceed severely against offenders.

1593   35 Eliz. c.7

An Act which, on the grounds that sufficient land was now in tillage, repealed the clause in the Act of 1563 concerning conversion to pasture.

1597   39 Eliz. c.1

An Act ordering all houses of husbandry which had decayed in the past seven years to be rebuilt, as well as half of those which had decayed in the previous seven years.

This was a period of very high prices, some famine and a great outcry against enclosures which had increased since the legislation of 1593.

THE POOR LAW

INTRODUCTION

The sixteenth century saw far-reaching developments in the legislation concerning poor relief. Early Tudor statutes were punitive and deterrent, primarily concerned with the repression of beggars as they were a force for disorder. Throughout the century there was a gradual understanding that social and economic forces could determine poverty, and that it was not necessarily man's idleness which was its cause. A distinction was made in later legislation between the deserving and undeserving poor, and between those who were unemployed through economic circumstances and those who genuinely could not work through age or infirmity. Rising prices made the problem of poverty particularly severe at a time when the traditional channels of poor relief – the monasteries – were removed. Thus the State assumed the concern which had been that of the Church. New machinery was provided to administer relief by use of J.P.s and by the selection of the parish as the administrative unit. The establishment of the poor rate meant that the cost of relief was met locally. This sphere of economic activity by the central government provides a particularly good illustration of the way that the Tudor government adopted ideas from local government. The whole development of the Poor Law was a process of adopting and spreading initiatives which had begun locally.

SUMMARY OF THE MAIN LEGISLATION

1495 11 Hen. VII c.2
An Act ordering local officials to set vagabonds or idle persons in the stocks and then to eject them. All beggars were to return to their own hundreds and beg there.

1531 22 Hen. VIII c.12
An Act ordering J.P.s to search out for the impotent poor in their district and give them letters authorising them to beg within certain limits. Any beggar who begged outside the specified area or without a license was to be put in the stocks. This Act set a precedent by making the J.P.s responsible for its enforcement.

1536 27 Hen. VIII c.25
An Act ordering the authorities of parishes to 'charitably receive' beggars and to relieve them with voluntary alms. Alms were to be collected every Sunday and preachers were to exhort liberality. Vagrant children between the ages of 5 and 14 years were to be apprenticed.

This was an extremely important Statute in that it established the parish as the administrative unit for poor relief and it was the first Act in which the government had accepted that the State was responsible for poor relief.

1547 1 Edw. VI c.3
A particularly severe Act providing that a sturdy beggar might be made a slave for two years, and if he ran away, a slave for life. (This clause was repealed in 1549.) The Act also laid down that cottages were to be erected for the impotent poor.

1551–2 5 & 6 Edw. VI c.2
An Act ordering municipal or parochial officers to call the local householders

together and to nominate two collectors to gather the alms for the parish. These were to 'gentellie aske' what every man would give, and anyone who refused alms was to be sent to the Bishop.

1563   5 Eliz. c.3

An Act charging that if a person refused to give alms after being exhorted by the Bishop, he could be bound by £10 to appear before the J.P.s. If he still refused, they were empowered to imprison him.

This Act was a first step towards a compulsory poor rate, but as yet care was taken to make contributions as voluntary as possible, and only to resort to force when persuasion was quite ineffectual.

1572   14 Eliz. c.5

This was an important codification of the law which ran heavily against the 'professional poor' as it provided very severe penalties for vagrants. The impotent and aged however were to have relief arranged in their home parish. The J.P.s were ordered to make a register of all the names of their local poor, to find habitations for them. To do this they were to estimate the cost and then to assess and tax all the parish inhabitants accordingly.

1576   18 Eliz. c.3

An Act supplementing that of 1572 with the extremely important order that a stock of wool, flax, hemp, iron or other stuff was to be provided in every city and corporate town, and every market town where it was thought by the J.P.s to be necessary to enable the able-bodied poor to work. Houses of correction were to be built in every county and those who refused to work were to be sent there.

This was the first expression in government legislation of the realisation that unemployment was not necessarily due to the wickedness and idleness of men, and that to provide work for the able-bodied poor was a positive and practical approach to the problem.

1598   39 Eliz. c.3

This was the most comprehensive statute, and one which remained in force until 1834. It placed the responsibility for poor relief in the hands of four overseers of the poor, to be chosen every Easter by the J.P.s. They were to set children to work as apprentices, to provide the adult unemployed with work, and to relieve the aged and infirm, for which they were empowered to build hospitals. The funds for their work were to be raised by a compulsory rate on every inhabitant and could be raised by distress, i.e. by seizing of goods. The assessments were to be made by parochial officers, and wealthier parishes were expected to aid the poorer ones.

1598   39 Eliz. c.4

An Act empowering J.P.s to take measures for houses of correction for rogues and vagabonds. Earlier statutes providing for punishment were repealed;

rogues were now to be whipped and then returned to their parish or placed in a house of correction.

1601   43 Eliz. c.2
This did little more than repeat and codify the legislation of 1598.

GILDS, TOWNS AND INDUSTRIES, WAGES

GILDS
The increasing complexity of economic life and the extension of the local market to a national one meant that the gilds, traditionally the protector of both producer and consumer, were no longer equipped to cope with their tasks. The central government was therefore frequently passing legislation to protect the consumer, to maintain good standards of craftsmanship and the stability of manufacturers, and to prevent exploitation of the worker. These measures were designed to protect the declining gild system, not to attack it; but they did include legislation aimed at remedying certain abuses within the gild system.

SUMMARY OF THE MAIN LEGISLATION
1503–4   19 Hen. VII c.7
An Act claiming that craft gilds had been making unlawful ordinances, and ordering gild bye-laws to be examined, and approved by the Chancellor, Treasurer and Chief Justices or by the Justices of Assize. One motive for this was the desire to take away from the Companies the power of determining the price of commodities since their commodites were being sold nationally rather than locally.

1531   22 Hen. VIII c.4
An Act claiming that gilds had been charging apprentices almost prohibitive fees for entry and fixing 2s 6d as the maximum an apprentice was to pay.

1537   28 Hen. VIII c.5
An Act forbidding masters to make their apprentices swear not to set up separate establishments without the assent and licence of the Master Wardens or Fellowships. This was partly designed to prevent craftsmen from being driven into the countryside, but also to adapt the gild to the needs of the new developments, which were transforming numbers of journeymen into small masters.

1547   1 Edw. VI c.14
An Act confiscating possessions of the gilds which had been devoted to religious purposes. This was a corollary to the 1545 Act which dissolved chantries.

1550   3 & 4 Edw. VI c.22
An Act which sought to prevent employers from hiring journeymen by the

week and for other short periods, and which demanded a one-to-three journeyman/apprentice ratio. This was to prevent too many apprentices being employed merely as a form of cheap labour, and it was hoped it would provide some security of employment and maintain high standards.

1563   5 Eliz. c.4 (Statute of Artificers: see also p. 187)
The apprenticeship clauses in this statute took the gild system already developed by industry and made it statutory and nation-wide, to apply to all industries. It made the seven-year term of apprenticeship universal, and extended compulsory apprenticeship to all urban crafts. It also established a detailed list of property qualifications – gilds had in fact long charged expensive premiums – which barred the sons of the very poor from admission to any gild. To prevent the apprenticeship system from being used as a form of cheap labour, masters were limited in the number of apprentices they might employ together with hired journeymen.

TOWNS AND INDUSTRIES
There was a great deal of government concern over maintenance of standards in industry and an enormous number of statutes were passed concerning this. They ranged from the favourite subject, wool (for details see 'Overseas Trade'), to leather, the next most frequent topic, and then to such matters as the making of hats and caps, malt, pins and many other artefacts. It is impossible to list all of these – suffice it to say that the promotion of good craftsmanship stretched over a wide range of items.

One particularly important concern of the government was to arrest the decay of the corporate towns. There was a tendency, partly because of the restrictive gild system, for industries to shift to the countryside. The ensuing struggle between the established seats of industry and the villages was one of the main economic features of the sixteenth century. The former sought by legislation to curb the activities of the latter, and claimed that the decline in standard of certain industries was because the rural employer employed men not properly trained.

SUMMARY OF THE MAIN LEGISLATION

1523   14 & 15 Hen. VIII c.3
An Act forbidding any worsteds woven in Norfolk or Suffolk to be shorn, dyed or calendared except in Norwich. It was for the protection of the shearmen, dyers and drapers of Norwich who had bitterly complained about the competition of the county capitalist.

1534   25 Hen. VIII c.18
An Act on behalf of Worcester and four other towns which forbade the manufacture of cloth elsewhere in the county.

1543   34 & 35 Hen. VIII c.10
An Act giving York a monopoly in the county of making coverlets and conferring on the gild of coverlet makers the power to search for offenders throughout the county.

1551   5 & 6 Edw. VI c.8
An Act forbidding anyone to weave unless he had been apprenticed for seven years.

1551–2   5 & 6 Edw. VI c.24
An Act concerning the making of hats and coverlets at Norwich which referred to 'evil and covetous disposed' individuals who had left the city for the countryside, and although not fully trained had been manufacturing goods 'deceitfully and insufficiently without controlment' to the decay both of the craft and the city.

1554   1 Mary c.7
An Act confining 5 & 6 Edw. VI c.8 to the countryside. Its ruling had affected the town clothiers as well as the rural ones and they had agitated for its repeal.

1554   1 & 2 Ph. and M. c.7
A general act to remedy the decay of corporate towns.

1555   2 & 3 Ph. and M. c.11
The Antwerp market was glutted (see 'Overseas Trade') and this famous Weaver's Act further limited the number of apprentices and looms which a rural manufacturer was to employ.

1557   4 & 5 Ph. and M. c.5
An Act forbidding anyone to manufacture certain cloths outside corporate or market towns where manufacture had been carried on for the last ten years, though certain districts were exempted.

1559   1 Eliz. c.9
An Act exempting certain areas of Essex from the Act of 1557.

1575–6   18 Eliz. c.16
An Act exempting areas of Wiltshire, Somerset and Gloucestershire from the Act of 1557. The 1557 Act was repealed in 1623–4 (21 Jac. I c.28).

REGULATION OF WAGES
1495   11 Hen. VII c.22
An Act closely following one of 1445 (23 Hen. VI c.12) which limited payments for holiday times and permitted reductions in wages for laziness. It fixed maximum rates of pay and permitted lower rates to be paid where these were usual. It was later repealed because of its severity.

1512   3 Hen. VIII c.6
An Act ordering payment to be made in money not in victuals.

1514   6 Hen. VIII c.3

An Act fixing the hours for labour. From mid-March to mid-September men were to work from 5 a.m. until 7 or 8 p.m. with half an hour free for breakfast, and one-and-a-half hours free for dinner and a rest. In the winter they were to work during daylight hours only. The statute fixed labourer's wages at 3*d* a day for half the year and 4*d* a day for the other half, with opportunities for extra earning at harvest time. Skilled artisans were to receive 6*d* a day for half the year and 5*d* a day for the other half.

1549   2 & 3 Edw. VI c.15

The rise in prices had led to a demand for higher wages and this statute claimed that some labourers had conspired together to fix a rate of pay or to limit the hours of work they would do. They were, by this Act, forbidden to combine together to improve the conditions of labour under severe penalties.

1563   5 Eliz. c.4 (Statute of Artificers: see also p. 185).

This was a comprehensive statute which represented an attempt to provide a labour code, and in particular, an industrial labour code. Its preamble declared that it aimed to codify the existing law especially that concerning wage assessments in order to promote employment, foster agriculture and adjust wages to prices. The Act fixed a maximum wage though not a minimum one, but the standard wage was to be assessed by J.P.s who were to meet annually at Easter to discuss and settle the rate of wages for each occupation within their county. They were to take into account the plenty or scarcity of the time, that is to calculate wages relative to prices. Their lists were then to be sent to the Privy Council for approval, after which they would be legally enforceable the following year.

This was a form of wage control which had been adopted in England after the Black Death but since then, as we have seen above, the central government had generally fixed a national scale of pay without reference to local authority. The scheme now established had the great advantage of flexibility, taking local variations and prices into account.

1598   39 Eliz. c.12

There was some doubt to whom exactly the Statute of Artificers referred, and this Act gave J.P.s authority to rate the wages 'of any labourers, weavers, spinsters and workmen or workwomen whatsoever'.

OVERSEAS TRADE AND COMMERCE

NAVIGATION ACTS

Tudor monarchs were aware of the importance of England's maritime independence, and were particularly concerned to promote native shipping and seamanship. This aim was behind a number of statutes passed in the sixteenth century.

1485   1 Hen. VII c.8

The preamble to this Act lamented the decay of the navy, and it ordered the wines of Gascony and Guinne to be imported only in ships from England, Ireland, Wales or Calais; it added that the majority of the crew must be of these nationalities.

1488   4 Hen. VII c.10

An Act adding to that of 1485 with the proviso that masters and mariners must be English subjects. The prohibition was extended to cover Toulouse woad and the King's subjects were forbidden to use foreign shipping for any exports or imports where English shipping was available.

1532   23 Hen. VIII c.7

This merely renewed the Navigation Acts of Henry VII.

1540   32 Hen. VIII c.14

An extremely comprehensive Act passed for the 'maintenance of the navy' which, the preamble stressed, had greatly decayed because people were infringing the statutes in force against importing goods in foreign ships. The old laws were re-enacted and freights were strictly defined for goods of various sorts from different ports.

1549   2 & 3 Edw. VI c.19

An Act ordering abstention from meat on Fridays and Saturdays to encourage the fishing industry. The aim of this measure was to increase the size of the fishing fleet and to encourage seamanship.

1559   1 Eliz. c.13

The protectionist act of 1540 had provoked reprisals by the Emperor Charles V, who placed a ban on English ships. This led Elizabeth to repeal all previous legislation on shipping which had provided that goods imported in foreign vessels 'masts, pitch, tar and corn only excepted' should pay aliens customs.

1563   5 Eliz. c.5

An Act making it obligatory to employ native shipping in the coastal trade and for importing French wines and woad. It also required Wednesdays to be observed as an additional fish day 'for the increase of fishermen and mariners and the repairing of port towns and navigation'.

1585   27 Eliz. c.11

This repealed the Act of 1563 which had made Wednesday a fish day.

1593   35 Eliz. c.7

This reduced the penalties for eating flesh on Fish Days.

WOOL AND CLOTH EXPORTS

Two primary considerations guided government policy in this field. Firstly there was a genuine desire to keep English pieces at a high and uniform standard of quality and to maintain the good name of English fabrics both at home and abroad. The other consideration was financial. Since more English cloth was being worked at home, revenue which had been drawn from wool customs had now to be obtained from levies imposed upon the manufactured article.

SUMMARY OF THE MAIN LEGISLATION

1487   3 Hen. VII c.11

An Act which forbade the export of undyed and unfinished cloth above the limit of £2. This was intended to benefit the native cloth-finishing industry; a policy which was widely criticised by the merchant adventurers who claimed the market was much smaller for finished cloth.

1512   3 Hen. VIII c.6

An Act against the 'deceitful making of woollen cloth' which enacted that walkers and pullers 'shall truly walk, pull, thick and work every web of woollen yarn', and forbade carders and spinners to appropriate any of the wool delivered to them.

1536   27 Hen. VIII c.12

An 'Act for the true making of woollen cloths' which referred to slanders abroad that English cloth was not well made and this was a hindrance to its sale.

1552   5 & 6 Edw. VI c.6

This statute followed the collapse of the Antwerp market which the merchants blamed on the shoddiness of the clothiers' goods. It was a comprehensive attempt to bring all varieties of cloth under the power of the law and to establish a thorough scheme of regulation. It catered for 22 types of cloth, and in each case a full specification was laid down. There had been a large number of statutes specifying the dimensions of cloths but it was seen that this was insufficient and therefore this statute specified the weights for the cloths so that shoddy material could not be substituted. Searchers were to be appointed to enforce the Act. It did however only apply to towns.

1552   5 & 6 Edw. VI c.7

An Act to bring down the price of wool, which allowed complete liberty of purchasing wool only to manufacturers and merchants of the staple. It was a statute aimed at the middleman – always a focus of hostility in sixteenth-century England, as he was frequently blamed for price increases.

1557   4 & 5 Ph. and M. c.5

This extended 5 & 6 Edw. VI c.6 to apply to some rural areas.

1564   Patent of 6 Eliz.

A patent enabling Merchant Adventurers to export a certain amount of undressed cloth.

1566   8 Eliz. c.6

An Act ordering one cloth 'wrought and dressed' to be exported for every nine unfinished.

1597   39 Eliz. c.20

A sweeping enactment concerned with cloth made north of the River Trent. No one was to stretch or strain cloths on pain of £5 and local officials were instructed to search out offenders. All the specifications for cloth laid down in previous statutes were to be strictly kept. The use of tenters – the frame on which the clothier stretched the shrunk fabric after it had been fulled – was forbidden and this caused bitter complaints from manufacturers who claimed the tenter was essential machinery. In 1623 the tenter was once more allowed, but it was to be constructed differently.

EXPEDITIONS FOR COMMERCE AND DISCOVERY

1496   Henry VII issued a patent to a syndicate of British merchants headed by John Cabot and his sons, permitting them to annex and trade with any lands hitherto unknown to Christians. An expedition in 1497 reached the area of Novia Scotia, and returned with reports which led to the establishment of the Newfoundland fisheries. Nothing is known for certain of the fate of a second expedition in 1498.

1502   The King issued a new patent to a syndicate called the Company Adventurers to the New Found Lands. This allowed the syndicate to colonise and trade with lands not occupied by a Christian prince, even if previously known.

1509   Sebastian Cabot led an expedition to search for the North-West Passage to Asia. He entered Hudson Bay, but the crew insisted on turning back because of the ice. Cabot took up service as Chief Navigator of Spain in 1512.

1521   Henry VIII and Wolsey attempted to form a National Company for trade and discovery. The London Livery Companies were obstructive, and on the outbreak of war with France the plan was dropped.

1530–40   In spite of protests from the Portuguese, William Hawkins made a number of trading voyages to the coasts of Guinea and Brazil.

1551–2   Thomas Wyndham opened up a new trade with the Atlantic coast of Morocco. In 1553 he led the first expedition to the Gold Coast and Benin.

1552–3   The Company of Merchant Adventurers for the Discovery of New Trades was formed by Northumberland as the first joint-stock company in England. Sebastian Cabot, who had returned from Spain in 1548, was its first Governor.

1553   An expedition led by Sir Hugh Willoughby and Richard Chancellor attempted to find the North-East Passage to Asia. Willoughby died trying to winter on the coast of Lapland. Chancellor entered the White Sea and reached what is now Archangel. He then made the overland journey to Moscow to the court of Ivan the Terrible. His successful negotiations there led to the founding of the Muscovy Company in 1553.

1556 Stephen Borough led an expedition in search of the North-East Passage. He was forced to turn back by weather conditions at the entrance to the Kara Sea.

1557–62 Anthony Jenkinson made two overland journeys into Asia. On the second he concluded trade agreements with Persia.

1562–9 John Hawkins led three expeditions to take slaves from Africa to Hispaniola, returning to England with precious metals, sugar and other valuable commodities. The third expedition was attacked in September 1568 at San Juan de Ulloa by a Spanish fleet escorting the Viceroy of Mexico.

1576–8 Martin Frobisher led three expeditions in search of the North-West Passage. He failed to find it, and the rock he discovered, which he believed to contain gold, proved to be worthless. The Company of Cathay, formed in 1577 to exploit his discoveries, went bankrupt in 1578.

1577–80 Francis Drake accomplished the first circumnavigation by an Englishman. After sailing through the Straits of Magellan and plundering along the South American coast, he crossed the Pacific and reached Asia in July 1579. He returned to Plymouth in September 1580, and was knighted by the Queen. A similar expedition was undertaken by Thomas Cavendish, 1586–8.

1578 Sir Humphrey Gilbert was granted a royal patent to settle North America. His expedition in 1582 reached Newfoundland, but a number of ships were wrecked as they explored southwards. Gilbert himself was drowned when his ship *Squirrel* disappeared on the return journey.

1579 The Eastland Company was formed to trade with the Baltic.

1580 An expedition to find the North-East Passage was mounted by the Muscovy Company, which had lost the Persian trade when the Turks invaded Persia in 1579. The expedition was led by Arthur Pet and Charles Jackman, but again weather conditions made it unsuccessful.

1583–91 John Newbury and Ralph Fitch travelled overland to India, Burma and the Malay Peninsula. Newbery vanished, but Fitch returned to England in 1591.

1584–91 A new grant for settlement in North America was made to Sir Walter Raleigh. A settlement, which Raleigh named Virginia, was founded on Roanoke Island off the North Carolina coast, but the settlers chose to return with Drake in 1586. A further settlement established in 1587 had disappeared when its founder, John White, returned with supplies in 1591.

1585–87   John Davis made three unsuccessful attempts to find the North West Passage.

1585   The Barbary Company was formed.

1591–94   Voyage of George Raymond and James Lancaster to the East Indies. Raymond's ship was lost in the Indian Ocean, and Lancaster returned to England with less than a dozen men.

1592   The Levant Company was formed from an amalgamation of the Turkey and Venetian Companies.

1592–93   Thomas Cavendish and John Davis sailed to the Straits of Magellan. Cavendish turned back and died at sea, whilst Davis went on and discovered the Falkland Islands.

1595   Sir Walter Raleigh sailed to Trinidad and up the Orinoco in search of 'Eldorado'; on his return he wrote his 'Discovery of Guiana'.

1600   East India Company established. Its first fleet sailed in 1601 with Sir James Lancaster in command and John Davis as chief pilot.

COINAGE, PRICES, USURY AND MONOPOLIES

THE COINAGE
Regulation of the coinage was an important aspect of the Tudor monarch's prerogative. Henry VII issued a number of proclamations concerning the acceptance of English coins including 'thin and old pence'. In July 1504 he ordered the withdrawal at bullion value of all coins that were clipped and acceptance as legal tender at the full nominal value, of unclipped coins.

Henry VIII in 1522 issued the first of a series of proclamations setting new values on foreign gold coins. In August 1526 the face value of all English gold coins was raised by 10 per cent, and in December of that year this was altered to 12½ per cent. In 1542 an increased amount of alloy was introduced into each coin, and from 1544 there was a series of debasements by the Crown simply with the object of making money to finance the war against France.

After some attempt at counteracting the previous debasements of the currency Edward VI resumed the coinage policies evident in his father's proclamations. In April 1551 the value of the shilling was lowered to 9d and in August, to 6d.

As soon as Mary came to the throne a proclamation was issued ordering the reform of gold and silver coin (August 1553) but the low standards continued for some pence and halfpence, and possibly groats. On Elizabeth's accession a great deal of base silver coin remained in circulation, and it was decided to withdraw it. In September 1560 a proclamation announced that 'her majesty hath . . . determined by advice of her council . . . to abolish the said corrupt, base and copper moneys, and to restore the owners thereof to

192

fine moneys. . . .' People were ordered to bring their bad coins to the mint and collect new ones in their stead. The recoinage was completed by September 1562 and confidence in the currency was restored.

To eliminate badly worn coin, the principle of minimum legal weight was introduced. In October 1587 a proclamation ordered that no one should accept English gold coins which were below a certain weight.

REGULATION OF PRICES

A rise in population in a century which saw no development in agricultural production produced a real danger of food scarcity. A series of bad harvests could cause a great deal of suffering. The Tudor government, on grounds of humanity and equity plus an acute awareness of the attraction of revolt for hungry men, tended to take speedy action. Grain export was constantly prohibited unless it was below a certain price. Many proclamations were issued against middlemen – long blamed for high prices.

Commodities subject to sale and price control included meat, wood, coal, wine, armour, sugar and still more. The list below is merely a small sample of the statutes and proclamations relating to grain and victuals, focusing particularly on the 1540s when the effects of Henry VIII's manipulation of the coinage was evident (see 'Coinage' above).

1534   25 Henry VIII c.2
A statute forbidding anyone to export victuals without a licence unless it were to supply Calais or ships going to sea.

Nov 1534   Proclamation ordering punishment of grain hoarders, which blamed high prices on the 'subtle invention and craft of divers covetous persons'.

Jan 1544   Proclamation providing penalties for export of grain and victual.
Nov 1544   Proclamation ordering sale of grain. This claimed that persons had 'by divers and sundry means accumulated . . . a great number and multitude of corns and grains', and ordered Justices of the Peace to search for the surplus and bring it to the markets.

June 1546   Proclamation prohibiting unlicensed export of grain. The granting of such licences was an important source of revenue for the King.

May 1547   Proclamation permitting export of grain since there is now 'great plenty and abundance' in the realm.

Dec 1547   Proclamation limiting grain export. Prices now exceeded those set down as the upper limit in the proclamation of May 1547, and therefore a special licence was needed for export.

April 1548   Proclamation prohibiting the export of victuals because of scarcity and high prices.

July 1551   Proclamation enforcing statutes against 'regraters, forestallers and engrossers', which claimed that the 'great and excessive prices' of victuals 'groweth by the greedy and insatiable covetous desires' of these men. 'Engrossers' were men who either dealt in many types of commodities instead of only one or who monopolised the supply of any one commodity. 'Forestallers' were men who went outside their borough or market town to intercept and buy goods, thereby raising the price. 'Regraters' were men who bought up goods in their own or neighbouring markets to sell them again at a profit.

1555   1 & 2 Ph. and M. c.5
An Act which prohibited the export of grain, victuals and wood under heavy penalties. Grain could be exported only when wheat was under 6s 8d a quarter.

1563   5 Eliz. c.5
An Act raising the limit within which corn might be exported to 10s a quarter in the case of wheat.

1571   13 Eliz. c.13
This Act permitted the export of corn provided that prices were moderate in the country from which export was contemplated. Local authorities were instructed to consult with the inhabitants of the country and then issue a proclamation as to whether the local supply was such as would permit export.

1593   35 Eliz. c.7
A reversal of the Act of 1571, taking control out of the hands of the local authorities. Corn was to be exported only when the price was under 20s a quarter.

THE TUDOR PRICE RISE[1]

Food prices, 1501–1602*

	Food	% increase or decrease on previous decade
1501–10	100	
1511–20	101	+1
1521–30	138	+37
1531–40	131	−5
1541–50	179	+37
1551–60	290	+62
1561–70	260	−10
1571–82	296	+14
1583–92	318	+7½
1593–1602	438	+38

* Food = wheat, beans, barley malt, cheese, butter, oxen or beef, sheep, pigs, hens, pigeons, eggs, herrings.

*Prices of building materials**

1501–10	100	1541–50	115
1511–20	98	1551–60	175
1521–30	114	1561–70	234
1531–40	99	1571–82	238

* Defined as laths, plain tiles, slates and bricks.

*Wage rates (building trades)**

1501–10	100	1541–50	121
1511–20	103	1551–60	169
1521–30	104	1561–70	178
1531–40	109	1571–82	194

* Includes carpenters, masons, sawyers and tilers.

[1] These statistics are derived from P. Mathias op. cit.

USURY

1487   3 Hen. VII c.5
An Act forbidding the taking of interest on loans – a practice long frowned upon by Church and State – under penalty of £100 for every transaction. Since the practice was more common in the boroughs cases were not to be tried by borough magistrates – who might be sympathetic – but by Chancery or County Justices of the Peace.

1495   11 Hen. VII c.8
An Act to remove certain ambiguities in that of 1487. It expressly forbade the selling of wages and repurchasing of them within four months at a lower price, and the practice of loans advanced on the security of land on condition that part of revenue from the land should go to the lender.

1545   37 Hen. VIII C.9
This reversed earlier policy by sanctioning interest on loans up to 10 per cent. This was a time when the Government needed money extremely badly.

1552   5 & 6 Edw. VI c.20
This repealed the Act of 1545 and repeated the injunctions against usury which had been accepted for centuries.

1571   13 Eliz. c.8
An Act repealing that of 1552, and reviving the Act of 1545. Persons taking more than 10 per cent interest were to forfeit the treble value of their profits, and to be imprisoned. To take interest of 10 per cent or less was no longer a criminal offence but a debtor who chose could undertake legal proceedings to recover the interest since the creditor was given no legal security.

MONOPOLIES

Patents granted by the Crown for new inventions and particularly those for the protection of foreign workmen coming to England, had been in use before the sixteenth century. New economic conditions, however, now encouraged the government to increase the extent and effectiveness of its former policy. Under Elizabeth, more than her predecessors, numerous patents were issued. Some were for genuine introductions of chemical products or processes, or for mechanical inventions. Another form of patent was that of export licences, enabling the recipient to export produce, for example, grain, contrary to existing legislation. There were also issued dispensing patents which gave an individual a dispensation from adhering to particular legislation, e.g. the penal laws. Although the Crown had a genuine desire to encourage invention and regulate industry, financial considerations and the need to reward servants and favourites were additional motivations for a practice of monopoly by the Crown which came to be abused by unscrupulous suitors. In the Parliament of 1601 long-standing grievances came to a head, and Elizabeth was forced to promise reform.

10 POPULATION AND THE GROWTH OF TOWNS

POPULATION

Population estimates for the sixteenth century are, in an age before national censuses were taken, by their very nature incomplete. The best estimate puts England's population at 2·3 million in 1522–35, 2·8 million in 1545, and 3·75 million in 1603.[1] Wales' population hovered around 250,000 in 1500[2] and probably increased little in the succeeding century. Scotland had a population of c.750,000 in 1500 but it grew to 850,000 by the end of the Tudor period.[3] Ireland's population, because of the paucity of the records, is the most difficult of all to calculate. The best estimate puts it at little more than half a million by 1603.[4]

The British people as a whole lived in the countryside, probably more than three-quarters of them living in villages. What urban life there was was mainly in England, with Scotland and Ireland having a few major towns and Wales only a few boroughs – little more than overgrown villages.

England's population in 1600, compared to other European countries, is set out below:

European Population in 1600 (millions, approx.)	
England and Wales	4
Scotland and Ireland	2
The Netherlands	3
Scandinavia	1·4
Poland and Lithuania	8
Germany	20
France	16
Italy	13
Spain and Portugal	9
Turkey (Europe and Asia)	18–30

THE GROWTH OF TOWNS

'We know surprisingly little about the economy, social structure, and physical growth of English towns before the latter part of the eighteenth century.' So

Professor Hoskins wrote in 1956.[5] Since that date, much research has been devoted to the subject and in several areas our knowledge greatly increased.[6] Although *The Italian Relation of England* declared that 'there are scarcely any towns of importance in the kingdom' except for London, Bristol and York, this is an exaggerated statement.[7] Although small compared to some French and Italian cities, by the time of Henry VIII we have fairly reliable estimates of the population of a variety of towns.

Estimated Population of major towns in 1524[8]

London	60,000	York	8,000—
Norwich	12,000+	Coventry	6,600
Bristol	9,500+	Worcester	6,000
Exeter	8,000	Gloucester	4,000+
Salisbury	8,000	Shrewsbury	4,000

London was the great metropolis. In 1539, it had 60,000–80,000 inhabitants; by 1559, 90,000; and by 1605 it had grown to 224,000. In addition to the largest towns listed above there were various towns, such as Plymouth, Taunton, Northampton, Leeds and Wakefield, with just over 3000 inhabitants. Meanwhile, the majority of market towns sustained a population of between 1,000 and 1,500. Even smaller were a number of towns that were nevertheless considered significant enough to be incorporated during the course of the century, towns such as Banbury, Bideford and Sutton Coldfield, with only six or seven hundred inhabitants each.

Interesting evidence on the relative importance of the Tudor towns in the national economy can be seen from the relative tax yields of London and the leading provincial towns in 1523–7.

Tax Yield of London and 25 Leading Provincial Towns
in the Subsidy of 1523–7 (to nearest pound)

London	£16,675	Lavenham	402
Norwich	1,704	York	379
Bristol	1,072	Totnes	c.317
Coventry	974	Worcester	312
Exeter	855	Gloucester	c.307
Salisbury	852	Lincoln	298
Ipswich	657	Hereford	273
Lynn	576	Yarmouth	260
Canterbury	532	Hull	256
Reading	c.470	Boston	c.240
Southwark	455	Southampton	224
Colchester	426	Hadleigh	c.224
Bury St Edmunds	405	Shrewsbury	c.220

NOTES
1. Julian Cornwall, 'English Population in the Early Sixteenth Century', *Economic History Review*, 2nd series, XXIII, No. 1 (1970), 32–44.
2. David Williams, *A History of Modern Wales* (London: repr., 1951) p. 13.
3. William Croft Dickinson, *Scotland from the Earliest Times to 1603*, 2nd ed. revised, (London, 1965) pp. 251, 373.
4. J. C. Beckett, *The Making of Modern Ireland* (London, 1966) p. 25.
5. 'English Provincial Towns in the early sixteenth century', *Transactions of the Royal Historical Society*, Vol. XX, 1956.
6. Of the more recent material, see in particular: Slack and Clark's *Crisis and Order in English Towns 1500–1700* (1972). This contains, apart from excellent contributions (especially those on Coventry and York) a good introduction summarising recent work in the field. Palliser has written several important articles on York including 'Epidemics in Tudor York' in *Northern History* (1973) and 'York under the Tudors' in *Perspectives in English Urban History* ed. Alan Everitt (Macmillan, 1973).
7. *A relation, or rather a true account, of the isle of England, about 1500*, translated from the Italian by C. A. Sneyd (Camden Society, O. S. XXXVII, 1847).
8. J. C. Russell, *British Medieval Population*, p. 298, suggests a population for London of 67,744 on the basis of the chantry certificates of 1545.

TUDOR TOWNS: INCORPORATION AS BOROUGHS

The desire by even quite small towns to gain incorporation as boroughs was a phenomenon of the Tudor period. The statistics of this process are summarised below:

Period	Boroughs obtaining charters of 'privileges' or 'incorporation'	No. of charters obtained
1485–1509	51	61
1509–47	72	104
1547–53	75	84
1553–8	67	70
1558–1603	123	156
	388	475

The vast increase after Henry VIII's death can best be seen in the figures below:

1485–1547 (62 years)	123	165
1547–1603 (56 years)	265	310

The dates of incorporation of the main boroughs for the period 1345 to 1485 are set out below:

1345	Coventry		1404	Norwich
1373	Bristol		1409	Lincoln
1393	Basingstoke		1439	Plymouth
1396	York		1440	Kingston-upon-Hull
1400	Newcastle upon Tyne		1445	Southampton

1446	Ipswich	1463	Grantham
	Rochester		Rye
1448	Canterbury	1466	Windsor
1449	Nottingham	1467	Doncaster
	Tenterden and Rye	1468	Bridgwater
1451	Chichester		Wenlock
1453	Woodstock	1472	Bewdley
1458	Wainfleet	1481	Kingston-upon-Thames
1460	Northampton	1483	Gloucester
1461	Ludlow	1484	Huntingdon
1462	Colchester		Pontefract
	Stamford		

During the Tudor period, the pace of borough incorporations expanded considerably. The dates of incorporation of the major boroughs are set out below:

1485	Llandovery	1549	Maidstone
	Pembroke		Monmouth
	Scarborough		Newark-upon-Trent
1488	Guildford		Saffron Walden
1489	Dunwich		Wisbech
1490	Southwold	1550	Newport (Salop)
1495	Criccieth	1551	Stafford
1505	Totnes		Louth
1506	Chester	1553	St Albans
1508	Ruthin		Stratford-upon-Avon
1524	King's Lynn	1554	Aylesbury
1528	Sutton Coldfield		Banbury
1537	Exeter		Buckingham
1539	Hemel Hempstead		Chippenham
1542	Cardigan		Droitwich
	Reading		Hertford
1543	Beccles		Leominster
	Colnbrook		Maldon
1544	Romsey		Sheffield
	Seaford		Sudbury
1545	Boston		Torrington
	Warwick	1555	Abingdon
1546	Bridgnorth		Great Dunmow
	Carmarthen		Launceston
	Faversham		Worcester
1547	Aldeburgh (Suffolk)	1556	Brecon
1548	Lichfield		Higham Ferrers

1557	Axbridge	1576	Marlborough
	Barnstaple	1577	Richmond
	Thaxted	1579	Orford
1558	St Ives (Cornwall)	1581	Tenby
	Wallingford		Thetford
	Wycombe	1582	Maidenhead
1559	Lyme Regis	1584	Congleton
1560	Tamworth	1585	Helston
1562	Beaumaris	1586	Arundel
	Gravesend		Shrewsbury
	Radnor	1587	Liskeard
1563	Bodmin		Looe East
1565	Durham	1588	Romford
1566	Farnham		Winchester
	Preston	1589	Hastings
1568	Henley-on-Thames		Leicester
	Nantwich		Truro
	Poole	1590	Bath
1571	Weymouth and		Newcastle-under-Lyme
	Melcombe Regis		South Molton
1573	Beverley	1593	Hartlepool
	Bideford	1594	Marazion
	Bishop's Castle	1595	Macclesfield
1574	Eye		Penzance
	Looe West	1596	Newbury
	Wells	1597	Hereford
1575	Godalming	1598	Chesterfield
	Hythe	1599	Andover
	Kendal	1600	Portsmouth
	Tewkesbury	1602	Plympton
1576	Daventry		

THE TUDOR BOROUGHS: CONSOLIDATED LIST

Cities and Boroughs	Date of first record as a borough	Date of grant of first charter of definite municipal privileges	Date of first charter of definite incorporation
Abingdon	1551	1557	1557
Andover	1307	1154	1599
Arundel	Domesday	—	—
Banbury	1553	1553	1553

Barnstaple	Domesday	1422	—
Basingstoke	1227	—	
Bath	Domesday	1256	1589
Beaumaris	1295	1295	—
Beccles	1542	1542	—
Bedford	Domesday	1156	—
Berwick-upon-Tweed	1200	1301	—
Beverley	1121	1121	1573
Bewdley	1472	1472	1472
Bideford	1583	1583	—
Blandford	1350	—	—
Bodmin	1216	1362	—
Boston	1352	1545	1545
Brecon	1531	1556	—
Bridgnorth	1220	1215	—
Bridgwater	1200	1200	1470
Bridport	Domesday	1252	—
Bristol	1164	1164	—
Buckingham	Domesday	1553	1553
Bury St Edmunds	1297	1100	—
Calne	Domesday	—	—
Cambridge	Domesday	1102	—
Canterbury	Domesday	1154	1448
Cardiff	1531	1338	—
Carlisle	1216	1154	—
Carmarthen	1531	1546	—
Carnarvon	1531	1224	—
Chester	Domesday	1200	—
Chesterfield	—	1599	—
Chichester	Domesday	1135	—
Chippenham	1216	1553	1553
Chipping Norton	1297	—	—
Chipping Wycombe	1236	1236	—
Clitheroe	1329	1147	—
Colchester	Domesday	1189	—
Congleton	—	1282	1583
Coventry	1267	1154	1445
Dartmouth	1216	1331	1463
Daventry	—	1200	—
Deal	—	—	—
Denbigh	1531	1272	—
Derby	Domesday	1205	—
Devizes	Domesday	1130	—

Doncaster	1194	1194	1467
Dorchester	Domesday	1327	—
Dover	Domesday	1229	—
Droitwich	Domesday	1199	—
Durham	1189	1189	1575
Evesham	1295	1603	1603
Exeter	Domesday	1154	—
Eye	Domesday	1200	—
Faversham	—	1252	—
Flint	1531	1284	—
Folkestone	—	1313	—
Glastonbury	1338	—	—
Gloucester	Domesday	1154	—
Godalming	—	1575	—
Godmanchester	—	1213	—
Grantham	1200	1462	1462
Gravesend	—	1562	—
Grimsby	1200	1200	—
Guildford	1135	1338	—
Harwich	1343	1320	1604
Hastings	Domesday	1589	—
Haverfordwest	1531	1377	—
Helston	1200	1200	1584
Hereford	Domesday	—	—
Hertford	Domesday	—	1553
Hull	1303	1299	1439
Huntingdon	Domesday	1206	1483
Hythe	Domesday	1575	—
Ipswich	Domesday	1199	1446
Kendal	—	1575	—
Kidderminster	1295	1154	—
King's Lynn	1200	1200	1524
Kingston-upon-Thames	1199	1199	1542
Lancaster	1193	1193	—
Launceston	1190	1250	1555
Leicester	Domesday	1199	1588
Leominster	1297	1554	—
Lichfield	1310	1547	1547
Lincoln	Domesday	1154	—
Liskeard	1230	1230	1586
Liverpool	1200	1207	—
Llandovery	—	1485	—
Louth	—	1551	—

Ludlow	1300	1461	1461
Lyme Regis	1311	1283	—
Lymington	1535	—	1605
Macclesfield	—	1261	—
Maidenhead	—	1581	—
Maidstone	—	1549	1549
Maldon	Domesday	1155	—
Marlborough	1200	1205	—
Monmouth	1255	1550	—
Morpeth	1553	1188	—
Newark	1674	1549	—
Newbury	1301	1596	—
Newcastle-under-Lyme	1215	1235	—
Newcastle upon Tyne	1116	1158	1588
Newport (I. of W.)	1294	1154	—
Northampton	Domesday	1189	1446
Norwich	Domesday	1159	—
Nottingham	Domesday	1154	1448
Oswestry	—	1397	—
Oxford	Domesday	1154	—
Pembroke	1531	1168	—
Penryn	1216	—	—
Southwold	—	1488	—
Stafford	Domesday	1203	1549
Stamford	Domesday	1461	1461
Stockport	—	1260	—
Stockton-on-Tees	—	—	—
Stratford-upon-Avon	—	1553	1553
Sudbury	Domesday	1558	1558
Sunderland	—	1634	—
Swansea	—	1305	—
Tamworth	Domesday	1560	1560
Tenby	—	1330	—
Tenterden	—	1600	1447
Tewkesbury	Domesday	1574	—
Thetford	Domesday	1573	—
Tiverton	1615	1615	—
Torrington (Great)	1301	1554	1554
Totnes	Domesday	1200	1595
Truro	1154	1250	1588
Wallingford	Domesday	1100	—
Walsall	—	1627	—
Warwick	Domesday	1546	—

Wells	1200	1200	1588
Welshpool	—	1323	—
Wenlock	1468	1468	—
Weymouth and Melcombe Regis	1257	1252	—
Wigan	1399	1246	—
Winchester	Domesday	1189	1587
Windsor	1267	1277	1466
Wisbech	—	1549	—
Worcester	Domesday	1189	—
Yarmouth	Domesday	1209	—
York	Domesday	1154	—

11 SELECTED TUDOR BIOGRAPHIES

This section does not attempt comprehensive entries for all major figures of the Tudor period. Rather, it is intended as a guide to a representative cross-section of persons who had influence during this period.

William Allen (1532–94)   A successful career at Oxford, where he became Principal of St Mary Hall in 1556, was terminated abruptly by the accession of Elizabeth in 1559. A staunch Roman Catholic, Allen went abroad and was ordained as a priest in 1565. He was one of the founders of the English seminary at Douai and the English College in Rome, where he lived at the end of his life. He was created a cardinal in 1587. Allen's many polemical writings vainly urged English Catholics to rise in rebellion against the 'usurper' Elizabeth. At the time of the attempted Spanish invasion of 1588 he published an *Admonition* urging rebellion, but the vast majority of his co-religionists in England remained loyal subjects of the Queen.

Roger Ascham (1514–68)   During the reign of Edward VI Ascham was persuaded to leave Cambridge, where he was Fellow of St John's College, and to become tutor to the Princess Elizabeth, the King's sister. Although a Protestant, he served Mary as Latin Secretary. His famous discourse on education, *The Schoolmaster*, was published in 1570. His other well-known work, *Toxophilus*, appeared in 1545.

Robert Aske (?–1537)   Aske was leader of the Yorkshire rebels in the Pilgrimage of Grace of 1536. He was a conservative country gentleman who opposed the Henrician Reformation. Despite the grant of a pardon by the King, Aske was tried for treason and executed at York.

Anne Askew (1521?–46)   Anne Askew was the daughter of a Lincolnshire knight. Her violent Protestantism led her to desert her husband and move to London, where she was arrested for attacking the Mass. After trial before the Privy Council, she was burned for heresy at Smithfield in July 1546.

John Aylmer (1521–94)   A Cambridge graduate, one of many Cambridge men who fled abroad during Mary's reign. After 1559, he found rapid promotion in the Church, becoming Bishop of London in 1577. He became a fervent persecutor of Puritanism and defender of the Elizabethan settlement.

Anthony Babington (1561–86)   Babington was a fervent Catholic who formed a group pledged to kill Queen Elizabeth. The plot was known to the government who allowed Mary, Queen of Scots, to become implicated before the arrest and execution of the plotters in 1586.

John Bale (1495–1563)   Bale was among the most active and most bitter Protestant controversialists of the Reformation period. He was given an Irish bishopric by Edward VI, fled to the Continent in Mary's reign, and died as a Canterbury prebendary. His dramatic works included *King John*.

Richard Bancroft (1544–1610)   A Lancashire man and a Cambridge graduate, Bancroft was one of the leading lights among the younger leaders of the Elizabethan Church. As Bishop of London from 1597, he was a determined opponent of Puritanism. He was a prominent participant in the Hampton Court conference and James I appointed him Archbishop of Canterbury in 1604.

Robert Barnes (1495?–1540)   Barnes was one of the earliest English Lutherans – like Luther he was an Augustinian friar. After being prosecuted for heresy by Wolsey in 1525, he fled to Germany, whence he was recalled by Thomas Cromwell and employed as ambassador to the German Protestants. After Cromwell's fall in 1540, he was arrested and burned for heresy at Smithfield.

Henry Barrow (?–1593)   Barrow was a founder of religious separatism. In 1586 he and his collaborator John Greenwood were arrested. After some years in gaol, they were tried on charges of sedition and hanged at Tyburn on 6 April 1593.

Elizabeth Barton (1506?–1534)   The 'Nun of Kent', as she became known, acquired some fame as a visionary before she came to national prominence in 1527 with forthright denunciations of the King's intended divorce. Barton's patron, Thomas More, disowned her and she and her supporters were arrested and hanged at Tyburn.

Lady Margaret Beaufort (1441–1509)   The mother of Henry VII was one of the key figures in the political manoeuvrings surrounding the coup of 1485. Her piety and interest in education moved her to found chairs of divinity at both universities and she generously endowed the Cambridge colleges of Christ's and St John's, working in close collaboration with her friend John Fisher.

Thomas Bilney (?-1531)   John Foxe claimed Bilney as the proto-martyr of the English Reformation. But Bilney, although a critic of the Church and a powerful influence on many young Cambridge Protestants, was never fully a Protestant. His trial before Wolsey in 1527 was the result of attacks on image worship: he remained loyal to the Church. When, after arrest for distributing English New Testaments in Norfolk, he was sentenced to burn in 1531, he declared his orthodoxy and received the last rites.

Edmund Bonner (c.1500-69)   'Bloody Bonner' was an Oxford lawyer who entered Wolsey's entourage and served Henry VIII at the time of the divorce, for which he campaigned at Rome, and later as ambassador to France and Spain. Bonner was rewarded with ecclesiastical offices, becoming Bishop of Hereford (1538) and London (1539). Bonner's conservative views led to his deprivation in 1549 and subsequent imprisonment. Mary restored him to his London bishopric, where he earned a not undeserved reputation as a vicious persecutor of heresy. On Elizabeth's succession, he refused to swear the Oath of Supremacy and was gaoled. He died in prison in 1569.

Robert Browne (c.1550-1633?)   Browne has been described as 'the earliest separatist from the Church of England after the Reformation'. At Cambridge he had come under Puritan influence and had resolved to become a minister. But he refused to be ordained by a bishop and believed that the Church should consist of free and self-governing congregations. He formed such a congregation at Norwich and was soon arrested, but was released by the intervention of Lord Burghley. After a period of exile he returned to England in 1584 and became a country parson for the rest of his life.

Sebastian Cabot (c.1472-1557)   Born in Bristol, the son of a Venetian navigator, Cabot served Ferdinand of Spain and the Emperor Charles V before settling in England with a pension from Edward VI. He was one of the founders of the Company of Merchant Venturers (1551) and the Muscovy Company (1555) and strongly supported the contemporary movement for exploration and discovery.

William Camden (1551-1623)   Camden was one of the greatest historians of the Elizabethan age. His *Annals* is the most important source of the contemporary history of Elizabethan England and was published in 1615.

Edmund Campion (1540-81)   The most celebrated of Elizabethan Catholic martyrs was a precocious scholar in his youth, the protégé of the Queen and Lord Leicester. Rejecting the Elizabethan religious settlement, Campion went to Douai and Rome and became a Jesuit. In 1580 he returned to England as a missionary priest but was arrested in July 1581 and, refusing to recant his faith, was executed for treason at Tyburn in December of the same year.

Thomas Cartwright (1535–1603)   Cartwright was a central figure of Elizabethan Puritanism. His opposition to the ecclesiastical establishment, especially over the issue of vestments, led to his dismissal from the Lady Margaret Chair of Divinity at Cambridge and he was later imprisoned for his views.

George Cavendish (c.1500–62)   A close confidant of Thomas Wolsey, whom he served as gentleman-usher. He wrote a famous biography of Wolsey, which was not published until 1641.

Thomas Cavendish (1560–92)   After a lucrative career as a privateer, Cavendish set out on a South American expedition in 1586 and during the next two years circumnavigated the globe, the second Englishman to do so. He died during a second expedition in 1592.

William Caxton (c.1420–91)   Caxton was a successful merchant at Bruges before, in 1471, he entered the household of Margaret of Burgundy, Edward IV's sister. During the next two years he learned the art of printing at Cologne and produced the first English printed book, *The Recuyell of the Historyes of Troye*, at Bruges. He moved his press to England in 1476 and the first book printed in England was *The Dictes or Sayengis of the Philosophres* (1477).

Robert Cecil (1563?–1612)   A younger son of Lord Burghley, whom he succeeded as Elizabeth's chief minister, thus ensuring proper continuity in government. He went on to serve James I, whose unimpeded accession he had carefully managed. He was created Viscount Cranborne (1604) and Earl of Salisbury (1605).

William Cecil (1520–98)   Queen Elizabeth's greatest minister, '*pater pacis patriae*', entered Royal service under Edward VI and became a Secretary of State. He continued to serve Mary, although he was a moderate Protestant, but came to the centre of the political stage in 1559 as chief Secretary of State to Elizabeth I. He served the Queen for forty years, being created Lord Burghley in 1571 and appointed Lord Treasurer in 1572.

Richard Chancellor (?–1556)   A seasoned explorer, Chancellor pioneered trade with Russia and made several journeys to Moscow via Archangel. He died when his ship was wrecked off Scotland in 1556.

John Cheke (1514–57)   As a distinguished classical scholar he was brought to Court in 1544 as tutor to the future Edward VI. He was a humanist and a moderate Protestant and an important influence on Edward, who rewarded him with lands and offices. His support for Jane Grey led to his arrest for treason in 1553 but he was released and went abroad. He was later kidnapped near Brussels, taken to England, and forced to recant his faith.

John Colet (1467?–1519)   His humanism led him to travel to France and Italy to study and on his return he emerged as a controversial interpreter of the Scriptures, on which he based forthright criticisms of the faults of the Church. He became Dean of St Paul's, London, in 1504 and five years later began to plan a new school to be attached to the cathedral. His advisers in this project included Erasmus and Thomas More and the school's first head-master was the notable scholar William Lily.

Miles Coverdale (1488–1569)   This great Biblical translator was a Yorkshire-man who had studied at Cambridge and become a friar. His version of the English Bible (1535) was based on that of Tyndale but was officially licensed. Coverdale supervised the production of the 'Great Bible' of 1539. He was Bishop of Exeter 1551–3, but was deprived by Mary and went abroad. He refused episcopal office in 1559 and became a major influence in Puritan circles and a noted preacher.

Thomas Cranmer (c.1490–1556)   He entered the service of Henry VIII after a distinguished academic career and when he was over forty years of age. In 1533 he was made Archbishop of Canterbury and gave his blessing to the King's divorce. A sincere Protestant, he suffered in silence the slow religious progress of Henry's reign and dutifully approved even the most obnoxious actions of that monarch. Under Edward VI, Cranmer was able to realise his plans for Church reform. The first Prayer Book appeared in 1549 and the second, incorporating more extreme Protestant doctrines, three years later. Cranmer was hated by Mary, whose mother he had divorced, and he was arrested for treason, tried for heresy and died (an affirmed Protestant after some wavering) at the stake in Oxford in March, 1556.

Thomas Cromwell (c.1485–1540)   In his youth Cromwell visited the Low Countries and Italy and gained wide experience of trade and the law. His talents brought him into Wolsey's service. He entered Parliament in 1523 and became a Privy Councillor in 1531. Within two years he was Henry VIII's principal minister and the effective ruler of England. He ruthlessly crushed all opposition to the destruction of the monasteries, the Royal supremacy in the Church and the imposition of firm, not to say tyrannical government. He reconstructed and modernised the government and brought into its service the best talents from the universities. His own beliefs were moderately Protestant and he supported the English Bible and the campaign against 'superstitions'. He was created Earl of Essex in 1540 but fell into disfavour and was executed for treason with the approval of the ungrateful Henry.

John Dee (1527–1608)   One of the first Fellows of Henry VIII's Trinity College, Cambridge, he left to study abroad. A noted mathematician and astronomer, Dee was highly valued by Queen Elizabeth as an astrologer, and his work was a strange mixture of serious science and superstitious 'conjury'.

He wasted years in a fruitless search for the so-called 'philosopher's stone' and fell into disfavour for his supposed practice of black magic. He died in extreme poverty, rejected by James I.

Robert Devereux, Earl of Essex (1567–1601)   Essex, who was stepson of the Earl of Leicester, was a favourite of Elizabeth I and joined the Privy Council in 1593. His successful Spanish raid of 1596 made him a popular hero but he offended the Queen by his impetuous behaviour and mismanaged the Irish campaign of 1599 in such a gross fashion that he was put on trial for dis-obeying the Queen's orders. His attempt to dominate the government had been effectively foiled, much to the satisfaction of Robert Cecil, and he was exiled from Court. He foolishly plotted to seize power and attempted to raise a revolt in London early in 1601. He was captured and put to death.

Francis Drake (c.1540–96)   Born in Devon, Drake came to fame with his lucrative raid on the Spanish colonies of Central America in 1572–3. A further expedition of 1577 was backed by the Queen and when Drake arrived home in 1580 he had circumnavigated the world – the first Englishman to do so. His successes against Spain made him a national hero. He was knighted by Elizabeth on board the *Golden Hind* at Deptford. Drake's continued raids on the Spanish and his part in the defeat of the Armada maintained his reputation, but he died of fever on a Panama raid in 1596.

Edmund Dudley (1462?–1510)   A talented young lawyer brought into the Privy Council by Henry VII. With Richard Empson he organised the 'king's legal counsel' as an important element in Henry's strict financial administra-tion. Both men were highly unpopular and were sacrificed as victims to popular hatred by Henry VIII, being executed for treason in 1510.

John Dudley, Duke of Northumberland (1502?–53)   Son of Edmund Dudley, Henry VII's minister. He was brought to Court by Henry VIII and served the King ably as a soldier. He entered the Privy Council in 1543, was created Earl of Warwick and named as one of Henry's executors. In 1549 he was able to remove the Duke of Somerset from power (Somerset was later executed) and became Duke of Northumberland in 1551, being strongly backed by extreme reformers (like John Hooper) who wanted further Church reform. When Edward died, Northumberland tried to set up Jane Grey, his son's wife, as Queen, but he was arrested and condemned for treason.

Robert Dudley, Earl of Leicester (1532?–88)   A younger son of the Duke of Northumberland. His influence with Elizabeth I was great and, when his wife died mysteriously, it was rumoured that he would marry the Queen, who heaped lands and offices on him. He became Earl of Leicester in 1564. His massive political influence was exercised in alliance with opposition elements in Church and State, but he remained a favourite of the Queen and a source

211

of patronage and promotion. He died in 1588, much mourned by Elizabeth, but Edmund Spenser wrote: 'His name is worn already out of thought.'

John Fisher (1459–1535)   A prominent humanist scholar and educationalist who became Chancellor of Cambridge in 1504. As Bishop of Rochester he emerged as a stout opponent of Henry VIII's divorce and was imprisoned for denying the Royal supremacy. He was beheaded in June 1535.

Richard Fox (c.1448–1528)   A trusted servant of Henry VII, Fox was given high office in the Church and in 1501 became Bishop of Winchester, the richest see in England, while continuing as chief minister to the King. Displaced from power by Wolsey, Fox devoted the last years of his life to the running of his diocese and to various educational schemes, the most ambitious of which was the foundation of Corpus Christi College, Oxford, a new humanistic foundation.

John Foxe (1516–87)   An Oxford graduate, he was ordained in 1550 and became a noted Protestant preacher and publicist. It was in exile, during the reign of Mary, that Foxe began work on his Latin version of the famous *Actes and Monuments* (popularly known as the 'Book of Martyrs'), which appeared in English in 1563. This great and influential work traced the history of the true (i.e. Protestant) Church throughout history and found its heirs in the English Protestants of the 1560s. A reticent man and a staunch Puritan, Foxe found no preferment in the Church but died in relative poverty in 1587.

John Frith (1503–33)   One of the most brilliant of the many young Protestant scholars who emerged from Cambridge in the 1520s. A talented writer, his radical view of the Eucharist and denial that eucharistic doctrine was an essential matter of faith were both novel. Frith was burned for heresy in July, 1533.

Martin Frobisher (1535–94)   He made a number of expeditions to Greenland and Newfoundland in search of the North-west Passage to the East. At Hudson's Bay he believed he had found the northern extremity of America but the 'gold' he discovered was found to be worthless and he fell into disgrace. Frobisher later served actively in the war against Spain. He died of wounds received in an attack on Brest in 1594.

Stephen Gardiner (1483?–1555)   A Cambridge lawyer who, like Thomas Cromwell, rose through the service of Wolsey and came to serve Henry VIII. He was rewarded with the see of Winchester in 1531. His *De Vera Obedientia* was a most competent defence of the Royal Supremacy in the Church. Gardiner was fervently opposed to Protestantism and his influence in government after Cromwell's fall was exercised in favour of religious reaction. He was imprisoned by Edward VI, but appointed Lord Chancellor by Mary, who forgave his previous views on Church government. He was the most competent of Mary's advisers and his death hastened the decline in the credibility and effectiveness of her regime.

John Gerard (1564–1637)   The autobiography of Gerard is a vivid source for the history of Elizabethan and Jacobean Catholic history. He became a Jesuit in 1588 and spent many years in England as a missionary priest. His dramatic exploits included an escape from the Tower in 1597. The last thirty years of Gerard's life were spent in the Low Countries and in Rome.

Humphrey Gilbert (1539?–83)   Gilbert had established a notable reputation as a soldier when, in 1578, he got the approval of Elizabeth I for his planned English settlement in Newfoundland. His first attempt at colonisation failed but Gilbert set out again in 1583. The voyage ended in disaster when his ship was sunk off the Azores and all on board lost.

Richard Grenville (c.1540–91)   A Cornishman and an experienced soldier who collaborated with Walter Raleigh in the Virginia colonisation of 1585–6, which was a total failure. Neither was Grenville a very successful wartime commander. He died when his ship *Revenge* attacked a large Spanish squadron and was quickly sunk.

Thomas Gresham (1519?–79)   A Londoner, the son of a great merchant, highly educated and financially acute, Gresham became Royal agent at Antwerp (the financial centre of Europe) in 1551. His skill in arranging loans was often crucial in the stability of government in England. War in the Netherlands brought Gresham to England. He founded an exchange (or 'bourse') in London in 1568 and left money in his will for the foundation of Gresham College.

Edmund Grindal (1519?–83)   A typical member of the large intellectual and religious community which went into exile during Mary's reign. Under Elizabeth he became Bishop of London, Archbishop of York and, in 1576, Archbishop of Canterbury (he was strongly backed for the primacy by Burghley). Grindal's desire to further reform and to renew the Church caused him to support 'prophesyings' (theological debates involving clergy and laity). The Queen opposed such meetings and suspended Grindal from office. His death in 1583 brought to Canterbury a very different personality, John Whitgift.

Richard Hakluyt (1552–1616)   A keen advocate of English colonies in America who published *Divers Voyages touching the Discovery of America* in 1582. His *Principal Navigations, Voyages, and Discoveries of the English Nation*, a history of the achievements of English explorers and navigators, appeared in 1589.

213

Christopher Hatton (1540–91)   Regarded by his enemies as 'a mere vegetable of the Court', and a firm favourite of Elizabeth I from the time he came to Court in 1564. Hatton was a rival of Leicester and a religious moderate. He was Lord Chancellor from 1587 until his death.

John Hawkins (1532–95)   He made his name and fortune in the slave trade. He became Treasurer of the Navy in 1577 and his reorganisation of English sea forces was an important factor in the victory against the Armada, where he served notably. He died during a voyage to the West Indies with Drake.

Nicholas Hilliard (1537–1619)   Official painter to Elizabeth I and one of the greatest artists of the age. His portraits of the Queen are important evidence of Tudor visual propaganda.

Hans Holbein (1497–1543)   A Swabian who acquired Protestant ideas at Basle, where he became friendly with Erasmus. The latter suggested a visit to England, where Holbein lived after 1532. He entered the service of Henry VIII and produced many portraits of the King, his Queens and Court.

Richard Hooker (1554–1600)   His *Laws of Ecclesiastical Polity* was recognised from the time of its appearance 1594–7 as an outstanding defence of the Elizabethan Church and State. His use of natural law marks him as an important figure in the development of political theory.

John Hooper (?–1555)   An ex-monk who acquired extreme Protestant views during exile in Strasbourg and Zurich after 1539. Under Edward VI, he became Bishop of Gloucester and Worcester, carrying out his episcopal duties with exceptional zeal. Hooper was an influential figure in government and strongly favoured sweeping changes in worship and theology. He was arrested by the Marian régime and was burned for heresy at Gloucester in February, 1555.

Charles, Lord Howard of Effingham (1536–1624)   'Howard of Effingham', who was created Earl of Nottingham in 1597, was Lord High Admiral from 1585 and commanded the English forces against the Armada. From 1599 he was also Lord-Lieutenant General of England.

Thomas Howard, Third Duke of Norfolk (1473–1554)   He earned his reputation as an able and ruthless soldier in French, Scottish and Irish campaigns. His fierce anti-clericalism made him Wolsey's greatest enemy and he was a staunch Henrician. But he strongly opposed the spread of Protestantism, and became, for a brief period, the King's chief adviser after Cromwell's fall in 1540. The disgrace of Norfolk's niece, Catherine Howard, brought about his own fall from favour and at the time of Henry's death he was in the Tower, convicted of treason. He lived to be released by Mary, but died soon after.

John Jewel (1522–71)   His hostility, while a Marian exile, to the extreme reforming party of Knox and others made him a natural candidate for a bishopric after 1559. This former Oxford academic became Bishop of Salisbury in 1560 and published his *Apology* (i.e. defence) of the Church of England in Latin in 1562 and in English in 1564. This seminal work was highly significant in the gradual emergence of 'Anglican' doctrines, opposed to Puritanism as well as to Romanism.

John Knox (1505–72)   His thorough-going Protestantism won him the patronage of Edward VI and he came from imprisonment in France to be an official preacher at Berwick and Newcastle and chaplain to the King. Knox went to Switzerland at Mary's accession, whence he was called to Frankfurt as pastor to the English exiles there. His refusal to use the Prayer Book (which he condemned as superstitious) led to his expulsion. He went to Geneva and from there to Scotland, where he emerged as the leader of the reforming forces. Knox's *First Blast of the Trumpet* . . . (1558), an attack on rule by women, made him anathema to Elizabeth I.

Hugh Latimer (c.1485–1555)   A Cambridge man and one of the great founders of English Protestantism, he was an outspoken and highly controversial critic of the Henrician Church. For four years (1535–9) he was Bishop of Worcester but resigned after the passing of the Six Articles Act and was gaoled on more than one occasion for his views. He was one of the greatest preachers of the Tudor age and frequently attacked the luxury and selfishness of the rich, believing that the Reformation should be accompanied by social reform. He was arrested by Mary's government and burned for heresy at Oxford in October 1555.

Thomas Linacre (c.1460–1524)   A distinguished humanist, Oxford academic and physician to Henry VII and Henry VIII. He was the founder of the Royal College of Physicians.

Walter Mildmay (c.1520–89)   A highly talented financier and administrator who served successive Tudor governments in a variety of important offices, becoming Chancellor of the Exchequer in 1566. His piety and interest in education were both evident in his foundation of Emmanuel College, Cambridge, a noted centre of Puritanism.

Thomas More (1478–1535)   Trained as a lawyer in his native London, he became a prominent member of the humanist circles of the city before entering Parliament in 1504. Wolsey recognised his great talents and brought him to the attention of Henry VIII. In 1518 More became a Privy Councillor and was knighted in 1521. He was the natural choice to succeed Wolsey as Lord Chancellor in 1529 but his opposition to Henry's divorce led him to resign the office in 1532. Two years later, he refused to subscribe to the Succession

Act and was gaoled. His refusal to accept the Royal Supremacy led to his indictment for high treason in 1535. He was beheaded on 5 July of that year. More's *Utopia* (1516) was a radical critique of contemporary Christian society, reflecting the influence of his friend Erasmus. But More stoutly opposed the spread of Lutheran ideas into England and became embroiled in a dreary controversy with Tyndale which reflected little credit on either of the two great participants.

John Morton (c.1420–1500)   He served both Henry VI and Edward IV with great ability and Edward made him Master of the Rolls and Bishop of Ely. He fell into disfavour under Richard III and was imprisoned. Henry VII created him Lord Chancellor and Archbishop of Canterbury and he became a cardinal in 1493.

John Norris (c.1547–97)   Having commanded English forces in the Low Countries and in Ireland, he was appointed Lord President of Munster in 1584. He served again in the Low Countries in 1585–6 and later commanded expeditions to Portugal and France. The last years of his life were spent in Ireland.

Matthew Parker (1504–75)   Queen Elizabeth's choice as primate of the Church of England in 1559. Parker's early career had been stimulated by the patronage of Elizabeth's mother, Anne Boleyn, and his rise in the Church was steady. He was a scholar and a moderate Protestant, determined to enforce firm Royal control over the Church, and he clashed with the Puritan party over the controversial issue of vestments. Parker's scholarly patronage was exercised particularly towards the revival of Anglo-Saxon studies.

Robert Parsons (1546–1610)   He was obliged to leave Oxford, where he was a Fellow of Balliol College, because of his Catholicism. In 1575 he became a Jesuit and in 1580 was sent with Edmund Campion on a mission to England. He avoided arrest and escaped abroad, becoming a prominent figure in the Society of Jesus and an active ally of Spain. He supported the attempted invasion of 1588 and was rejected as a traitor by many English Catholics.

William Perkins (1558–1603)   He was a Fellow of Christ's College, Cambridge, 1584–92, and one of the most important and widely read of English Calvinist writers. He provided a detailed doctrinal basis for English Puritanism and his works were translated into many other languages.

Reginald Pole (1500–58)   Of Royal descent, a favourite of Henry VIII, and widely admired for his humanistic learning. He looked set for a brilliant career in the Church but broke with Henry over the divorce and went abroad. He was created a cardinal in 1536, was a prominent participant in the Council of Trent and was nominated Papal Legate to England at the accession of Mary. Pole came to England, where he became Archbishop of Canterbury in

1556. His primacy was marked by an unhappy breach with Pope Paul IV (who cancelled his legation) and by the bloody and futile persecution of Protestant heretics, a policy Pole fully endorsed. He died in November, 1558.

John Ponet (1514–56) Ponet was successively Bishop of Rochester (1550) and Winchester (1551) under Edward VI. His important political tract, *A Short Treatise of Politic Power*, appeared in 1556.

Walter Raleigh (1554?–1618) His heroic military exploits brought him to the notice of Elizabeth I and he became a firm favourite of the Queen, who knighted him and made him captain of her guards. His privateering activities against the Spaniards, rather than his involvement in the colonising of North America, made him a popular hero. James I's policy of peace with Spain made Raleigh an embarrassing presence and he was imprisoned. Released to lead an expedition to Guiana (which was a dismal failure) he was rearrested on his return and beheaded for treason in October 1618.

Nicholas Ridley (c.1500–55) A Cambridge intellectual who became chaplain to the King and Master of Pembroke College under Henry VIII. In the reign of Edward VI he was successively Bishop of Rochester and London. As a leading figure in the Protestant movement, Ridley was arrested by Mary's government. He was burned for heresy at Oxford, with Latimer, in 1555.

William Salesbury (1520?–84?) The most prolific Welsh scholar of his day. He published what was probably the first Welsh printed book – an English/Welsh dictionary – in 1547. Converted to Protestantism at Oxford, he translated the Prayer Book and New Testament into Welsh (1563–7) and produced many other translations.

Edward Seymour, Duke of Somerset (1506?–52) He rose to supreme power – as Protector under the young Edward VI – via the favour of Henry VIII, who brought him to the Council, created him Earl of Hertford and, in 1544, gave him charge of the kingdom during his own absence in France. He was created Duke of Somerset in 1547. A sincere religious and social reformer, Somerset fell from power in the crisis of 1549 and was imprisoned. He was released by Northumberland, but the rise of the latter to total domination of the government resulted in Somerset's arrest on charges of treason. He was executed early in 1552.

Philip Sidney (1554–86) Perhaps the most universally admired of all the younger courtiers at the Elizabethan Court. A soldier and a poet (his *Arcadia* was published after his death), he was also a fervent Protestant. In 1585 he assumed a command in the army in the Netherlands but was wounded at Zutphen and died, much lamented, in October 1586.

Lambert Simnel (1473?–1525) A youth of humble birth who was persuaded to impersonate the Earl of Warwick, son of the Duke of Clarence, and was crowned as 'Edward VI' at Dublin in 1487. Leading a Yorkist army, he was defeated by Henry VII at Stoke and was kept as a humble servant at Court for many years.

Robert Southwell (c.1560–95) Educated at Douay and Paris, Southwell became a Jesuit in 1580 and in 1586 was sent to England with Fr. Henry Garnett. He was a notable poet. Arrested in June 1592, in Middlesex, he was kept in gaol for three years before being executed.

Thomas Starkey (1499?–1538) A distinguished humanist who was the author of the important political tract *The Dialogue between Pole and Lupset*, a defence of Royal supremacy.

Thomas Stucley (1525?–78) Stucley was an unscrupulous adventurer who became something of a folk-hero. An adherent of the Duke of Somerset, he later served the Emperor, was a successful pirate, and fought against the Turks at the battle of Lepanto. He died fighting the Moors in 1578.

Walter Travers (c.1548–1635) Travers acquired Calvinist views at Geneva and advocated the adoption of Presbyterianism by the Church of England. He was unacceptable to the Elizabethan Church because of his extreme views but Burghley employed him as tutor to the young Robert Cecil and later secured his appointment as Provost of Trinity College, Dublin. Banned from preaching, Travers spent the last thirty years of his life in quiet retirement in London.

Cuthbert Tunstal (1474–1559) Tunstal was a man of great learning and wide ability who served Henry VIII as an ambassador and was appointed Master of the Rolls in 1516. He was rewarded with the see of London in 1522 and in 1523 became Keeper of the Privy Seal. In 1530 he was made Bishop of Durham and became President of the Council in the North in 1537. A loyal Henrician but a religious conservative, he was deprived of his see in 1552 but was restored by Mary. He died, again deprived, in 1559.

William Turner (?–1568) Often described as the founder of English botany, Turner was a native of Northumberland who was converted to militant Protestantism at Cambridge and went on to study medicine in Italy. He was physician and chaplain to the Duke of Somerset, who secured for him the deanery of Wells. He was in exile under Mary, returning to Wells under Elizabeth. He was suspended from office in 1564 for nonconformity. His *Herbal*, one of many scientific and theological works, appeared in 1551.

William Tyndale (c.1495–1536) His radical Erasmianism, his criticism of the clergy and support for the idea of a vernacular Bible brought him into conflict with the Church authorities. He became a Lutheran and went to Germany, where he worked on his English translation of the New Testament. Tyndale's controversial works, issued from a variety of European bases, caused him to be regarded as 'the captain of our English heretics'. His life was ever at risk and he was betrayed and imprisoned at Vilvorde, near Antwerp, in 1536. He was put to death in October 1536.

Nicholas Udall (1505?–56) A prominent humanist, translator and Protestant who translated Erasmus's *Paraphrases* for Queen Catherine Parr. He is now best remembered as a founder of the English drama and especially for his play *Ralph Roister Doister*.

Francis Vere (1560–1609) One of the great military veterans of Elizabeth's reign, serving with distinction in the Low Countries, at Cadiz and in the Azores. In 1601–2 he conducted the defence of Ostend.

Polydore Vergil (c.1470–1555) Born in Urbino, Vergil was a noted scholar long before his despatch to England as a Papal tax collector in 1501. Henry VIII encouraged his work on English history and the *Anglica Historia* appeared in 1534.

Francis Walsingham (c.1530–90) He had a legal training and, on return from exile in 1559, entered William Cecil's service. Brilliant as a diplomatist and organiser of espionage, he rose rapidly to become Secretary of State in 1573 and held the office until his death. For nearly two decades Walsingham was second only to Cecil in the government. A staunch Puritan and promoter of anti-Spanish policies, he campaigned for English intervention in the Netherlands and for the execution of Mary Stuart. But he was no narrow bigot and Spenser, a recipient of his wide patronage, described him as 'the great Maecenas of this age'.

Perkin Warbeck (1475–99) A naïve tool of the Yorkist plotting which disrupted the first part of Henry VII's reign. After an abortive invasion attempt in 1495 Warbeck – supposedly the Duke of York – reappeared in 1497, landing with an army in Cornwall and attacking Exeter. He was captured and kept in captivity until his involvement in a foolhardy plot obliged Henry to order his execution.

William Warham (c.1450–1532) Trained as a civil lawyer, Warham became Master of the Rolls in 1494 and served Henry VII ably as an ambassador. He became Bishop of London in 1501 and Archbishop of Canterbury in 1503, being Keeper of the Great Seal from 1502 and Lord Chancellor from 1504. With the scholarly but unassertive Warham at its head, the Church fell under the domination of Wolsey and then succumbed to the Royal attack.

John Whitgift (c.1530–1604)   He became a radical Protestant at Cambridge, to which university he returned in 1563 as Lady Margaret Professor of Divinity, becoming subsequently Master of Trinity College and Vice-Chancellor. Whitgift's increasingly anti-Puritan views brought him to the notice of the Queen and he became Bishop of Worcester (1577) and Archbishop of Canterbury (1583). His fierce persecution of nonconformity widened the rift in the Elizabethan Church.

Thomas Wolsey (c.1475–1532)   He came to prominence as an aide to Bishop Fox and Royal chaplain. Rapid promotion in the Church followed and by 1512 Wolsey was Henry VIII's chief adviser. He became Archbishop of York and in 1515 was created a Cardinal by the Pope and Lord Chancellor by Henry. Wolsey's diplomatic failures and his inability to secure a divorce for his master led to his downfall. Disgraced and driven from office, he died at Leicester, on his way to trial in London, in 1532.

BIBLIOGRAPHICAL NOTE

The following list of books provides only a short introduction to the very large literature now available on the Tudor period. For a detailed bibliography, students should consult Conyers Read, *Bibliography of British History: Tudor Period 1485–1603* (2nd ed., Oxford, 1959).

In addition to the books cited below, two works have been indispensable for compiling a reference book of this type. They are M. Powicke and E. B. Fryde (eds.), *Handbook of British Chronology* (2nd ed., London, 1961) and G. R. Elton, *The Tudor Constitution* (Cambridge, 1972). In addition to the books cited below, readers are referred to the detailed footnote references in the appropriate chapter.

CROWN AND CENTRAL GOVERNMENT

THE PRIVY COUNCIL
Elton, G. R., 'Why the History of the Early Tudor Council Remains Unwritten' in *Studies in Tudor and Stuart Politics and Government*, I (Cambridge, 1974).
—'Henry VII's Council' in ibid.
Hoak, D. E., *The King's Council in the Reign of Edward VI* (Cambridge, 1976).
Hurstfield, J., 'The Succession Struggle in Late Elizabethan England' in *Elizabethan Government and Society* ed. S. T. Bindoff *et al.* (London, 1961).
Pulman, M. B., *The Elizabethan Privy Council in the Fifteen-seventies* (Berkeley, California, 1971).

THE SEALS AND THE SECRETARY
Dewar, M., *Sir Thomas Smith* (London, 1964).
Elton, G. R., *Policy and Police: the Enforcement of the Reformation in the Age of Thomas Cromwell* (Cambridge, 1972).
—*Studies in Tudor and Stuart Politics and Government* (Cambridge, 1974).
Emmison, F. G., *Tudor Secretary* (London, 1961).
Evans, F. M. G., *The Principle Secretary of State* (Manchester, 1923).
Hearder, H. and Loyn, H. R. (eds), *BritishG overnment and Administration: Studies Presented to S. B. Chrimes.*

221

Read, C., *Mr Secretary Walsingham and the Policy of Queen Elizabeth*, 3 vols (Oxford, 1925).

ROYAL FINANCE

Bell, H. E., *An Introduction to the History and Records of the Court of Wards and Liveries* (Cambridge, 1953).

Dietz, F. C., *English Public Finance 1558-1642* (New York, 1932).

—*English Government Finance 1485-1558* (University of Illinois Studies in the Social Sciences, IX, 1920, no. 3).

Gras, N., *The Early English Customs System* (Cambridge, Massachusetts, 1918).

Hooker, J. R., 'Some Cautionary Notes on Henry VII's Household and Chamber "System" ', *Speculum*, XXXIII (1958).

Hurstfield, J., *The Queen's Wards* (London, 1958).

Newton, A. P., 'The Establishment of the Great Farm of the English Customs', *Transactions of the Royal Historical Society*, 4th series (1918).

Richardson, W. C., *Tudor Chamber Administration* (Baton Rouge, 1952).

PARLIAMENT

Elton, G. R., 'The Commons' Supplication against the Ordinaries: Parliamentary Manoeuvres in the Reign of Henry VIII', *English Historical Review*, LXVI (1951).

Hinton, R. W. K., 'The Decline of Parliamentary Government under Elizabeth I and the Early Stuarts', *Cambridge Historical Journal*, XIII (1957).

McKisack, M., *The Parliamentary Representation of the English Boroughs during the Middle Ages* (Oxford, 1932).

Neale, J. E., The Commons' Privilege of Free Speech in Parliament, *Tudor Studies presented . . . to A. F. Pollard* (London, 1924).

—*The Elizabethan House of Commons* (London, 1949).

—*Elizabeth I and her Parliaments* (London, 1957).

—*Essays in Elizabethan History* (London, 1958).

—'Peter Wentworth', *English Historical Review*, XXXIX (1924).

Notestein, W., *The Winning of the Initiative by the House of Commons* (London, 1924).

Pike, L. O., *A Constitutional History of the House of Lords* (London, 1894).

Pollard, A. F., *The Evolution of Parliament* (2nd ed., London, 1934).

LOCAL GOVERNMENT

GENERAL

Hassell Smith, A., *County and Court: Government and Politics in Norfolk 1558-1603* (Oxford, 1974).

Hurstfield, J., 'County Government c. 1530–c. 1660' in *V.C.H. Wiltshire*, v (1957).
Smith, A. G. R., *The Government of Elizabethan England* (London, 1967).
Willcox, W. B., *Gloucestershire: a study in local government, 1590–1640* (New Haven, 1940).

REGIONAL COUNCILS
Brooks, F. W., *The Council of the North* (Historical Association series, 1953).
Reid, R. R., *The King's Council of the North* (London, 1921).
Williams, P., *The Council in the Marches of Wales under Elizabeth I* (Cardiff, 1958).
Youings, J., 'The Council of the West' *Transactions of the Royal Historical Society*, 5th series (1960).

ASSIZES
Cockburn, J. S., *A History of English Assizes 1558–1714* (Cambridge, 1972).

QUARTER SESSIONS AND THE J.P.S
Forster, G. C. F., *The East Riding Justices of the Peace in the Seventeenth Century* (East Yorkshire Local History Society, 1973).

LORDS LIEUTENANTS AND DEFENCE
Boynton, L., *The Elizabethan Militia 1558–1638* (London and Toronto, 1967).
Cruickshank, C. G., *Elizabeth's Army* (2nd ed., Oxford, 1966).
Sainty, J. C., *Lieutenants of Counties 1585–1642* (*Bulletin of the Institute of Historical Research*, Special Supplement, VIII, 1970).
Scott Thomson, G., *Lords Lieutenants in the Sixteenth Century* (London, 1923)

TOWNS
Dyer, A. D., *The City of Worcester in the Sixteenth Century* (Leicester, 1973).
MacCaffrey, W. T., *Exeter 1540–1640* (2nd ed., Cambridge, Massachusetts, 1976).
Phythian-Adams, C., 'Ceremony and the Citizen: the Communal Year at Coventry, 1450–1550' in P. Clark (ed.), *The Early Modern Town* (London, 1976).

JUDICATURE

GENERAL
Elton, G. R., *The Tudor Constitution* (Cambridge, 1960).
—*The Tudor Revolution in Government*, (Cambridge, 1953).
—'The Rule of Law in Sixteenth-Century England' in *Studies in Tudor and Stuart Politics and Government*, I (Cambridge, 1974).

Harding, A., *The Law Courts of Medieval England* (London, 1973).

Holdsworth, W. H., *A History of English Law* (13 vols., London, 1903 onwards): vol. I describes the courts.

Hurstfield, J., 'Was there a Tudor Despotism after all?' in *Freedom, Corruption and Government* (London, 1973).

ANCIENT COURTS

Hastings, M., *The Court of Common Pleas in Fifteenth-Century England* (Ithaca, 1947).

Jones, W. J., *The Elizabethan Court of Chancery* (Oxford, 1967).

STAR CHAMBER AND CONCILIAR COURTS

Elton, G. R., *Star Chamber Stories* (London, 1958).

Leadam, I. S., *Select Cases in the Court of Requests, 1467–1569* (Selden Society, XII, London, 1898): introduction describes the court.

Ruddock, A. A., 'The Earliest Records of the High Court of Admiralty, 1515–58' in *Bulletin of the Institute of Historical Research*, XXII (1949).

THE CHURCH AND RELIGION

THE PRE-REFORMATION CHURCH AND THE RELIGIOUS ORDERS

Heath, P., *The English Parish Clergy on the Eve of the Reformation* (London and Toronto, 1969).

Knowles, D., *The Religious Orders in England: III, The Tudor Age* (Cambridge, 1959).

Pollard, A. F., *Wolsey* (London, 1929 [Fontana, 1965]).

Smith, H. M., *Pre-Reformation England* (London, 1938).

Thomson, J. A. F., *The Later Lollards, 1414–1520* (Oxford, 1965).

THE REFORMATION AND THE GROWTH OF PROTESTANTISM

Dickens, A. G., *The English Reformation* (Revised ed., London, 1967).

—*Lollards and Protestants in the Diocese of York, 1509–1558* (Oxford, 1959).

—*Thomas Cromwell and the English Reformation* (London, 1959).

Elton, G. R., *Policy and Police: the Enforcement of the Reformation in the Age of Thomas Cromwell* (Cambridge, 1972).

McConica, J. K., *English Humanists and Reformation Politics* (Oxford, 1965).

Palliser, D. M., *The Reformation in York, 1534–1553* (York, Borthwick Papers, 1971).

Rupp, E. G., *Studies in the Making of the English Protestant Tradition* (Cambridge, 1947).

Scarisbrick, J. J., *Henry VIII* (London, 1968).

Smith, L. B., *Tudor Prelates and Politics 1536–1558* (Princeton, New Jersey, 1953).

Williams, G., 'The Protestant Experiment in the Diocese of St. David's, 1534–1555', in *Welsh Reformation Essays* (Cardiff, 1967), pp. 111–39.

THE MARIAN REACTION

Dickens, A. G., *The Marian Reaction in the Diocese of York* (York, Borthwick Papers, 1957).
Loades, D. M., 'The Enforcement of Reaction, 1553–58', *Journal of Ecclesiastical History*, XVI, 1965, pp. 54–66.
—*The Oxford Martyrs* (London, 1970).
Powell, K. G., *The Marian Martyrs and the Reformation in Bristol* (Bristol, Historical Association series, 1972).

PURITANISM, CATHOLICISM AND THE ELIZABETHAN CHURCH

Bossy, J., 'The Character of Elizabethan Catholicism', in *Crisis in Europe 1560–1660*, ed. T. Aston (London, 1965) pp. 223–46.
Collinson, P., *The Elizabethan Puritan Movement* (London, 1967).
Cross, C. *The Royal Supremacy in the Elizabethan Church* (London, 1969).
Hill, C., *Economic Problems of the Church, from Whitgift to the Long Parliament* (Oxford, 1956).
Knappen, M. M., *Tudor Puritanism* (Chicago, 1939 [Phoenix, 1970]).
McGrath, P. V., *Papists and Puritans under Elizabeth I* (London, 1967).
Porter, H. C., *Reformation and Reaction in Tudor Cambridge* (Cambridge, 1958).
—*Puritanism in Tudor England* (London, 1970).

THE ENGLISH BIBLE

Mozley, J. F., *Coverdale and his Bibles* (London, 1953).
Pollard, A. W., *Records of the English Bible* (Oxford, 1911).

EDUCATION

GENERAL

Charlton, K., *Education in Renaissance England* (London, 1965).
Simon, J., *Education and Society in Tudor England* (Cambridge, 1966).
Stone, L., 'The Educational Revolution in England, 1560–1640' in *Past and Present*, XXVIII (1964).

SCHOOLS

Baldwin, T. W., *William Shakespeare's small Latine and lesse Greeke* (Oxford, 1944).
Lawson, J., *The Endowed Grammar Schools of East Yorkshire* (York, 1962).
Leach, A. F., *English Schools at the Reformation* (London, 1896).
Orme, N., *English Schools in the Middle Ages* (London, 1973).

Orme, N., *Education in the West of England 1066–1548* (Exeter, 1977).
Simon, J., 'The Reformation and English Education' in *Past and Present*, XI, (1957): a critique of A. F. Leach.

UNIVERSITIES AND INNS OF COURT

Curtis, M. H., *Oxford and Cambridge in Transition 1558–1642* (Oxford, 1959).
Hexter, J. H., 'The Education of the Aristocracy in the Renaissance', in *Reappraisals in History* (London, 1961).
Kearney, H., *Scholars and Gentlemen: Universities and Society in Pre-Industrial Britain* (London, 1970).
McConica, J. K., 'Scholars and Commoners in Renaissance Oxford' in L. Stone (ed.) *The University in Society*, I (Princeton, New Jersey, 1974).
Prest, W. R., *The Inns of Court under Elizabeth I and the Early Stuarts 1590–1640* (London, 1972).

BOOKS AND READERS

Bennett, H. S., *English Books and Readers 1475–1557* (Cambridge, 1952).
Clark, P., 'The Ownership of Books in England 1560–1640: the Example of some Kentish Townsfolk', in L. Stone (ed.), *Schooling and Society* (Baltimore, 1976).
Eisenstein, E. L., 'The Advent of Printing and the Problem of the Renaissance' *Past and Present*, XLV (1969).
Wright, L. B., *Middle Class Culture in Elizabethan England* (Chapel Hill, 1935).

WAR, REBELLION AND DIPLOMACY

THE ARMY

Boynton, L., *The Elizabethan Militia* (London, 1967).
Cruickshank, C. G., *Elizabeth's Army* (2nd ed., Oxford, 1966).
Davies, C. S. L., 'Provisions for Armies 1509–1560', *Economic History Review*, XVII.
Falls, C., *Elizabeth's Irish Wars* (London, 1950).
Fortescue, Sir J., *A History of the British Army*, vol. I (London, 1899–1930).
Goring, J., *The Military Obligations of the English People, 1511–1558* (unpublished Ph.D. thesis, London, 1955).
Hattaway, H. M., Some Aspects of Tudor Military History, *Army Quarterly* (April, 1969).
Neale, Sir J., 'Elizabeth and the Netherlands 1586–7', *English Historical Review*, vol. 45 (1930).
Oman, Sir C., *A History of the Art of War in the Sixteenth Century* (London, 1937).
Roberts, M., *The Military Revolution 1560–1660* (Inaugural Lecture at

Queen's University, Belfast, 1956).

Rogers, Col. H. C. B., *Weapons of the British Soldier* (London, 1960).

Rowse, A. L., *The Expansion of Elizabethan England* (London, 1955).

Stone, L., *The Crisis of the Aristocracy 1558–1641* (Oxford, 1965).

Webb, H. H., *Elizabethan Military Science* (University of Wisconsin Press, 1965).

Wernham, R. B., 'Queen Elizabeth and the Portugal Expedition of 1589', *English Historical Review*, vol. 66 (1951).

—'Elizabethan War Aims and Strategy', in *Elizabethan Government and Society: Essays Presented to Sir John Neale* (London, 1961).

—*Before the Armada: the Growth of English Foreign Policy 1485–1588* (London, 1966).

THE NAVY

Clowes, Sir W. L., *The Royal Navy, a History from the Earliest Times to the Present* (London, 1897–1903).

Corbett, Sir J., *Drake and the Tudor Navy* (London, 1898).

—*The Sucessors of Drake* (London, 1900).

Davies, C. S. L., 'The Administration of the Royal Navy under Henry VIII', *English Historical Review*, vol. 80 (1965).

Goldingham, Capt. C. S., 'The Navy under Henry VII', *English Historical Review*, vol. 33 (1918).

Lewis, M. A., *The History of the British Navy* (Harmondsworth, 1957).

Marcus, G. J., *A Naval History of England*, vol. I (London, 1961).

Mattingly, G., *The Defeat of the Spanish Armada* (London, 1959).

Oppenheim, M., *A History of the Administration of the Royal Navy* (London, 1896).

Richmond, Admiral Sir H., *Statesmen and Seapower* (Oxford, 1946).

—*The Navy as an Instrument of Policy 1585–1727* (Cambridge, 1953).

Williamson, J. A., *The Age of Drake* (London, 1938).

—*The Tudor Age* (London, 1953).

TREATIES

Parry, C. and Hopkins, C., *An Index of British Treaties, 1101–1968* (London, 1970).

THE TUDOR ECONOMY

Bowden, P. J., *The Wool Trade in Tudor and Stuart England* (London, 1962).

Cornwall, J., 'English Population in the Early Sixteenth Century', *Economic History Review*, 2nd series, XXII (1970).

Craig, J., *The Mint* (Cambridge, 1953).

Cunningham, W., *The Growth of English Industry and Commerce* (Cambridge, 1922).

Everitt, A. (ed.), *Perspectives in English Urban History* (London, 1973).

Fisher, F. J., 'Commercial Trends in 16th-Century England', in *Economic History Review* (1940).

Gras, N. S. B., *The Evolution of the English Corn Market* (Cambridge, Massachusetts, 1915).

Kramer, S., *The English Craft Gilds and the Government* (New York, 1905).

Jones, W. R. D., *The Tudor Commonwealth 1529–1559* (London, 1970).

Leonard, E. M., *The Early History of English Poor Relief* (Cambridge, 1900).

Lipson, E., *The Economic History of England*, (3 vols.) (London, 1915, 1931).

Price, W. H., *The English Patents of Monopoly* (Harvard, 1906).

Ramsey, P., *Tudor Economic Problems* (London, 1963).

Slack, P. and Clark, P., *Crisis and Order in English Towns 1500–1700* (London, 1972).

Slater, G., *The English Peasantry and the Enclosure of Common Fields*, Appendix D, (1907).

Tawney, R. H., *The Agrarian Problem in the 16th Century* (London, 1912).

—*Introduction to T. Wilson's 'A Discourse upon Usury'* (London, 1925).

Thirsk, J., *Tudor Enclosures* (Historical Association no. 41 1959).

Unwin, G., *Industrial Organisation in the 16th and 17th Centuries* (Oxford, 1904).